1000 Recipes Cupcakes

Published in 2012
by Igloo Books Ltd
Cottage Farm
Sywell
Northants
NN6 0BJ
www.igloobooks.com

Food photography and recipe development: PhotoCuisine UK
Front and back cover images © PhotoCuisine UK

SHE001 0912
2 4 6 8 10 9 7 5 3
ISBN: 978-0-85780-726-7

Printed and manufactured in China

1000 Recipes Cupcakes

CONTENTS

CUPCAKES

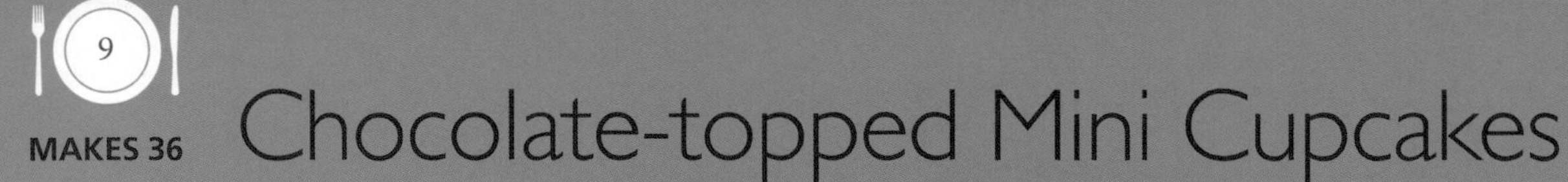

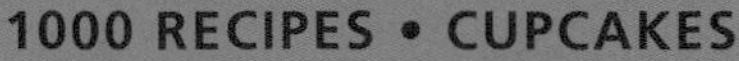

9

MAKES 36

Chocolate-topped Mini Cupcakes

PREPARATION TIME: 25 MINUTES

COOKING TIME: 15 MINUTES

INGREDIENTS

110 g / 4 oz / ½ cup self-raising flour, sifted
110 g / 4 oz / ½ cup caster (superfine) sugar
110 g / 4 oz / ½ cup butter, softened
2 large eggs
1 tsp vanilla extract

TO DECORATE

110 g / 4 oz / ½ cup dark chocolate, minimum 60% cocoa solids, chopped
2 tbsp hazelnuts, chopped

- Preheat the oven to 190°C (170° fan) / 375 F / gas 5 and line a 36-hole mini cupcake tin with paper cases.
- Combine the flour, sugar, butter, eggs and vanilla extract in a bowl and whisk together for 2 minutes or until smooth.
- Divide the mixture between the paper cases and bake for 10 – 15 minutes.
- Test with a wooden toothpick, if it comes out clean, the cakes are done.
- Transfer the cakes to a wire rack and leave to cool.
- Melt the chocolate in a microwave or bain-marie.
- Dip the top of each cake in the chocolate and sprinkle with nuts, then leave to set.

Double Chocolate Mini Cupcakes

10

Replace the vanilla extract in the cake mixture with 2 tbsp of unsweetened cocoa powder and add 75 g of chocolate chips. Sprinkle the cakes with white chocolate chips instead of chopped hazelnuts.

White Chocolate Mini Cupcakes

11

Replace the dark chocolate with white chocolate.

Chocolate-topped Coconut Cupcakes

12

Add 2 tbsp of desiccated coconut to the mixture before cooking.

13

MAKES 24

Raspberry Mini Cupcakes

- Preheat the oven to 180°C (160° fan) / 350 F / gas 4 and line a 24-hole silicone mini muffin tin with paper cases.
- Beat the egg in a jug with the oil and milk. Mix the flour, baking powder, sugar and raspberries in a bowl, then pour in the egg mixture and stir to combine.
- Divide the mixture between the moulds then bake in the oven for 15 – 20 minutes. Transfer the cakes to a wire rack and leave to cool.
- Beat the butter with a wooden spoon until light and fluffy then beat in the icing sugar a quarter at a time.
- Use a whisk to incorporate the raspberry syrup, then whisk for 2 minutes.
- Spoon the icing onto the cupcakes and scatter over the cake sprinkles.

PREPARATION TIME: 25 MINUTES

COOKING TIME: 15-20 MINUTES

INGREDIENTS

1 large egg
120 ml / 4 fl. oz / ½ cup sunflower oil
120 ml / 4 fl. oz / ½ cup milk
375 g / 12 ½ oz / 2 ½ cups self-raising flour, sifted
1 tsp baking powder
200 g / 7 oz / ¾ cup caster (superfine) sugar
150 g / 5 oz / 1 cup raspberries

TO DECORATE
110 g / 4 oz / ½ cup butter, softened
225 g / 8 oz / 2 cups icing (confectioners') sugar
1 tbsp raspberry syrup
red cake sprinkles

Orange Mini Cupcakes

14

Try adding 1 tbsp of finely grated orange zest to the muffin mixture and buttercream.

15

MAKES 12

Baby Girl Cupcakes

- Preheat the oven to 190°C (170° fan) / 375 F / gas 5 and line a 12-hole cupcake tin with pink paper cases.
- Combine the flour, sugar, butter, eggs and vanilla extract in a bowl and whisk together for 2 minutes.
- Divide the mixture between the cases, then transfer to the oven and bake for 15 – 20 minutes. Transfer the cakes to a wire rack and leave to cool.
- To make the buttercream, beat the butter with a wooden spoon until light and fluffy then beat in the icing sugar a quarter at a time.
- Use a whisk to incorporate the milk and vanilla extract, then whisk for 2 minutes.
- Spoon the buttercream into a piping bag fitted with a star nozzle and pipe a swirl on top of each cake.
- Sprinkle with edible glitter and top each cake with a sugar baby girl head.

PREPARATION TIME: 30 MINUTES

COOKING TIME: 20 MINUTES

INGREDIENTS

110 g / 4 oz / 1 cup self-raising flour, sifted
110 g / 4 oz / ½ cup caster (superfine) sugar
110 g / 4 oz / ½ cup butter, softened
2 large eggs
1 tsp vanilla extract

TO DECORATE
110 g / 4 oz / ½ cup butter, softened
225 g / 8 oz / 2 cups icing (confectioners') sugar
2 tbsp milk
1 tsp vanilla extract
Edible glitter
sugar baby girl heads

Strawberry Baby Cupcakes

16

Replace the milk with 2 tbsp of strawberry syrup to add a pink tint to the cakes and give a fruity flavour.

17

MAKES 12

Simple Vanilla Cupcakes

PREPARATION TIME: 25 MINUTES

COOKING TIME: 20 MINUTES

INGREDIENTS

110 g / 4 oz / 1 cup self-raising flour, sifted
110 g / 4 oz / ½ cup caster (superfine) sugar
110 g / 4 oz / ½ cup butter, softened
2 large eggs
1 tsp vanilla extract

- Preheat the oven to 190°C (170° fan) / 375 F / gas 5 and line a 12-hole cupcake tin with paper cases.
- Combine the flour, sugar, butter, eggs and vanilla extract in a bowl and whisk together for 2 minutes.
- Divide the mixture between the paper cases, then transfer to the oven and bake for 15 – 20 minutes.
- Test with a wooden toothpick, if it comes out clean, the cakes are done.
- Transfer the cakes to a wire rack and leave to cool.

Vanilla Cupcakes with Buttercream Frosting

18

Decorate these cakes with a simple buttercream frosting.

19

MAKES 12

Sugar Pearl Cupcakes

PREPARATION TIME: 25 MINUTES

COOKING TIME: 20 MINUTES

INGREDIENTS

110 g / 4 oz / 1 cup self-raising flour, sifted
110 g / 4 oz / ½ cup caster (superfine) sugar
110 g / 4 oz / ½ cup butter, softened
2 large eggs
1 tsp vanilla extract

TO DECORATE

110 g / 4 oz / ½ cup butter, softened
225 g / 8 oz / 2 cups icing (confectioners') sugar
28 g / 1 oz / ¼ cup unsweetened cocoa powder, sifted
2 tbsp milk

- Preheat the oven to 190°C (170° fan) / 375 F / gas 5 and line a 12-hole cupcake tin with paper cases.
- Combine the flour, sugar, butter, eggs and vanilla extract in a bowl and whisk together for 2 minutes.
- Divide the mixture between the paper cases, then transfer to the oven and bake for 15–20 minutes. Transfer the cakes to a wire rack and leave to cool.
- Beat the butter with a wooden spoon until light and fluffy then beat in the icing sugar and cocoa a quarter at a time.
- Use a whisk to incorporate the milk, then whisk for 2 minutes.
- Spoon the chocolate buttercream into a piping bag fitted with a small star nozzle and pipe small stars to fill the surface of the cupcakes.
- Top with the sugar pearls.

Sugar Pearl Fruit Cupcakes

Add 75 g / 3 oz of dried fruit to the cupcake mixture before cooking.

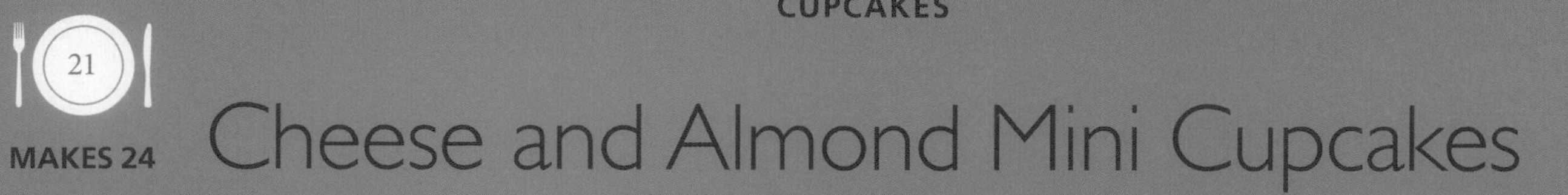

21

MAKES 24

Cheese and Almond Mini Cupcakes

PREPARATION TIME: 25 MINUTES

COOKING TIME: 15 MINUTES

INGREDIENTS

2 large eggs
120 ml / 4 fl. oz / ½ cup sunflower oil
180 ml / 6 fl. oz / ¾ cup Greek yogurt
75 g / 2 ½ oz / ½ cup flaked (slivered) almonds
110 g / 4 oz / 1 cup Reblochon cheese, cubed
225 g / 8 oz / 1 ½ cups plain (all purpose) flour
2 tsp baking powder
½ tsp bicarbonate of (baking) soda
½ tsp salt

- Preheat the oven to 180°C (160° fan) / 350 F / gas 4 and oil a 24-hole silicone muffin tin.
- Beat the egg in a jug with the oil, yoghurt, almonds and cheese until well mixed.
- Mix the flour, raising agents and salt in a bowl, then pour in the egg mixture and stir just enough to combine.
- Divide the mixture between the moulds, then bake in the oven for 10 – 15 minutes.
- Test with a wooden toothpick, if it comes out clean, the cupcakes are done.
- Serve warm.

Cheese and Nut Mini Cupcakes

22

Try this recipe with Roquefort and walnuts instead of Reblochon and almonds.

Cheese and Tomato Cupcakes

23

Add 2 finely chopped sun-dried tomatoes to the mixture before cooking.

Cheese and Bacon Cupcakes

24

Add 100 g / 4 oz of cooked chopped bacon pieces before cooking.

25

MAKES 36

Chocolate Caramel Mini cupcakes

Chocolate Fruit and Caramel Cupcakes

26

Add 75 g / 3 oz dried fruit to the cupcake mixture.

Peanut and Caramel Cupcakes

27

Add chopped peanuts to the mixture and sprinkle on top.

Pecan and Caramel Cupcakes

28

Add chopped pecans to the mixture and sprinkle on top.

PREPARATION TIME: 20 MINUTES

COOKING TIME: 15 MINUTES

INGREDIENTS

110 g / 4 oz / ½ cup self-raising flour, sifted
28 g / 1 oz / ¼ cup unsweetened cocoa powder, sifted
110 g / 4 oz / ½ cup caster (superfine) sugar
110 g / 4 oz / ½ cup butter, softened
2 large eggs
36 chocolate caramels

- Preheat the oven to 190°C (170° fan) / 375 F / gas 5 and line a 36 hole mini cupcake tin with paper cases.
- Combine the flour, cocoa, sugar, butter and eggs in a bowl and whisk together for 2 minutes.
- Divide the mixture between the paper cases and press a chocolate caramel into the top of each, then transfer to the oven and bake for 10 – 15 minutes.
- Serve warm

29

MAKES 36

Red Iced Mini Cupcakes

- Preheat the oven to 190°C (170° fan) / 375 F / gas 5 and line a 36-hole cupcake tin with paper cases.
- Combine the flour, sugar, butter, eggs and vanilla extract in a bowl and whisk together for 2 minutes.
- Divide the mixture between the paper cases and bake for 10 – 15 minutes.
- Test with a wooden toothpick, if it comes out clean, the cakes are done.
- Transfer the cakes to a wire rack and leave to cool.
- Sieve the icing sugar into a bowl, then slowly stir in the food colouring and boiling water a few drops at a time until you have a thick icing.
- Spoon the icing over the cakes and sprinkle with hundreds and thousands and cake sprinkles.

PREPARATION TIME: 25 MINUTES

COOKING TIME: 15 MINUTES

INGREDIENTS

110 g / 4 oz / ½ cup self-raising flour, sifted
110 g / 4 oz / ½ cup caster (superfine) sugar
110 g / 4 oz / ½ cup butter, softened
2 large eggs
1 tsp vanilla extract

TO DECORATE

225 g / 8 oz / 2 cups icing (confectioners') sugar
red food colouring
boiling water, to mix
coloured sprinkles

Mini Rainbow Cupcakes

30

Use lots of different food colouring and make small amounts of icing in each colour. Drizzle a bit of each coloured icing onto the cupcakes to create a rainbow effect.

31

MAKES 12

Chocolate and Cream Cupcakes

- Preheat the oven to 190°C (170° fan) / 375 F / gas 5 and line a 12-hole cupcake tin with paper cases.
- Combine the flour, cocoa, sugar, butter and eggs in a bowl and whisk together for 2 minutes.
- Divide the mixture between the paper cases, then transfer to the oven and bake for 15 – 20 minutes.
- Test with a wooden toothpick, if it comes out clean, the cakes are done.
- Transfer the cakes to a wire rack and leave to cool.
- Whisk the cream with the icing sugar and vanilla until thick then spoon on top of the cakes.
- Top each cake with a cherry and some chocolate flakes.

PREPARATION TIME: 25 MINUTES

COOKING TIME: 20 MINUTES

INGREDIENTS

110 g / 4 oz / ½ cup self-raising flour, sifted
28 g / 1 oz / ¼ cup unsweetened cocoa powder, sifted
110 g / 4 oz / ½ cup caster (superfine) sugar
110 g / 4 oz / ½ cup butter, softened
2 large eggs

TO DECORATE

225 ml / 8 fl. oz / 1 cup double cream
2 tbsp icing (confectioners') sugar
½ tsp vanilla extract
12 glace cherries
chocolate flakes

Double Chocolate and Cream Cupcakes

32

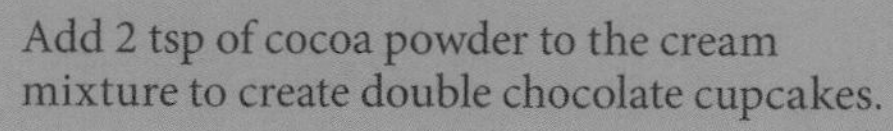

Add 2 tsp of cocoa powder to the cream mixture to create double chocolate cupcakes.

33

MAKES 12

Peanut Butter Cupcakes

PREPARATION TIME: 30 MINUTES

COOKING TIME: 20 MINUTES

INGREDIENTS

110 g / 4 oz / ½ cup self-raising flour, sifted
110 g / 4 oz / ½ cup caster (superfine) sugar
110 g / 4 oz / ½ cup butter, softened
2 large eggs
2 tbsp crunchy peanut butter

TO DECORATE
110 g / 4 oz / ½ cup butter, softened
2 tbsp smooth peanut butter
225 g / 8 oz / 2 cups icing (confectioners') sugar
2 tbsp milk
2 tbsp chopped peanuts

- Preheat the oven to 190°C (170° fan) / 375 F / gas 5 and line a 12-hole cupcake tin with paper cases.
- Combine the flour, sugar, butter, eggs and crunchy peanut butter in a bowl and whisk together for 2 minutes.
- Divide the mixture between the paper cases, then transfer to the oven and bake for 15 – 20 minutes.
- Transfer the cakes to a wire rack and leave to cool.
- To make the buttercream, beat the butter and smooth peanut butter together with a wooden spoon until light and fluffy then beat in the icing sugar a bit at a time.
- Use a whisk to incorporate the milk, then whisk for 2 minutes.
- Spoon the buttercream into a piping bag fitted with a star nozzle and pipe a swirl on top of each cake.
- Sprinkle with chopped peanuts.

Cupcakes with Caramel Sauce

34

Put 2 tbsp each, of: butter, double cream, golden syrup and brown sugar in a pan and boil for 2 minutes, stirring. Leave to cool before drizzling over the iced cakes.

35

MAKES 12

Cinnamon Cupcakes

PREPARATION TIME: 30 MINUTES

COOKING TIME: 20 MINUTES

INGREDIENTS

110 g / 4 oz / ½ cup self-raising flour, sifted
110 g / 4 oz / ½ cup caster (superfine) sugar
110 g / 4 oz / ½ cup butter, softened
2 large eggs
2 tsp ground cinnamon

TO DECORATE
225 ml / 8 fl. oz / 1 cup double (heavy) cream
2 tbsp icing (confectioners') sugar
1 tsp ground cinnamon

- Preheat the oven to 190°C (170° fan) / 375 F / gas 5 and line a 12-hole cupcake tin with paper cases.
- Combine the flour, sugar, butter, eggs and cinnamon in a bowl and whisk together for 2 minutes.
- Divide the mixture between the paper cases, then transfer to the oven and bake for 15 – 20 minutes.
- Test with a wooden toothpick, if it comes out clean, the cakes are done.
- Transfer the cakes to a wire rack and leave to cool.
- To make the topping, whisk the cream with the icing sugar until it forms soft peaks.
- Spoon the whipped cream into a piping bag fitted with a large star nozzle and pipe a swirl on top of each cake.
- Use a small sieve to dust each cake with cinnamon.

Cinnamon Cupcakes in Syrup

36

Put the juice of 2 lemons in a pan with 2 tbsp of caster sugar and 1 tsp of ground cinnamon and heat until the sugar dissolves. Spoon the syrup over the cakes as soon as they come out of the oven.

37

MAKES 12

Blackberry and Raspberry Cupcakes

- Preheat the oven to 180°°C (160° fan) / 350 F / gas 4 and oil 12 muffin tins.
- Beat the egg in a jug with the oil and milk until well mixed.
- Mix the flour, baking powder, sugar, raspberries and blackberries in a bowl, then pour in the egg mixture and stir just enough to combine.
- Divide the mixture between the tins, then bake in the oven for 20 – 25 minutes.
- Test with a wooden toothpick, if it comes out clean, the cakes are done.
- Transfer the cakes to a wire rack and leave to cool completely before dusting with icing sugar.

PREPARATION TIME: 25 MINUTES

COOKING TIME:
20 – 25 MINUTES

INGREDIENTS

1 large egg
120 ml / 4 fl. oz / ½ cup sunflower oil
120 ml / 4 fl. oz / ½ cup milk
375 g / 12 ½ oz / 2 ½ cups self-raising flour, sifted
1 tsp baking powder
200 g / 7 oz / ¾ cup caster (superfine) sugar
75 g / 2 ½ oz / ½ cup raspberries
75 g / 2 ½ oz / ½ cup blackberries

Blackberry and Blueberry Cupcakes

38

Replace the raspberries with the same amount of blueberries.

39

MAKES 24

Wholemeal Almond Mini Cupcakes

- Preheat the oven to 180°C (160° fan) / 350 F / gas 4 and oil a 24-hole silicone mini muffin mould.
- Beat the egg in a jug with the oil, milk and almond essence until well mixed.
- Mix the flour, baking powder, sugar and ground almonds in a bowl, then pour in the egg mixture and stir just enough to combine.
- Divide the mixture between the moulds and sprinkle with chopped almonds, then bake in the oven for 15 – 20 minutes.
- Test with a wooden toothpick, if it comes out clean, the cakes are done.
- Transfer the cakes to a wire rack and leave to cool.

PREPARATION TIME: 25 MINUTES

COOKING TIME: 20 MINUTES

INGREDIENTS

1 large egg
120 ml / 4 fl. oz / ½ cup sunflower oil
120 ml / 4 fl. oz / ½ cup milk
1 tsp almond essence
375 g / 12 ½ oz / 2 ½ cups wholemeal flour
2 tsp baking powder
200 g / 7 oz / ¾ cup caster (superfine) sugar
55 g / 2 oz / ½ cup ground almonds
75 g / 2 ½ oz / ½ cup blanched almonds, chopped

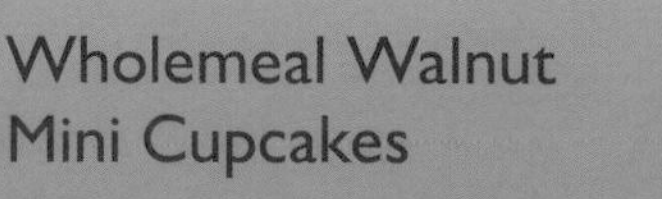

Wholemeal Walnut Mini Cupcakes

40

Replace the almonds with the same amount of crushed walnuts and the almond essence with vanilla essence.

41

MAKES 6

Chocolate and Hazelnut Cupcakes

PREPARATION TIME: 45 MINUTES

COOKING TIME: 25 MINUTES

INGREDIENTS

110 g / 4 oz / ½ cup self-raising flour, sifted
28 g / 1 oz / ¼ cup unsweetened cocoa powder, sifted
110 g / 4 oz / ½ cup caster (superfine) sugar
110 g / 4 oz / ½ cup butter, softened
2 large eggs
110 g / 4 oz / ½ cup chocolate and hazelnut spread

TO DECORATE
whole hazelnuts
summer berries
strawberry and caramel sauce

- Preheat the oven to 190°C (170° fan) / 375 F / gas 5 and oil a 6-hole silicone large cupcake tin
- Combine the flour, cocoa, sugar, butter and eggs in a bowl and whisk together for 2 minutes.
- Divide half of the mixture between the moulds, then add 2 tsp of chocolate spread in the centre of each one.
- Top with the rest of the cake mixture then transfer the mould to the oven and bake for 20 – 25 minutes.
- Serve the cakes warm, garnished with your choice of summer fruits and strawberry sauce or whole hazelnuts and caramel sauce.

Fruity Chocolate and Hazelnut Cupcakes

42

Add 75 g / 2 ½ oz / ½ cup of raisins to the cupcake batter before cooking, to add a fruity flavour.

43

MAKES 12

Strawberry and Rose Cupcakes

PREPARATION TIME: 30 MINUTES

COOKING TIME: 20 MINUTES

INGREDIENTS

110 g / 4 oz / ½ cup self-raising flour, sifted
110 g / 4 oz / ½ cup caster (superfine) sugar
110 g / 4 oz / ½ cup butter, softened
2 large eggs
110 g / 4 oz / ½ cup strawberry jam (jelly)

TO DECORATE
110 g / 4 oz / ½ cup butter, softened
225 g / 8 oz / 2 cups icing (confectioners') sugar
2 tbsp rose water
pink food colouring
flower-shaped cake sprinkles

- Preheat the oven to 190°C (170° fan) / 375 F / gas 5 and line a 12-hole cupcake tin with paper cases.
- Combine the flour, sugar, butter, eggs and strawberry jam in a bowl and whisk together for 2 minutes.
- Divide the mixture between the paper cases, then transfer to the oven and bake for 15 – 20 minutes.
- Test with a wooden toothpick, if it comes out clean, the cakes are done.
- Transfer the cakes to a wire rack and leave to cool.
- To make the buttercream, beat the butter with a wooden spoon until light and fluffy then beat in the icing sugar a quarter at a time.
- Use a whisk to incorporate the rose water and food colouring, then whisk for 2 minutes.
- Spoon the buttercream into a piping bag fitted with a star nozzle and pipe a swirl on top of each cake.
- Sprinkle with flower-shaped cake sprinkles.

Raspberry and Rose Cupcakes

44

To maximise the rose flavour of these cakes, replace the strawberry jam with rose petal jam and decorate with a single fresh rose petal instead of the cake sprinkles.

45

MAKES 12

Mixed Pepper Cupcakes

Mixed Pepper and Pesto Cupcakes

46

Add 2 tbsp of pesto to the mixture before baking.

Cheesy Mixed Pepper Cupcakes

47

Add 5 tbsp of cubed mozzarella to the batter before baking to add a cheesy flavour. Sprinkle with Parmesan before serving.

Courgette and Mixed Pepper Cupcakes

48

Replace one of the peppers with grated courgette to add extra flavour.

PREPARATION TIME 25 MINUTES

COOKING TIME 25 MINUTES

INGREDIENTS

1 red pepper, deseeded and sliced
1 orange pepper, deseeded and sliced
1 green pepper, deseeded and sliced
2 tbsp olive oil
2 large eggs
120 ml / 4 fl. oz / ½ cup sunflower oil
180 ml / 6 fl. oz / ¾ cup Greek yogurt
110 g / 4 oz / 1 cup Parmesan, grated
225 g / 8 oz / 1 ½ cups plain (all purpose) flour
2 tsp baking powder
½ tsp bicarbonate of (baking) soda
½ tsp salt

- Preheat the oven to 180°C (160° fan) / 350 F / gas 4 and line a 12-hole muffin tin with paper cases.
- Fry the peppers in the olive oil for 10 minutes or until soft.
- Beat the egg in a jug with the oil, yogurt and cheese until well mixed then stir in the peppers.
- Mix the flour, raising agents and salt in a bowl, then pour in the egg mixture and stir just enough to combine.
- Divide the mixture between the paper cases, then bake in the oven for 20 – 25 minutes.
- Test with a wooden toothpick, if it comes out clean, the cupcakes are done.
- Serve warm.

90

MAKES 12

Hot Chocolate Cupcakes

PREPARATION TIME: 45 MINUTES

COOKING TIME: 20 MINUTES

INGREDIENTS

110 g / 4 oz / ½ cup self-raising flour, sifted
28 g / 1 oz / ¼ cup unsweetened cocoa powder, sifted
110 g / 4 oz / ½ cup caster (superfine) sugar
110 g / 4 oz / ½ cup butter, softened
2 large eggs
225 g / 8 oz / 1 cup dark chocolate, minimum 60% cocoa solids

TO DECORATE
225 ml / 8 fl. oz / 1 cup double (heavy) cream
2 tbsp icing (confectioners') sugar
Mixed summer berries

- Preheat the oven to 190°C (170° fan) / 375 F / gas 5 and oil 12 small mugs.
- Combine the flour, cocoa, sugar, butter and eggs in a bowl and whisk together for 2 minutes.
- Divide half the mixture between the mugs.
- Break the chocolate into squares and divide between the mugs, then spoon the rest of the cake mixture on top.
- Sit the mugs on a baking tray and bake in the oven for 15 – 20 minutes.
- Test with a wooden toothpick, if it comes out clean, the cakes are done.
- While the cakes are cooking, make the topping. Whisk the cream with the icing sugar until thick and spoon into a piping bag fitted with a large star nozzle.
- When the cakes are ready, pipe a swirl of cream on top and scatter over a few summer berries.

Marshmallow Hot Chocolate Cupcakes

91

For an extra indulgent treat, replace the berries with marshmallows and finish with a dusting of cocoa powder.

92

MAKES 12

Bacon Cupcakes

PREPARATION TIME: 25 MINUTES

COOKING TIME: 25 MINUTES

INGREDIENTS

12 rashers of bacon
2 large eggs
120 ml / 4 fl. oz / ½ cup sunflower oil
180 ml / 6 fl. oz / ¾ cup Greek yogurt
110 g / 4 oz / 1 cup Parmesan, grated
225 g / 8 oz / 1 ½ cups plain (all purpose) flour
2 tsp baking powder
½ tsp bicarbonate of (baking) soda
½ tsp salt

TO DECORATE
225 g / 8 oz / 1 cup cream cheese
12 little gem lettuce leaves
4 rashers of bacon, chopped and fried
1 tbsp balsamic glaze

- Preheat the oven to 180°C (160° fan) / 350 F / gas 4 and oil a 12-hole silicone muffin mould.
- Cut a long strip down one side of each bacon rasher and use them to line the inside of the cupcakes moulds.
- Chop the rest of the bacon.
- Beat the egg in a jug with the oil, yoghurt, cheese and chopped bacon until well mixed.
- Mix the flour, raising agents and salt in a bowl, then pour in the egg mixture and stir to combine.
- Divide the mixture between the moulds, then bake in the oven for 20 – 25 minutes.
- Transfer the cupcakes to a wire rack and leave to cool.
- Spoon the cream cheese into a piping bag fitted with a large star nozzle and pipe a swirl on top of each muffin.
- Top with a little gem leaf, fill with bacon pieces and drizzle with balsamic glaze.

Sour Cream and Bacon Cupcakes

Add a spoonful of soured cream to the top of each cupcake and sprinkle with chopped pistachios.

94

MAKES 12

Colourful Cupcakes

- Preheat the oven to 190°C (170° fan) / 375 F / gas 5 and line a 12-hole cupcake tin with paper cases.
- Combine the flour, sugar, butter, eggs and vanilla extract in a bowl and whisk together for 2 minutes.
- Divide the mixture between the paper cases, then transfer to the oven and bake for 15 – 20 minutes.
- Test with a wooden toothpick, if it comes out clean, the cakes are done.
- Transfer the cakes to a wire rack and leave to cool.
- Sift the icing sugar into a bowl, then slowly stir in the boiling water a few drops at a time until you have a thick icing.
- Divide the icing into 3 bowls and colour each with a different food colouring.
- Ice 4 cakes with each of the coloured icings, then sprinkle with your choice of toppings.

Rainbow Cupcakes

95

To make these cakes even more colourful, divide the cake mixture before it is cooked into 3 bowls and colour each one with a different food colouring.

PREPARATION TIME: 45 MINUTES

COOKING TIME: 20 MINUTES

INGREDIENTS

110 g / 4 oz / ½ cup self-raising flour, sifted
110 g / 4 oz / ½ cup caster (superfine) sugar
110 g / 4 oz / ½ cup butter, softened
2 large eggs
1 tsp vanilla extract

TO DECORATE
225 g / 8 oz / 2 cups icing (confectioners') sugar
boiling water, to mix
yellow, pink and green food colouring
coloured sprinkles
small sweets

96

MAKES 24

Sun-dried Tomato and Brie Mini Cupcakes

- Preheat the oven to 180°C (160° fan) / 350 F / gas 4 and oil a 24-hole silicone muffin tin.
- Beat the egg in a jug with the oil, yoghurt, tomatoes and cheese until well mixed.
- Mix the flour, raising agents, salt and herbs in a bowl, then pour in the egg mixture and stir just enough to combine.
- Divide the mixture between the moulds, then bake in the oven for 10 – 15 minutes.
- Test with a wooden toothpick, if it comes out clean, the cupcakes are done.
- Serve warm.

Tomato, Brie and Pesto Cupcakes

Marble 4 tbsp of pesto through the muffin mix before filling the moulds.

PREPARATION TIME: 25 MINUTES

COOKING TIME: 15 MINUTES

INGREDIENTS

2 large eggs
120 ml / 4 fl. oz / ½ cup sunflower oil
180 ml / 6 fl. oz / ¾ cup Greek yogurt
75 g / 2 ½ oz / ½ cup sundried tomatoes, chopped
110 g / 4 oz / 1 cup Brie, cubed
225 g / 8 oz / 1 ½ cups plain (all purpose) flour
2 tsp baking powder
½ tsp bicarbonate of (baking) soda
½ tsp salt
2 tsp dried herbs de Provence

98

MAKES 12

Polka Dot Cupcakes

PREPARATION TIME: 45 MINUTES

COOKING TIME: 20 MINUTES

INGREDIENTS

110 g / 4 oz / ½ cup self-raising flour, sifted
110 g / 4 oz / ½ cup caster (superfine) sugar
110 g / 4 oz / ½ cup butter, softened
2 large eggs
1 tsp vanilla extract

TO DECORATE
225 g / 8 oz / 2 cups icing (confectioners') sugar
boiling water, to mix
white cake sprinkles

- Preheat the oven to 190°C (170° fan) / 375 F / gas 5 and line a 12-hole cupcake tin with paper cases.
- Combine the flour, sugar, butter, eggs and vanilla extract in a bowl and whisk together for 2 minutes.
- Divide the mixture between the paper cases, then transfer to the oven and bake for 15 – 20 minutes.
- Test with a wooden toothpick, if it comes out clean, the cakes are done.
- Transfer the cakes to a wire rack and leave to cool.
- Sift the icing sugar into a bowl, then slowly stir in the boiling water a few drops at a time until you have a thick icing.
- Spoon the icing onto the cakes then scatter over the cake sprinkles.

Colourful Dotty Cupcakes

99

Spread the icing to the edge of the cakes and dip the tops of them in colourful sprinkles, for maximum coverage.

100

MAKES 36

Mini Sweetie Cupcakes

PREPARATION TIME: 30 MINUTES

COOKING TIME: 15 MINUTES

INGREDIENTS

110 g / 4 oz / ½ cup self-raising flour, sifted
110 g / 4 oz / ½ cup caster (superfine) sugar
110 g / 4 oz / ½ cup butter, softened
2 large eggs
1 tsp vanilla extract

TO DECORATE
225 g / 8 oz / 2 cups icing (confectioners') sugar
boiling water, to mix
1 tube of sweets

- Preheat the oven to 190°C (170° fan) / 375 F / gas 5 and line a 36 hole mini cupcake tin with paper cases.
- Combine the flour, sugar, butter, eggs and vanilla extract in a bowl and whisk together for 2 minutes.
- Divide the mixture between the paper cases, then transfer to the oven and bake for 10 – 15 minutes.
- Test with a wooden toothpick, if it comes out clean, the cakes are done.
- Transfer the cakes to a wire rack and leave to cool.
- Sift the icing sugar into a bowl, then slowly stir in the boiling water a few drops at a time until you have a thin icing.
- Dip the top of the cakes in the icing and decorate with the sweets.

Mini Sweetie and Buttercream Cupcakes

101

Pipe the top with a small rosette of buttercream before decorating with the sweets.

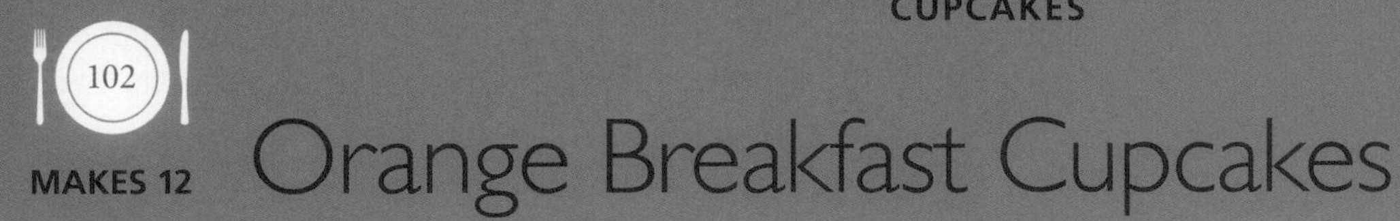

102

MAKES 12

Orange Breakfast Cupcakes

Orange and Muesli Cupcakes

103

Add 75 g / 3 oz / ⅓ cup of your favourite muesli to the mixture for extra crunch.

Lemon and Muesli Cupcakes

104

Add 75 g / 3 oz / ⅓ cup of muesli to the mixture for extra crunch and replace the orange with a lemon.

PREPARATION TIME: 25 MINUTES

COOKING TIME: 25 MINUTES

INGREDIENTS

1 large egg
120 ml / 4 fl. oz / ½ cup sunflower oil
120 ml / 4 fl. oz / ½ cup milk
1 orange, juiced
375 g / 12 ½ oz / 2 ½ cups self-raising flour, sifted
1 tsp baking powder
200 g / 7 oz / ¾ cup caster (superfine) sugar
1 orange, zest finely pared

- Preheat the oven to 180°C (160° fan) / 350 F / gas 4 and oil a 12-hole silicone muffin tin.
- Beat the egg in a jug with the oil, milk and orange juice until well mixed.
- Mix the flour, baking powder, sugar and orange zest in a bowl, then pour in the egg mixture and stir just enough to combine.
- Divide the mixture between the moulds, then bake in the oven for 20 – 25 minutes.
- Test with a wooden toothpick, if it comes out clean, the cakes are done.
- Transfer the cakes to a wire rack and leave to cool.

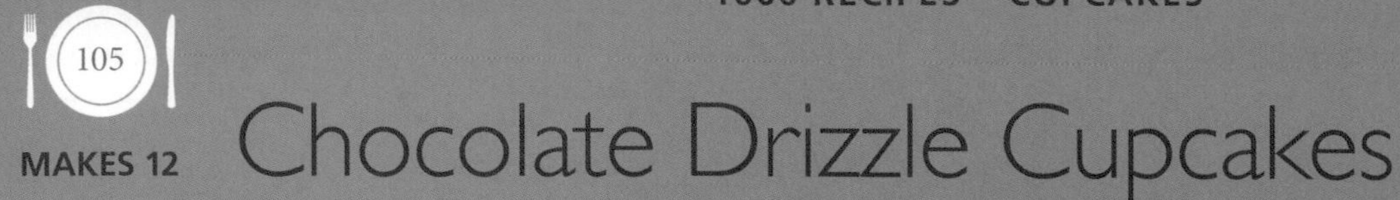

105

MAKES 12

Chocolate Drizzle Cupcakes

PREPARATION TIME: 25 MINUTES

COOKING TIME: 25 MINUTES

INGREDIENTS

1 large egg
120 ml / 4 fl. oz / ½ cup sunflower oil
120 ml / 4 fl. oz / ½ cup milk
375 g / 12 ½ oz / 2 ½ cups self-raising flour, sifted
55 g / 2 oz / ½ cup cocoa powder, sifted
1 tsp baking powder
200 g / 7 oz / ¾ cup caster (superfine) sugar
110 g / 4 oz / ½ cup dark chocolate, chopped

TO DECORATE
225 g / 8 oz / 2 cups icing (confectioners') sugar
28 g / 1 oz / ¼ cup unsweetened cocoa powder, sifted
boiling water, to mix

- Preheat the oven to 180°C (160° fan) / 350 F / gas 4 and line a 12-hole muffin tin with paper cases.
- Beat the egg in a jug with the oil and milk until well mixed.
- Mix the flour, cocoa, baking powder, sugar and chocolate in a bowl, then pour in the egg mixture and stir just enough to combine.
- Divide the mixture between the paper cases, then bake in the oven for 20 – 25 minutes.
- Test with a wooden toothpick, if it comes out clean, the cakes are done.
- Transfer the cakes to a wire rack and leave to cool.
- Sift the icing sugar and cocoa into a bowl, then slowly stir in the boiling water a few drops at a time until you have a thin icing.
- Drizzle the icing over the cupcakes.

106

Almond and Chocolate Drizzle Cupcakes

Add 55 g / 2 oz of chopped almonds to the cupcake batter.

107

Walnut and Chocolate Drizzle Cupcakes

Add 55 g / 2 oz of chopped walnuts to the cupcake batter.

108

Raisin and Chocolate Drizzle Cupcakes

Add 75 g / 3 oz of raisins to the cupcake batter.

109

MAKES 24

Mini Pumpkin Cupcakes

- Preheat the oven to 180°C (160° fan) / 350 F / gas 4 and line a 24-hole muffin tin with paper cases.
- Beat the egg in a jug with the oil, yoghurt, pumpkin and cheese until well mixed.
- Mix the flour, raising agents and salt in a bowl, then pour in the egg mixture and stir just enough to combine.
- Divide the mixture between the paper cases and sprinkle with pumpkin seeds, then bake in the oven for 10 – 15 minutes.
- Test with a wooden toothpick, if it comes out clean, the cupcakes are done.
- Serve warm.

PREPARATION TIME: 25 MINUTES

COOKING TIME: 15 MINUTES

INGREDIENTS

2 large eggs
120ml / 4 fl. oz / ½ cup sunflower oil
180ml / 6 fl. oz / ¾ cup Greek yogurt
150 g / 5 oz pumpkin, coarsely grated
110 g / 4 oz / 1 cup Parmesan, grated
225 g / 8 oz / 1 ½ cups plain (all purpose) flour
2 tsp baking powder
½ tsp bicarbonate of (baking) soda
½ tsp salt
2 tbsp pumpkin seeds

110

Pumpkin and Sage Mini Cupcakes

Add 2 tbsp of chopped fresh sage to the mixture before baking.

111

MAKES 24

Ginger Cupcakes

- Preheat the oven to 190°C (170° fan) / 375 F / gas 5 and oil 24 small dariole moulds.
- Sieve the flour, bicarbonate of soda and ground ginger together into a bowl.
- Put the golden syrup, butter, brown sugar and stem ginger in a small saucepan and boil gently for 2 minutes, stirring to dissolve the sugar.
- Pour the butter and sugar mixture onto the flour with the eggs and milk and fold it all together until smooth.
- Divide the mixture between the dariole moulds, then sit them on a baking tray and bake in the oven for 20 – 25 minutes.
- Transfer the cakes to a wire rack and leave to cool.
- Top each cake with a piece of crystallised ginger.

PREPARATION TIME: 20 MINUTES

COOKING TIME: 20 MINUTES

INGREDIENTS

250 g / 9 oz / 1 ¼ cups self-raising flour
1 tsp bicarbonate of (baking) soda
2 tsp ground ginger
200 g / 8 ½ oz / ½ cup golden syrup
125 g / 4 ½ oz / ½ cup butter
125 g / 4 ½ oz / ¾ cup light brown sugar
4 pieces stem ginger, chopped
2 large eggs, beaten
240 ml / 8 fl. oz / 1 cup milk
24 pieces crystallised ginger

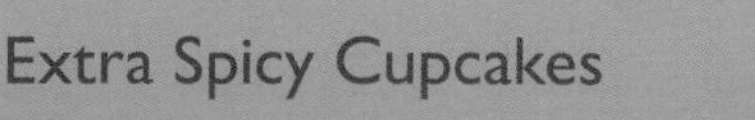

Extra Spicy Cupcakes

Add 1 tsp mixed spice and 1 tsp ground cinnamon to the cake mixture with the ground ginger.

113

MAKES 12

Baby Boy Cupcakes

PREPARATION TIME: 45 MINUTES

COOKING TIME: 20 MINUTES

INGREDIENTS

110 g / 4 oz / 1 cup self-raising flour
110 g / 4 oz / ½ cup caster sugar
110 g / 4 oz / ½ cup butter, softened
2 large eggs
1 tsp vanilla extract

TO DECORATE

110 g / 4 oz / ½ cup butter, softened
225 g / 8 oz / 2 cups icing sugar
2 tbsp milk
1 tsp vanilla extract
edible glitter
110 g / 4 oz / ½ cup ready-to-roll fondant icing
blue food colouring

- Preheat the oven to 190°C (170° fan) / 375 F / gas 5 and line a 12-hole cupcake tin with blue paper cases.
- Combine the flour, sugar, butter, eggs and vanilla extract in a bowl and whisk together for 2 minutes.
- Divide the mixture between the paper cases, then bake for 15 – 20 minutes. Transfer to a wire rack to cool.
- Beat the butter with a wooden spoon until light and fluffy then beat in the icing sugar. Use a whisk to incorporate the milk and vanilla extract, then whisk for 2 minutes.
- Spoon the buttercream into a piping bag fitted with a star nozzle and pipe a swirl on top of each cake.
- Sprinkle with edible glitter. To make the blue baby feet, knead the fondant icing with a little blue food colouring until pliable and evenly coloured.
- Make a flattened pear shape for each foot and 5 little balls to make the toes. Assemble two feet on the top of each cake, attaching the toes with a little water.

114

MAKES 12

Honey and Almond Cupcakes

PREPARATION TIME: 25 MINUTES

COOKING TIME: 20 MINUTES

INGREDIENTS

55 g / 2 oz / ½ cup self-raising flour
55 g / 2 oz / ½ cup ground almonds
55 g / 2 oz / ¼ cup caster sugar
110 g / 4 oz / ½ cup honey
110 g / 4 oz / ½ cup butter, softened
2 large eggs
1 tsp almond essence

TO DECORATE

Icing sugar for dusting
6 strawberries, halved
12 raspberries

- Preheat the oven to 190°C (170° fan) / 375 F / gas 5 and line a 12-hole cupcake tin with paper cases.
- Combine the flour, ground almonds, sugar, honey, butter, eggs and almond essence in a bowl and whisk together for 2 minutes.
- Divide the mixture between the paper cases, then transfer to the oven and bake for 15 – 20 minutes.
- Test with a wooden toothpick, if it comes out clean, the cakes are done.
- Transfer the cakes to a wire rack to cool.
- Dust the cakes with icing sugar then top each one with half a strawberry and a raspberry.

115

MAKES 12

Purple Party Cupcakes

PREPARATION TIME: 30 MINUTES

COOKING TIME: 20 MINUTES

INGREDIENTS

110 g / 4 oz / ½ cup self-raising flour
110 g / 4 oz / ½ cup caster sugar
110 g / 4 oz / ½ cup butter, softened
2 large eggs
1 tsp vanilla extract
175 g / 6 oz fresh blueberries

TO DECORATE

110 g / 4 oz / ½ cup butter, softened
225 g / 8 oz / 2 cups icing sugar
2 tbsp milk
5 drops purple food colouring
edible glitter
silver balls

- Preheat the oven to 190°C (170° fan) / 375 F / gas 5 and line a 12-hole cupcake tin with paper cases.
- Combine the flour, sugar, butter, eggs and vanilla extract in a bowl and whisk together for 2 minutes.
- Fold in the blueberries and divide the mixture between the paper cases.
- Transfer the tin to the oven and bake for 15 – 20 minutes.
- Transfer the cakes to a wire rack and leave to cool.
- Beat the butter with a wooden spoon until light and fluffy then beat in the icing sugar.
- Use a whisk to incorporate the milk and food colouring, then whisk for 2 minutes.
- Spoon the buttercream into a piping bag fitted with a star nozzle and pipe a swirl on top of each cake.
- Sprinkle with edible glitter and silver balls and top with plastic cake novelties of your choice.

116

MAKES 12

Pink Iced Vanilla Cupcakes

- Preheat the oven to 190°C (170° fan) / 375 F / gas 5 and line a 12-hole cupcake tin with paper cases.
- Combine the flour, sugar, butter, eggs and vanilla extract in a bowl and whisk together for 2 minutes.
- Divide the mixture between the paper cases, then transfer to the oven and bake for 15 – 20 minutes.
- Transfer the cakes to a wire rack and leave to cool.
- Sieve the icing sugar into a bowl, then slowly stir in the boiling water a few drops at a time until you have a thick icing.
- Stir in the food colouring a drop at a time until you reach your desired colour.
- Spoon the icing onto the cakes and swirl with the back of the spoon.
- Scatter over the cake sprinkles.

PREPARATION TIME: 25 MINUTES

COOKING TIME: 20 MINUTES

INGREDIENTS

110 g / 4 oz / ½ cup self-raising flour, sifted
110 g / 4 oz / ½ cup caster (superfine) sugar
110 g / 4 oz / ½ cup butter, softened
2 large eggs
1 tsp vanilla extract

TO DECORATE

225 g / 8 oz / 2 cups icing (confectioners') sugar
boiling water, to mix
pink food colouring
pink heart-shaped cake sprinkles

Pink Iced Almond Cupcakes

117

Replace the vanilla extract with almond extract and top with flaked almonds instead of heart-shaped sprinkles.

118

MAKES 12

Sugar Nib Cupcakes

- Preheat the oven to 190°C (170° fan) / 375 F / gas 5 and line a 12-hole cupcake tin with paper cases.
- Combine the flour, sugar, butter, eggs and vanilla extract in a bowl and whisk together for 2 minutes.
- Divide the mixture between the paper cases.
- Sprinkle with sugar nibs.
- Transfer the tin to the oven and bake for 15 – 20 minutes.
- Test with a wooden toothpick, if it comes out clean, the cakes are done.
- Transfer the cakes to a wire rack and leave to cool.

PREPARATION TIME: 25 MINUTES

COOKING TIME: 20 MINUTES

INGREDIENTS

110 g / 4 oz / 1 cup self-raising flour, sifted
110 g / 4 oz / ½ cup caster (superfine) sugar
110 g / 4 oz / ½ cup butter, softened
2 large eggs
1 tsp vanilla extract
55 g / 2 oz sugar nibs

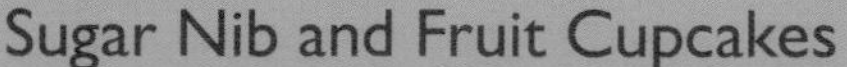

Sugar Nib and Fruit Cupcakes

119

Add 75 g / 3 oz of dried fruit to the cupcake batter, before baking.

120

MAKES 12

Almond and Rose Cupcakes

PREPARATION TIME: 20 MINUTES

COOKING TIME: 20 MINUTES

INGREDIENTS

55 g / 2 oz / ½ cup self-raising flour, sifted
55 g / 2 oz / ½ cup ground almonds
110 g / 4 oz / ½ cup caster (superfine) sugar
110 g / 4 oz / ½ cup butter, softened
2 large eggs
1 tsp rose water
1 tsp almond essence

TO DECORATE

225 g / 8 oz / 2 cups icing (confectioners') sugar
1 – 2 tsp rose water
3 drops pink food colouring
12 Icing roses
Pink silver balls

- Preheat the oven to 190°C (170° fan) / 375 F / gas 5 and line a 12-hole cupcake tin with paper cases.
- Combine the flour, ground almonds, sugar, butter, eggs, rose water and almond essence in a bowl and whisk together for 2 minutes.
- Divide the mixture between the paper cases, then transfer to the oven and bake for 15 – 20 minutes.
- Test with a wooden toothpick, if it comes out clean, the cakes are done.
- Transfer the cakes to a wire rack and leave to cool.
- Sieve the icing sugar into a bowl, then slowly stir in the rose water a few drops until you have a thick icing.
- Spoon the icing onto the cakes and decorate with icing roses and silver balls.

Orange Flower Water Cupcakes

121

These cakes work really well with orange flower water instead of rose water.

122

MAKES 12

Parmesan and Poppy Seed Cupcakes

PREPARATION TIME: 25 MINUTES

COOKING TIME: 25 MINUTES

INGREDIENTS

2 large eggs
120 ml / 4 fl. oz / ½ cup sunflower oil
180 ml / 6 fl. oz / ¾ cup Greek yogurt
110 g / 4 oz / 1 cup Parmesan, grated
225 g / 8 oz / 1 ½ cups plain (all purpose) flour
2 tsp baking powder
½ tsp bicarbonate of (baking) soda
½ tsp salt
2 tbsp poppy seeds

- Preheat the oven to 180°C (160° fan) / 350 F / gas 4 and line a 12-hole muffin tin with paper cases.
- Beat the egg in a jug with the oil, yoghurt and cheese until well mixed.
- Mix the flour, raising agents, salt and poppy seeds in a bowl, then pour in the egg mixture and stir just enough to combine.
- Divide the mixture between the paper cases, then bake in the oven for 20 – 25 minutes.
- Test with a wooden toothpick, if it comes out clean, the cupcakes are done.
- Serve warm.

Mixed Seed Cupcakes

Add 2 tbsp of pumpkin seeds and 2 tbsp of sunflower seeds for savoury mixed seed cupcakes.

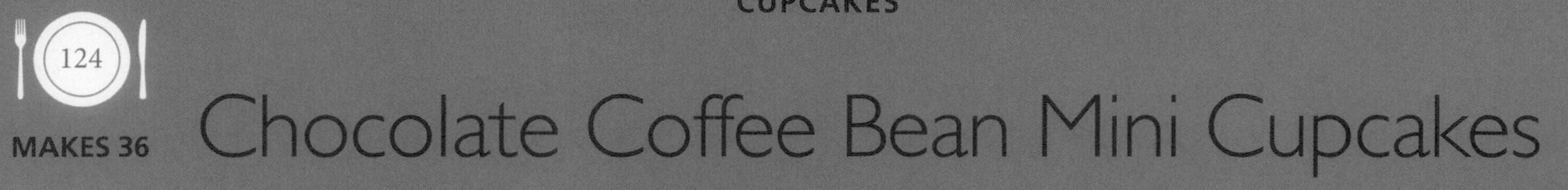

124

MAKES 36

Chocolate Coffee Bean Mini Cupcakes

White Chocolate Coffee Bean Cupcakes

125

Replace the chocolate coated coffee beans with white chocolate coated coffee beans.

PREPARATION TIME: 20 MINUTES

COOKING TIME: 15 MINUTES

INGREDIENTS

110 g / 4 oz / ½ cup self-raising flour, sifted
110 g / 4 oz / ½ cup caster (superfine) sugar
110 g / 4 oz / ½ cup butter, softened
2 large eggs
1 tsp vanilla extract
150 g / 5 oz / 1 cup chocolate coated coffee beans, chopped

TO DECORATE
36 chocolate coated coffee beans

- Preheat the oven to 190°C (170° fan) / 375 F / gas 5 and line a 36-hole mini cupcake tin with paper cases.
- Combine the flour, sugar, butter and eggs in a bowl and whisk together for 2 minutes.
- Fold in the chopped coffee beans then divide the mixture between the cases.
- Transfer the tin to the oven and bake for 15 – 20 minutes.
- Test with a wooden toothpick, if it comes out clean, the cakes are done.
- Transfer the cakes to a wire rack and leave to cool completely before topping each cake with a whole coffee bean.

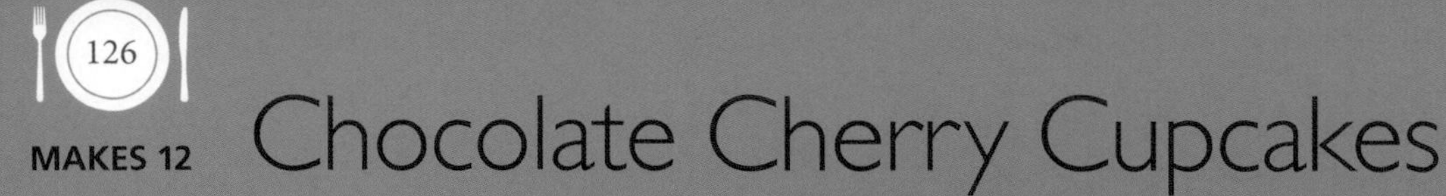

126

MAKES 12

Chocolate Cherry Cupcakes

PREPARATION TIME: 25 MINUTES

COOKING TIME: 20 MINUTES

INGREDIENTS

2 tbsp unsweetened cocoa powder
150 g / 6 oz / ⅔ cup dark chocolate, chopped
150 g / 6 oz / ⅔ cup butter, chopped
85 g / 3 oz / ⅓ cup caster (superfine) sugar
3 large eggs
3 egg yolks
1 tbsp plain (all purpose) flour
150 g / 5 oz / 1 cup black cherries in syrup, drained

TO DECORATE
12 black cherries in syrup, drained
Icing (confectioners') sugar to dust

- Line a 12-hole cupcake tin with paper cases.
- Melt the chocolate, butter and sugar together in a saucepan, stirring to dissolve the sugar.
- Leave to cool a little then beat in the eggs and egg yolks and fold in the flour.
- Divide half the mixture between the cake cases, and top with the black cherries.
- Top with the rest of the cake mixture then chill for 30 minutes.
- Preheat the oven to 180°C (160° fan) / 350 F / gas 4.
- Bake the cupcakes for 8 minutes then leave them to cool for 2 minutes before decorating each one with a whole black cherry and a dusting of icing sugar.

127

Chocolate, Cherry and Orange Cupcakes

Add the finely grated zest of an orange to the cake mixture.

128

Chocolate, Cherry and Lemon Cupcakes

Add the finely grated zest of a lemon to the cake mixture.

129

MAKES 24

Hazelnut and Pistachio Mini Cupcakes

- Preheat the oven to 190°C (170° fan) / 375 F / gas 5 and line a 24-hole mini cupcake tin with paper cases.
- Combine the flour, sugar, butter and eggs in a bowl and whisk together for 2 minutes.
- Divide the mixture between the paper cases and sprinkle liberally with the chopped nuts, then transfer to the oven and bake for 10 – 15 minutes.
- Test with a wooden toothpick, if it comes out clean, the cakes are done.
- While the cakes are cooking, make the soaking syrup. Put the honey and water in a small saucepan and boil for 2 minutes.
- When the cakes are ready, spoon over the soaking syrup and leave them to cool in their tin.

PREPARATION TIME: 35 MINUTES

COOKING TIME: 15 MINUTES

INGREDIENTS

110 g / 4 oz / 1 cup self-raising flour, sifted
110 g / 4 oz / ½ cup caster (superfine) sugar
110 g / 4 oz / ½ cup butter, softened
2 large eggs
75 g / 2 ½ oz / ½ cup hazelnuts (cobnuts), chopped
75 g / 2 ½ oz / ½ cup pistachio nuts, chopped

FOR THE SOAKING SYRUP
3 tbsp honey
2 tbsp water

Cupcakes with Spicy Syrup

130

To spice up the soaking syrup, add ½ tsp each of ground cinnamon and mixed spice.

131

MAKES 12

Orange Blossom Cupcakes

- Preheat the oven to 190°C (170° fan) / 375 F / gas 5 and line a 12-hole cupcake tin with paper cases.
- Combine the flour, sugar, butter, eggs and orange zest in a bowl and whisk together for 2 minutes.
- Divide the mixture between the paper cases and press an orange blossom flower face down into the top of each cake.
- Transfer the tin to the oven and bake for 15 – 20 minutes.
- While the cakes are cooking, make the soaking syrup. Put the lemon juice and caster sugar in a small saucepan and boil for 2 minutes, then turn off the heat and stir in the orange blossom water.
- When the cakes are ready, spoon over the soaking syrup and leave them to cool in their tin.

PREPARATION TIME: 1 HOUR

COOKING TIME: 20 MINUTES

INGREDIENTS

110 g / 4 oz / ½ cup self-raising flour, sifted
110 g / 4 oz / ½ cup caster (superfine) sugar
110 g / 4 oz / ½ cup butter, softened
2 large eggs
1 orange, zest finely grated
12 orange blossom flowers

FOR THE SOAKING SYRUP
1 lemon, juiced
2 tbsp caster (superfine) sugar
2 tsp orange blossom water

Cupcakes with Orange Blossom Syllabub

Whip 300ml / 10 fl. oz of double cream with 1 tsp orange blossom water and 1 tbsp orange liqueur until thick and ice the cupcakes.

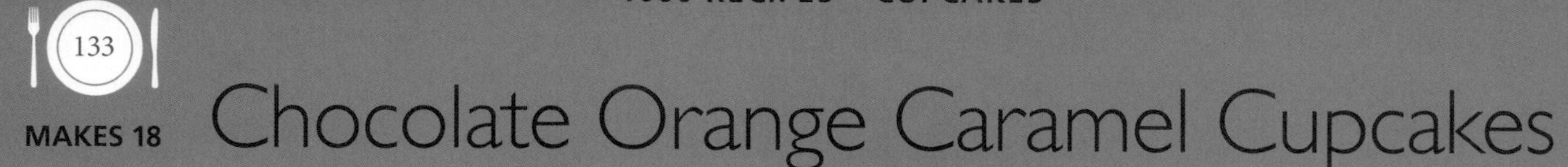

133

MAKES 18

Chocolate Orange Caramel Cupcakes

Chocolate and Fruit Caramel Cupcakes

134

Add 75 g / 3 oz of raisins to the cupcake batter.

Chocolate and Nut Caramel Cupcakes

135

Add 55 g / 2 oz of flaked almonds to the cupcake batter.

PREPARATION TIME: 40 MINUTE

COOKING TIME: 20 MINUTES

INGREDIENTS

110 g / 4 oz / ½ cup self-raising flour, sifted
28 g / 1 oz / ¼ cup unsweetened cocoa powder, sifted
110 g / 4 oz / ½ cup caster (superfine) sugar
110 g / 4 oz / ½ cup butter, softened
2 large eggs
1 orange, zest finely grated
Icing (confectioners') sugar, to dust

TO DECORATE
85 g / 3 oz / ½ cup butter
85 ml / 3 fl. oz / ⅓ cup double (heavy) cream
85 g / 3 oz / ¼ cup golden syrup
85 g / 3 oz / ½ cup dark brown sugar
2 chocolate flakes

- Preheat the oven to 190°C (170° fan) / 375 F / gas 5 and oil a 12-hole silicone cupcake mould.
- Combine the flour, cocoa, sugar, butter, eggs and orange zest in a bowl and whisk together for 2 minutes.
- Divide the mixture between the moulds, then transfer to the oven and bake for 15 – 20 minutes.
- Test with a wooden toothpick, if it comes out clean, the cakes are done.
- Transfer the cakes to a wire rack and leave to cool completely before dusting with icing sugar.
- Put the butter, cream, golden syrup and brown sugar in a small saucepan and boil for 2 minutes, stirring to dissolve the sugar.
- Leave to cool to room temperature, then spoon over the cupcakes and crumble over the chocolate flakes.

136

MAKES 12

Marmalade Cupcakes

Marmalade and Dark Chocolate Cupcakes

137

Add 110g / 4oz / ½ cup of dark chocolate chunks to the cupcake mixture for a chocolate orange taste.

Lime Marmalade Cupcakes

138

Replace the orange marmalade with lime marmalade for an extra citrus twist.

PREPARATION TIME: 25 MINUTES

COOKING TIME: 25 MINUTES

INGREDIENTS

1 large egg
120 ml / 4 fl. oz / ½ cup sunflower oil
120 ml / 4 fl. oz / ½ cup milk
375 g / 12 ½ oz / 2 ½ cups self-raising flour, sifted
1 tsp baking powder
200 g / 7 oz / ¾ cup caster (superfine) sugar
110 g / 4 oz / ½ cup marmalade

- Preheat the oven to 180°C (160° fan) / 350 F / gas 4 and oil a 12-hole silicone muffin tin.
- Beat the egg in a jug with the oil and milk until well mixed.
- Mix the flour, baking powder and sugar in a bowl, then pour in the egg mixture and stir just enough to combine.
- Divide half the mixture between the paper cases and add a big spoonful of marmalade on top.
- Top with the rest of the muffin mixture then bake in the oven for 20 – 25 minutes.
- Test with a wooden toothpick, if it comes out clean, the cakes are done.
- Transfer the cakes to a wire rack and leave to cool.

139

MAKES 12

Apricot Cupcakes

Apricot Cupcakes with Icing

140

Make a simple white icing from icing sugar mixed with a little boiling water and pipe it across the cakes in a zigzag motion.

Peach Cupcakes

141

Replace the apricot halves with peach halves.

PREPARATION TIME: 25 MINUTES

COOKING TIME: 20 MINUTES

INGREDIENTS

110 g / 4 oz / ½ cup self-raising flour, sifted
110 g / 4 oz / ½ cup caster (superfine) sugar
110 g / 4 oz / ½ cup butter, softened
2 large eggs
1 tsp vanilla extract
12 canned apricot halves, drained

- Preheat the oven to 190°C (170° fan) / 375 F / gas 5 and line a 12-hole cupcake tin with paper cases.
- Combine the flour, sugar, butter, eggs and vanilla extract in a bowl and whisk together for 2 minutes.
- Divide the mixture between the paper cases and press half an apricot into the top of each cake, then transfer to the oven and bake for 15 – 20 minutes.
- Test with a wooden toothpick, if it comes out clean, the cakes are done.
- Transfer the cakes to a wire rack and leave to cool.

142

MAKES 6

Chocolate and Walnut Cupcakes

- Melt the chocolate, butter and sugar together in a saucepan, stirring to dissolve the sugar.
- Leave to cool a little then beat in the eggs and egg yolks and fold in the flour and chopped walnuts.
- Divide the mixture between 6 deep cupcake cases, then chill them for 30 minutes.
- Preheat the oven to 180°C (160° fan) / 350 F / gas 4 and put a baking tray in to heat.
- Transfer the cupcakes to the heated baking tray and bake in the oven for 8 minutes.
- Leave to cool for 10 minutes then serve warm.

PREPARATION TIME: 50 MINUTES

COOKING TIME: 8 MINUTES

INGREDIENTS

2 tbsp unsweetened cocoa powder
150 g / 6 oz / ⅔ cup dark chocolate, minimum 60% cocoa solids, chopped
150 g / 6 oz / ⅔ cup butter, chopped
85 g / 3 oz / ⅓ cup caster (superfine) sugar
3 large eggs
3 egg yolks
1 tbsp plain (all purpose) flour
75 g / 2 ½ oz / ½ cup walnuts, chopped

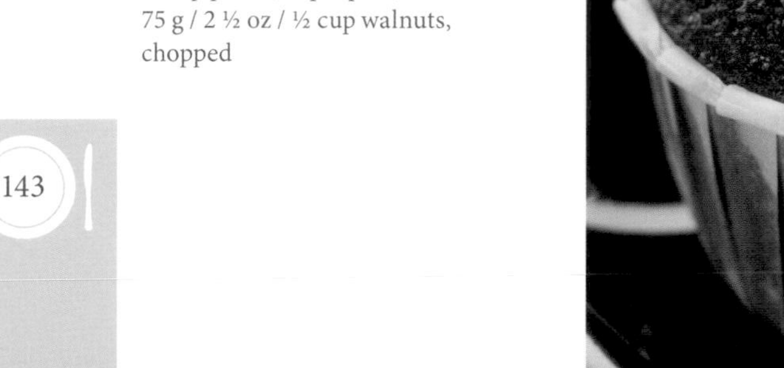

Chocolate and Pistachio Cupcakes

143

Replace the walnuts for the same amount of chopped pistachios.

144

MAKES 18

Lemon and Poppy Seed Cupcakes

- Preheat the oven to 190°C (170° fan) / 375 F / gas 5 and line a 12-hole cupcake tin with paper cases.
- Combine the flour, sugar, butter, eggs, lemon zest and poppy seeds in a bowl and whisk together for 2 minutes.
- Divide the mixture between the paper cases, then transfer to the oven and bake for 15 – 20 minutes.
- Test with a wooden toothpick, if it comes out clean, the cakes are done.
- Transfer the cakes to a wire rack and leave to cool.
- To make the icing, sieve the icing sugar into a bowl and stir in the lemon juice a little at a time until you have a thick pouring consistency.
- Drizzle the icing over the cakes and top with shreds of lemon zest.

PREPARATION TIME: 1 HOUR

COOKING TIME: 20 MINUTES

INGREDIENTS

110 g / 4 oz / ½ cup self-raising flour, sifted
110 g / 4 oz / ½ cup caster (superfine) sugar
110 g / 4 oz / ½ cup butter, softened
2 large eggs
1 lemon, zest finely grated
1 tbsp poppy seeds

TO DECORATE

225 g / 8 oz / 2 cups icing (confectioners') sugar
2-4 tsp lemon juice
1 lemon, zest finely pared

Orange and Poppy Seed Cupcakes

145

Replace the lemon zest with orange zest and instead of using lemon juice in the icing, use orange liqueur.

146

MAKES 12

Lavender Cupcakes

PREPARATION TIME: 25 MINUTES

COOKING TIME: 20 MINUTES

INGREDIENTS

110 g / 4 oz / ½ cup self-raising flour, sifted
110 g / 4 oz / ½ cup caster (superfine) sugar
110 g / 4 oz / ½ cup butter, softened
2 large eggs
5 drops lavender oil

TO DECORATE
225 g / 8 oz / 2 cups icing (confectioners') sugar
boiling water, to mix
purple and white ready to roll fondant icing

- Preheat the oven to 190°C (170° fan) / 375 F / gas 5 and line a 12-hole cupcake tin with paper cases.
- Combine the flour, sugar, butter, eggs and lavender oil in a bowl and whisk together for 2 minutes.
- Divide the mixture between the paper cases, then transfer to the oven and bake for 15 – 20 minutes.
- Transfer the cakes to a wire rack and leave to cool.
- Sieve the icing sugar into a bowl, then slowly stir in the boiling water a few drops at a time until you have a thick icing.
- Spoon the icing onto the cakes and tap the on the work surface to level the icing.
- Roll out the purple icing and cut out tiny petal shapes.
- Assemble the flowers on top of the cakes and make the centres from the white fondant icing.

Lavender and Chocolate Chip Cupcakes

Add 100 g / 4 oz of chocolate chips to the cupcake batter.

148

MAKES 12

Cheese and Chive Cupcakes

PREPARATION TIME: 25 MINUTES

COOKING TIME: 25 MINUTES

INGREDIENTS

2 large eggs
120 ml / 4 fl. oz / ½ cup sunflower oil
180 ml / 6 fl. oz / ¾ cup Greek yogurt
225 g / 8 oz / 2 cups Morbier cheese, cubed
225 g / 8 oz / 1 ½ cups plain (all purpose) flour
2 tsp baking powder
½ tsp bicarbonate of (baking) soda
½ tsp salt
2 tbsp chives, chopped

- Preheat the oven to 180°C (160° fan) / 350 F / gas 4 and oil 12 silicone muffin moulds.
- Beat the eggs in a jug with the oil, yogurt and half of the cheese until well mixed.
- Mix the flour, raising agents, salt and chives in a bowl, then pour in the egg mixture and stir just enough to combine.
- Divide the mixture between the moulds and top with the rest of the cheese, then bake in the oven for 20 – 25 minutes.
- Test with a wooden toothpick, if it comes out clean, the cupcakes are done.
- Serve warm.

Cheese, Chive and Shallot Cupcakes

149

Add a finely sliced shallot to the cupcake batter before baking.

150 MAKES 12 Sprinkle Cupcakes

- Preheat the oven to 190°C (170° fan) / 375 F / gas 5 and line a 12-hole cupcake tin with paper cases.
- Combine the flour, sugar, butter, eggs and lemon zest in a bowl and whisk together for 2 minutes.
- Divide the mixture between the paper cases, then transfer to the oven and bake for 15 – 20 minutes.
- Test with a wooden toothpick, if it comes out clean, the cakes are done.
- Transfer the cakes to a wire rack and leave to cool.
- Sift the icing sugar into a bowl, then slowly stir in the boiling water a few drops at a time until you have a thick icing.
- Divide the icing into 3 bowls and colour each with a different food colouring.
- Dip the top of 4 cakes in each of the coloured icings, then sprinkle with your choice of toppings.

Buttercream Sprinkle Cupcakes 151

To add height to your cupcakes, replace the icing with buttercream and apply a thick layer with a palette knife before dipping the tops in the cake sprinkles.

PREPARATION TIME: 45 MINUTES

COOKING TIME: 20 MINUTES

INGREDIENTS

110 g / 4 oz / ½ cup self-raising flour, sifted
110 g / 4 oz / ½ cup caster (superfine) sugar
110 g / 4 oz / ½ cup butter, softened
2 large eggs
1 lemon, zest finely grated

TO DECORATE

225 g / 8 oz / 2 cups icing (confectioners') sugar
boiling water, to mix
blue, pink and green food colouring
coloured sprinkles
heart-shaped cake sprinkles

152 MAKES 12 Orange and Hazelnut Cupcakes

- Preheat the oven to 190°C (170° fan) / 375 F / gas 5.
- Oil 12 small cups and divide the chopped hazelnuts between them.
- Shake to coat the inside of the cups with nuts and tip the excess into a mixing bowl.
- Combine the flour, sugar, butter, eggs and orange zest in the bowl and whisk together for 2 minutes.
- Divide the mixture between the cups and bake for 15 – 20 minutes.
- Test with a wooden toothpick, if it comes out clean, the cakes are done.
- Transfer the cakes to a wire rack to cool completely.
- Whip the cream with the icing sugar until thick.
- Spoon the cream into a piping bag fitted with a large star nozzle and pipe a small swirl on top of each cake.

Orange and Coconut Cupcakes 153

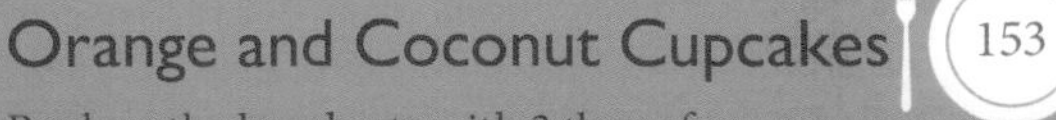

Replace the hazelnuts with 2 tbsp of desiccated coconut.

PREPARATION TIME: 30 MINUTES

COOKING TIME: 20 MINUTES

INGREDIENTS

75 g / 2 ½ oz / ½ cup hazelnuts, finely chopped
110 g / 4 oz / 1 cup self-raising flour, sifted
110 g / 4 oz / ½ cup caster (superfine) sugar
110 g / 4 oz / ½ cup butter, softened
2 large eggs
1 orange, zest finely grated

TO DECORATE

225 ml / 8 fl. oz / 1 cup double (heavy) cream
2 tbsp icing (confectioners') sugar

154

MAKES 12

Coconut and Strawberry Jam Cupcakes

PREPARATION TIME: 1 HOUR

COOKING TIME: 20 MINUTES

INGREDIENTS

110 g / 4 oz / 1 cup self-raising flour, sifted
110 g / 4 oz / ½ cup caster (superfine) sugar
110 g / 4 oz / ½ cup butter, softened
2 large eggs
28 g / 1 oz / ⅛ cup desiccated coconut
110 g / 4 oz / ½ cup strawberry jam (jelly)

TO DECORATE
1 tbsp desiccated coconut

- Preheat the oven to 190°C (170° fan) / 375 F / gas 5 and line a 12-hole cupcake tin with paper cases.
- Combine the flour, sugar, butter, eggs and coconut in a bowl and whisk together for 2 minutes.
- Divide half of the mixture between the paper cases, then add 1 tsp of strawberry jam in the centre of each one.
- Top with the rest of the cake mixture then transfer to the oven and bake for 15 – 20 minutes.
- Test with a wooden toothpick, if it comes out clean, the cakes are done.
- Transfer the cakes to a wire rack and sprinkle with desiccated coconut.

155

Coconut and Lime Marmalade Cupcakes

Replace the jam with lime marmalade for a zesty treat.

156

MAKES 18

Rhubarb Cupcakes

PREPARATION TIME: 25 MINUTES

COOKING TIME: 25 MINUTES

INGREDIENTS

1 large egg
120 ml / 4 fl. oz / ½ cup sunflower oil
120 ml / 4 fl. oz / ½ cup milk
375 g / 12 ½ oz / 2 ½ cups self-raising flour, sifted
1 tsp baking powder
200 g / 7 oz / ¾ cup caster (superfine) sugar
150 g / 5 oz / 1 cup rhubarb, finely chopped
2 tbsp demerara sugar

- Preheat the oven to 180°C (160° fan) / 350 F / gas 4 and line a 12-hole muffin tin with paper cases.
- Beat the egg in a jug with the oil and milk until well mixed.
- Mix the flour, baking powder, sugar and rhubarb in a bowl, then pour in the egg mixture and stir just enough to combine.
- Divide the mixture between the moulds and sprinkle with demerara sugar then bake in the oven for 20 – 25 minutes.
- Test with a wooden toothpick, if it comes out clean, the cakes are done.
- Transfer the cakes to a wire rack and leave to cool.

157

Orange, Ginger and Rhubarb Cupcakes

Try adding 1 tbsp finely grated orange zest and 2 tbsp chopped stem ginger to the cupcake mixture.

158

MAKES 12

Banana and Ginger Cupcakes

Banana, Ginger and Rum Cupcakes

159

Spoon ½ tsp of rum over each cake as they come out of the oven.

Banana and Coconut Cupcakes

160

Replace the ginger with 2 tsp of desiccated coconut.

PREPARATION TIME: 20 MINUTES

COOKING TIME: 20 MINUTES

INGREDIENTS

250 g / 9 oz / 1 ¾ cups self-raising flour
1 tsp bicarbonate of (baking) soda
2 tsp ground ginger
200 g / 8 ½ oz / ½ cup golden syrup
125 g / 4 ½ oz / ½ cup butter
125 g / 4 ½ oz / ¾ cup light brown sugar
4 pieces stem ginger, chopped
2 large eggs, beaten
240 ml / 8 fl. oz / 1 cup milk
6 small bananas, halved

- Preheat the oven to 190°C (170° fan) / 375 F / gas 5 and oil 12 small kugelhopf moulds.
- Sieve the flour, bicarbonate of soda and ground ginger together into a bowl.
- Put the golden syrup, butter, brown sugar and stem ginger in a small saucepan and boil gently for 2 minutes, stirring to dissolve the sugar.
- Pour the butter and sugar mixture onto the flour with the eggs and milk and fold it all together until smooth.
- Divide the mixture between the moulds and push half a banana into each one.
- Sit the moulds on a baking tray and bake in the oven for 20 – 25 minutes.
- Test with a wooden toothpick, if it comes out clean, the cakes are done.
- Transfer the cakes to a wire rack and leave to cool.

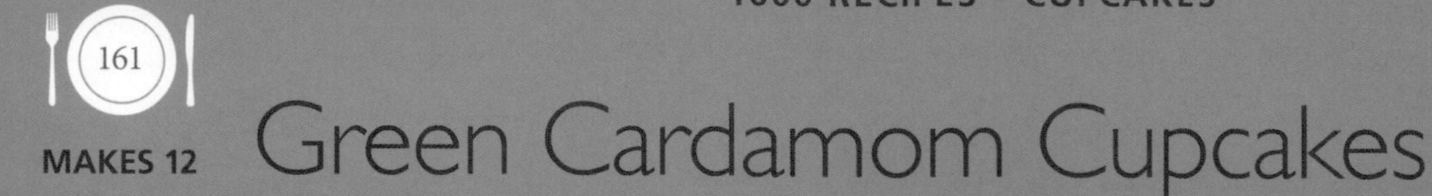

161

MAKES 12

Green Cardamom Cupcakes

Fragrant Cardamom Cupcakes

162

Add ½ tsp of orange flower water and ½ tsp rose water to the soaking syrup for extra fragrant cakes.

PREPARATION TIME: 1 HOUR

COOKING TIME: 20 MINUTES

INGREDIENTS

110 g / 4 oz / ½ cup self-raising flour, sifted
110 g / 4 oz / ½ cup caster (superfine) sugar
110 g / 4 oz / ½ cup butter, softened
2 large eggs
1 tsp ground cardamom

FOR THE SOAKING SYRUP
2 lemons, juiced
2 tbsp caster (superfine) sugar
3 green cardamom pods, crushed

- Preheat the oven to 190°C (170° fan) / 375 F / gas 5 and line a 12-hole cupcake tin with paper cases.
- Combine the flour, sugar, butter, eggs and ground cardamom in a bowl and whisk together for 2 minutes.
- Divide the mixture between the paper cases, then transfer to the oven and bake for 15 – 20 minutes.
- Test with a wooden toothpick, if it comes out clean, the cakes are done.
- While the cakes are cooking, make the soaking syrup. Put the lemon juice, caster sugar and crushed cardamom pods in a small saucepan and boil for 2 minutes, then strain through a sieve to remove the cardamom.
- When the cakes are ready, spoon over the soaking syrup and leave them to cool in their tin.

163

MAKES 12

Lemon and Nigella Seed Cupcakes

- Preheat the oven to 190°C (170° fan) / 375 F / gas 5 and line a 12-hole cupcake tin with paper cases.
- Combine the flour, sugar, butter, eggs and lemon zest in a bowl and whisk together for 2 minutes.
- Divide the mixture between the paper cases, then transfer to the oven and bake for 15 – 20 minutes.
- Test with a wooden toothpick, if it comes out clean, the cakes are done.
- Transfer the cakes to a wire rack and leave to cool.
- To make the icing, sieve the icing sugar into a bowl and stir in the lemon juice a little at a time until you have a thick pouring consistency.
- Stir in the lemon zest and nigella seeds then spoon the icing onto the cakes.

PREPARATION TIME: 1 HOUR

COOKING TIME: 20 MINUTES

INGREDIENTS

110 g / 4 oz / ½ cup self-raising flour, sifted
110 g / 4 oz / ½ cup caster (superfine) sugar
110 g / 4 oz / ½ cup butter, softened
2 large eggs
1 lemon, zest finely grated

TO DECORATE

225 g / 8 oz / 2 cups icing (confectioners') sugar
4 tsp lemon juice
1 tbsp lemon, zest finely grated
1 tsp nigella seeds

Crunchy Lemon Cupcakes

164

Add 2 tsp nigella seeds to the cake mixture before baking to add an extra crunch to the finished cakes.

165

MAKES 12

Chocolate and Raspberry Cupcakes

- Preheat the oven to 190°C (170° fan) / 375 F / gas 5 and line a 12-hole cupcake tin with paper cases.
- Combine the flour, cocoa, sugar, butter, eggs and raspberry syrup in a bowl and whisk together for 2 minutes.
- Divide the mixture between the paper cases, then transfer to the oven and bake for 15 – 20 minutes.
- Test with a wooden toothpick, if it comes out clean, the cakes are done.
- Transfer the cakes to a wire rack and leave to cool.
- To make the raspberry cream, whisk the cream with the raspberry syrup until thick.
- Spoon the cream into a piping bag fitted with a large star nozzle and pipe a generous swirl on top of each cake.
- Sprinkle with hundreds and thousands.

PREPARATION TIME: 30 MINUTES

COOKING TIME: 20 MINUTES

INGREDIENTS

110 g / 4 oz / ½ cup self-raising flour, sifted
28 g / 1 oz / ¼ cup unsweetened cocoa powder, sifted
110 g / 4 oz / ½ cup caster (superfine) sugar
110 g / 4 oz / ½ cup butter, softened
2 large eggs
2 tbsp raspberry syrup

TO DECORATE

225ml / 8 fl. oz / 1 cup double (heavy) cream
2 tbsp raspberry syrup
hundreds and thousands

Rose and Raspberry Cream Cupcakes

166

Replace the cocoa powder in the cake mixture with 1 tbsp rose water and add 2 tsp of rose water to the raspberry buttercream.

167

MAKES 12

Pear and Vanilla Cupcakes

PREPARATION TIME: 25 MINUTES

COOKING TIME:
20 – 25 MINUTES

INGREDIENTS

1 large egg
120 ml / 4 fl. oz / ½ cup sunflower oil
120 ml / 4 fl. oz / ½ cup milk
2 pears, peeled, cored and chopped
1 tsp vanilla extract
225 g / 7 ½ oz / 1 ½ cups self-raising flour, sifted
1 tsp baking powder
200 g / 7 oz / ¾ cup caster (superfine) sugar

- Preheat the oven to 180°C (160° fan) / 350 F / gas 4 and line a 12-hole muffin tin with paper cases.
- Beat the egg in a jug with the oil, milk, pears and vanilla extract until well mixed.
- Mix the flour, baking powder and sugar in a bowl, then pour in the egg mixture and stir just enough to combine.
- Divide the mixture between the paper cases and bake in the oven for 20 – 25 minutes.
- Test with a wooden toothpick, if it comes out clean, the cakes are done.
- Transfer the cakes to a wire rack and leave to cool.

Pear and White Chocolate Cupcakes

168

Add 100 g of white chocolate chips to the cupcake mixture.

169

MAKES 12

Mini Bacon and Broad Bean Frittata Cupcakes

PREPARATION TIME: 35 MINUTES

COOKING TIME: 10 MINUTES

INGREDIENTS

150 g / 5 oz / 1 cup baby broad beans, fresh or frozen
2 rashers streaky bacon, chopped
1 clove garlic, crushed
2 tbsp olive oil
4 large eggs

- Preheat the oven to 180°C (160° fan) / 350 F / gas 4 and oil a 12-hole silicone cupcake mould.
- Cook the broad beans in boiling salted water for 5 minutes then drain.
- Fry the bacon and garlic in the olive oil for 5 minutes or until soft, then stir in the broad beans.
- Beat the eggs in a jug and stir in the bacon and broad bean mixture.
- Season well with salt and black pepper.
- Pour the mixture into the prepared moulds then bake in the oven for 5 – 10 minutes or until set.

Mini Feta, Broad Bean and Dill Frittatas

170

Replace the bacon and garlic with 75g / 3 oz / ⅓ cup of crumbled feta cheese and 1 tbsp chopped fresh dill.

171

MAKES 12

Vanilla Buttercream Cupcakes

- Preheat the oven to 190°C (170° fan) / 375 F / gas 5 and line a 12-hole cupcake tin with paper cases.
- Combine the flour, sugar, butter, eggs and vanilla extract in a bowl and whisk together for 2 minutes.
- Divide the mixture between the paper cases, then transfer to the oven and bake for 15 – 20 minutes.
- Transfer the cakes to a wire rack and leave to cool.
- To make the buttercream, beat the butter with a wooden spoon until light and fluffy then beat in the icing sugar a quarter at a time.
- Use a whisk to incorporate the milk and vanilla extract, then whisk for 2 minutes.
- Spoon the buttercream into a piping bag fitted with a star nozzle and pipe a swirl on top of each cake.
- Sprinkle with sugar nibs.

PREPARATION TIME: 30 MINUTES

COOKING TIME: 20 MINUTES

INGREDIENTS

110 g / 4 oz / ½ cup self-raising flour,
110 g / 4 oz / ½ cup caster sugar
110 g / 4 oz / ½ cup butter, softened
2 large eggs
1 tsp vanilla extract

TO DECORATE

110 g / 4 oz / ½ cup butter, softened
225 g / 8 oz / 2 cups icing sugar
2 tbsp milk
1 tsp vanilla extract
2 tbsp sugar nibs

172

MAKES 12

Chocolate and Stout Cupcakes

PREPARATION TIME: 40 MINUTES

COOKING TIME: 20 MINUTES

INGREDIENTS

250 g / 9 oz / 1 ¼ cups self-raising flour
28 g / 1 oz / ¼ cup unsweetened cocoa powder, sifted
1 tsp bicarbonate of (baking) soda
200 g / 8 ½ oz / ½ cup golden syrup
125 g / 4 ½ oz / ½ cup butter
125 g / 4 ½ oz / ¾ cup brown sugar
2 large eggs, beaten
240 ml / 8 fl. oz / 1 cup stout

TO DECORATE

225 ml / 8 fl. oz / 1 cup double (heavy) cream
2 tbsp icing (confectioners') sugar
Silver sugar strands

- Preheat the oven to 190°C (170° fan) / 375 F / gas 5 and oil 12 small beer glasses or glass espresso cups.
- Sieve the flour, cocoa and bicarbonate of soda together into a bowl.
- Put the golden syrup, butter and brown sugar in a small saucepan and boil gently for 2 minutes, stirring to dissolve the sugar.
- Pour the butter and sugar mixture onto the flour with the eggs and stout and fold it all together until smooth.
- Divide the mixture between the glasses, then stand them on a baking tray and bake for 20 – 25 minutes.
- Test with a wooden toothpick, if it comes out clean, the cakes are done.
- Transfer the glasses to a wire rack and leave to cool completely.
- To make the topping, whisk the cream with the icing sugar until thick, then spoon onto the cakes and top with the sugar strands.

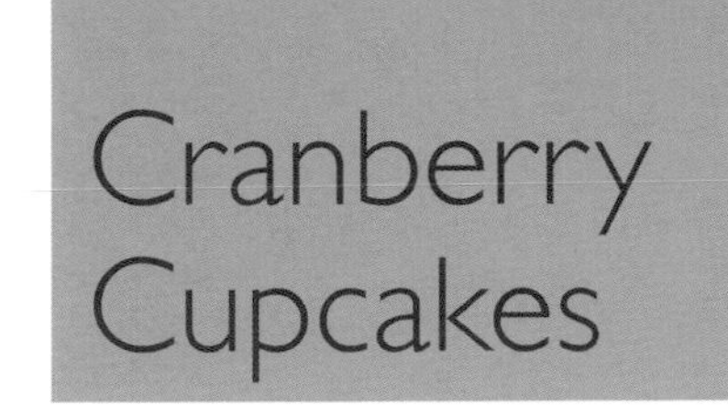

173

MAKES 12

Cranberry Cupcakes

PREPARATION TIME: 25 MINUTES

COOKING TIME: 25 MINUTES

INGREDIENTS

1 large egg
120 ml / 4 fl. oz / ½ cup sunflower oil
120 ml / 4 fl. oz / ½ cup milk
375 g / 12 ½ oz / 2 ½ cups self-raising flour, sifted
1 tsp baking powder
200 g / 7 oz / ¾ cup caster sugar
75 g / 2 ½ oz / ½ cup mixed candied peel, chopped
75 g / 2 ½ oz / ½ cup dried cranberries

TO DECORATE

75 g / 2 ½ oz / ½ cup dried cranberries
75 g / 2 ½ oz / ½ cup mixed candied peel, chopped
2 tbsp blanched almonds

- Preheat the oven to 180°C (160° fan) / 350 F / gas 4 and oil a 12-hole silicone muffin mould.
- Beat the egg in a jug with the oil and milk until well mixed.
- Mix the flour, baking powder, sugar, mixed peel and cranberries in a bowl, then pour in the egg mixture and stir just enough to combine.
- Divide the mixture between the moulds, then bake in the oven for 20 – 25 minutes.
- Test with a wooden toothpick, if it comes out clean, the cakes are done.
- Transfer the cakes to a wire rack and leave to cool.
- Mix together the cranberries, mixed peel and blanched almonds and spoon on top of the cupcakes.

174

MAKES 12

Lemon Meringue Cupcakes

PREPARATION TIME: 1 HOUR 15 MINUTES

COOKING TIME: 30 MINUTES

INGREDIENTS

110 g / 4 oz / ½ cup self-raising flour, sifted
110 g / 4 oz / ½ cup caster (superfine) sugar
110 g / 4 oz / ½ cup butter, softened
2 large eggs
1 lemon, zest finely grated
2 tsp ground cinnamon

TO DECORATE

225 g / 8 oz / 1 cup lemon curd
4 egg whites
110 g / 4 oz / 1 cup caster (superfine) sugar

- Preheat the oven to 190°C (170° fan) / 375 F / gas 5 and line a 12-hole cupcake tin with paper cases.
- Combine the flour, sugar, butter, eggs, lemon zest and cinnamon in a bowl and whisk together for 2 minutes.
- Divide the mixture between the paper cases, then transfer to the oven and bake for 15 – 20 minutes.
- Use a teaspoon to make a little hollow in the centre of each cake and fill with lemon curd.
- To make the meringue topping, whisk the egg whites until stiff, then gradually whisk in half the sugar until the mixture is very shiny. Fold in the remaining sugar then spoon the mixture into a large piping bag fitted with a plain nozzle.
- Pipe a swirl of meringue on top of each cake and return to the oven for 10 minutes or until the topping is golden brown. Serve warm.

Mini Queen of Puddings

175

Instead of filling the cakes with lemon curd, use raspberry jam (jelly) to make miniature Queen of Puddings.

MAKES 12

Mini Roquefort Frittata Cupcakes

PREPARATION TIME: 35 MINUTES

COOKING TIME: 10 MINUTES

INGREDIENTS

4 large eggs
110 g / 4 oz / 1 cup Roquefort, cubed
2 tbsp French tarragon, chopped

- Preheat the oven to 180°C (160° fan) / 350 F / gas 4 and oil a 12-hole silicone cupcake mould.
- Beat the eggs in a jug and stir in the cheese and tarragon.
- Season well with salt and black pepper.
- Pour the mixture into the prepared moulds then bake in the oven for 5 – 10 minutes or until set.

Mini Roquefort and Thyme Cupcakes

Replace the tarragon with fresh thyme leaves and sprinkle the tops with Parmesan.

178

MAKES 12

Cheese Cupcakes

Blue Cheese Cupcakes

179

Replace the Cheddar cheese with blue cheese, such as Stilton.

Dutch Cheese Cupcakes

180

Replace the Cheddar cheese with the same amount of Edam cheese.

Parmesan Cheese Cupcakes

181

Replace the Cheddar cheese with the same amount of Parmesan cheese.

PREPARATION TIME: 25 MINUTES

COOKING TIME: 25 MINUTES

INGREDIENTS

2 large eggs
120 ml / 4 fl. oz / ½ cup sunflower oil
180 ml / 6 fl. oz / ¾ cup Greek yogurt
110 g / 4 oz / 1 cup Cheddar cheese, grated
225 g / 8 oz / 1 ½ cups plain (all purpose) flour
2 tsp baking powder
½ tsp bicarbonate of (baking) soda
½ tsp salt

- Preheat the oven to 180°C (160° fan) / 350 F / gas 4 and oil a 12-hole silicone muffin tin.
- Beat the egg in a jug with the oil, yogurt and cheese until well mixed.
- Mix the flour, raising agents and salt in a bowl, then pour in the egg mixture and stir just enough to combine.
- Divide the mixture between the moulds, then bake in the oven for 20 – 25 minutes.
- Test with a wooden toothpick, if it comes out clean, the cupcakes are done.
- Transfer the cupcakes to a wire rack and leave to cool.

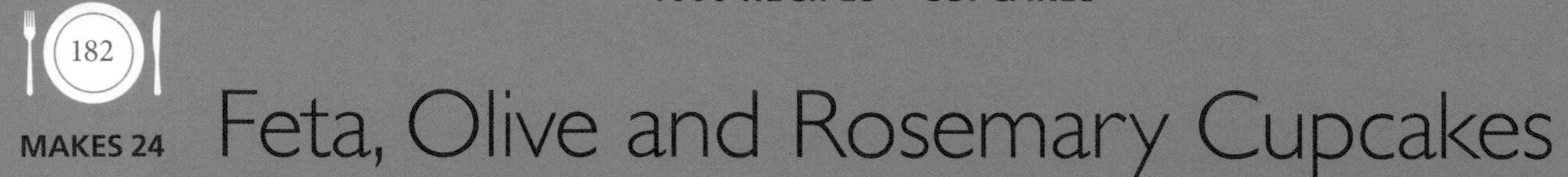

182

MAKES 24

Feta, Olive and Rosemary Cupcakes

Garlic and Onion Cupcakes

183

Add 1 tsp of crushed garlic and 1 sliced onion that have been fried in a little olive oil to the muffin mixture.

Ricotta, Olive and Rosemary Cupcakes

184

Replace the feta cheese with the same amount of ricotta cheese.

Feta, Tomato and Rosemary Cupcakes

185

Replace the olives with 75 g of sun-dried tomatoes.

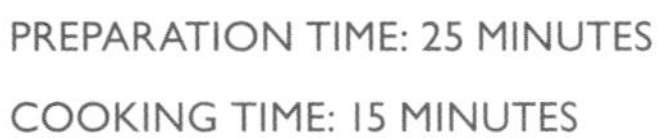

PREPARATION TIME: 25 MINUTES

COOKING TIME: 15 MINUTES

INGREDIENTS

2 large eggs
120 ml / 4 fl. oz / ½ cup sunflower oil
180 ml / 6 fl. oz / ¾ cup Greek yogurt
110 g / 4 oz / 1 cup feta cheese, cubed
225 g / 8 oz / 1 ½ cups plain (all purpose) flour
2 tsp baking powder
½ tsp bicarbonate of (baking) soda
½ tsp salt
75 g / 2 ½ oz / ½ cup black olives, stoned and chopped
2 tbsp fresh rosemary, chopped

- Preheat the oven to 180°C (160° fan) / 350 F / gas 4 and line a 24-hole mini muffin tin with paper cases.
- Beat the egg in a jug with the oil, yoghurt and cheese until well mixed.
- Mix the flour, raising agents, salt, olives and rosemary in a bowl, then pour in the egg mixture and stir just enough to combine.
- Divide the mixture between the paper cases, then bake in the oven for 10 – 15 minutes.
- Test with a wooden toothpick, if it comes out clean, the cupcakes are done.
- Serve warm.

186

MAKES 12

Blue Star Cupcakes

- Preheat the oven to 190°C (170° fan) / 375 F / gas 5 and line a 12-hole cupcake tin with blue paper cases.
- Combine the flour, sugar, butter and eggs in a bowl and whisk together for 2 minutes.
- Divide half of the mixture between the paper cases, then add 1 tsp of blueberry jam in the centre of each.
- Top with the rest of the cake mixture then transfer to the oven and bake for 15 – 20 minutes.
- Transfer the cakes to a wire rack and leave to cool.
- Beat the butter with a wooden spoon until light and fluffy then beat in the icing sugar a quarter at a time.
- Use a whisk to incorporate the rose water and food colouring, then whisk for 2 minutes.
- Spoon the buttercream into a piping bag fitted with a star nozzle and pipe a swirl on top of each cake.
- Sprinkle with star-shaped cake sprinkles.

PREPARATION TIME: 30 MINUTES

COOKING TIME: 20 MINUTES

INGREDIENTS

110 g / 4 oz / ½ cup self-raising flour, sifted
110 g / 4 oz / ½ cup caster (superfine) sugar
110 g / 4 oz / ½ cup butter, softened
2 large eggs
110 g / 4 oz / ½ cup blueberry jam (jelly)

TO DECORATE

110 g / 4 oz / ½ cup butter, softened
225 g / 8 oz / 2 cups icing (confectioners') sugar
2 tbsp milk
blue and white star-shaped cake sprinkles

Red Raspberry Cupcakes

187

Fill half of the cakes with raspberry jam instead of blueberry and top the cakes with fresh raspberries.

188

MAKES 12

Banana and Blueberry Cupcakes

- Preheat the oven to 200°C (180° fan) / 400 F / gas 6 and line a 12-hole cupcake tin with paper cases.
- Mash the bananas with a fork then whisk in the sugar, eggs and oil.
- Sieve the flour and bicarbonate of soda into the bowl and add the blueberries and stir just enough to evenly mix all the ingredients together.
- Divide the mixture between the paper cases, then transfer to the oven and bake for 15 – 20 minutes.
- Test with a wooden toothpick, if it comes out clean, the cakes are done.
- Transfer the cakes to a wire rack and leave to cool.

PREPARATION TIME: 25 MINUTES

COOKING TIME: 25 MINUTES

INGREDIENTS

3 very ripe bananas
110 g / 4 oz / ⅔ cup soft light brown sugar
2 large eggs
120 ml / 4 fl. oz / ½ cup sunflower oil
225 g / 8 oz / 1 ½ cups plain (all purpose) flour
1 tsp bicarbonate of (baking) soda
150 g / 5 oz / 1 cup blueberries

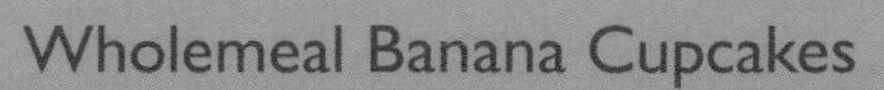

Wholemeal Banana Cupcakes

189

Replace the plain flour with wholemeal flour and double the quantity of bicarbonate of soda.

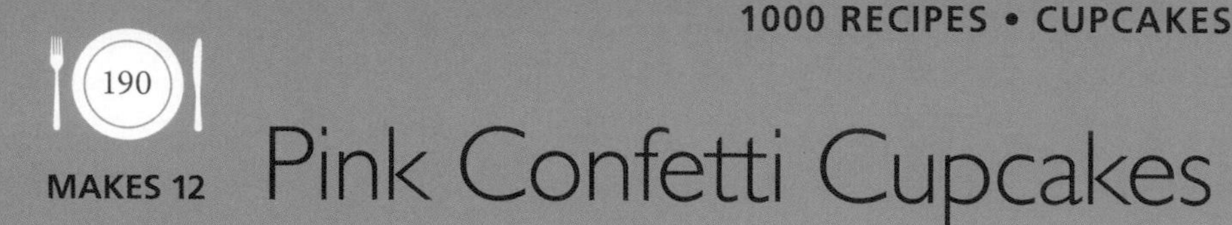

190

MAKES 12

Pink Confetti Cupcakes

PREPARATION TIME: 40 MINUTES

COOKING TIME: 20 MINUTES

INGREDIENTS

110 g / 4 oz / ½ cup self-raising flour, sifted
110 g / 4 oz / ½ cup caster (superfine) sugar
110 g / 4 oz / ½ cup butter, softened
2 large eggs
1 tsp vanilla extract

TO DECORATE

110 g / 4 oz / ½ cup butter, softened
225 g / 8 oz / 2 cups icing (confectioners') sugar
2 tbsp milk
pink food colouring
pink, red and white heart-shaped cake sprinkles

- Preheat the oven to 190°C (170° fan) / 375 F / gas 5 and line a 12-hole cupcake tin with paper cases.
- Combine the flour, sugar, butter, eggs and vanilla extract in a bowl and whisk together for 2 minutes.
- Divide the mixture between the paper cases then transfer to the oven and bake for 15 – 20 minutes.
- Transfer the cakes to a wire rack and leave to cool.
- To make the buttercream, beat the butter with a wooden spoon until light and fluffy then beat in the icing sugar a quarter at a time.
- Use a whisk to incorporate the milk and food colouring, then whisk for 2 minutes.
- Spoon the icing into a piping bag fitted with a large star nozzle and pipe a big swirl of icing on top of each cake.
- Scatter over the heart-shaped cake sprinkles to finish.

Purple Confetti Cupcakes

191

Replace the pink food colouring with purple food colouring and use purple, blue and white cake sprinkles to finish.

192

MAKES 12

Flower Cupcakes

PREPARATION TIME: 30 MINUTES

COOKING TIME: 20 MINUTES

INGREDIENTS

110 g / 4 oz / ½ cup self-raising flour, sifted
110 g / 4 oz / ½ cup caster (superfine) sugar
110 g / 4 oz / ½ cup butter, softened
2 large eggs
1 tsp vanilla extract

TO DECORATE

450 g / 1 lb / 2 cups ready-to-roll fondant icing
icing (confectioners') sugar

- Preheat the oven to 190°C (170° fan) / 375 F / gas 5 and line a 12-hole cupcake tin with paper cases.
- Combine the flour, sugar, butter, eggs and vanilla extract in a bowl and whisk together for 2 minutes.
- Divide the mixture between the paper cases, then transfer to the oven and bake for 15 – 20 minutes.
- Transfer the cakes to a wire rack and leave to cool completely, then remove the cases.
- Knead the fondant icing until pliable. Dust a work surface with icing sugar and roll out the fondant icing.
- Use a small flower-shaped cutter to cut out flowers for half of the cakes.
- Use a round scallop-edged cutter to cut tops for the other half of the cakes and press a pattern into the top using a sugar craft mould. Alternatively you can score in your own design with the end of a knitting needle.
- Transfer the flowers carefully to the top of the cakes.

Petal Cupcakes

193

Cut large individual petals out of fondant icing and attach them to the top of the cakes with a little buttercream for a 3D effect.

194

MAKES 12

Almond Cupcakes

Hazelnut Cupcakes

195

These cakes work really well with ground hazelnuts instead of almonds and a whole hazelnut pressed into the top.

Pistachio Cupcakes

196

Replace the ground almonds with pistachios and press a whole pistachio nut on top.

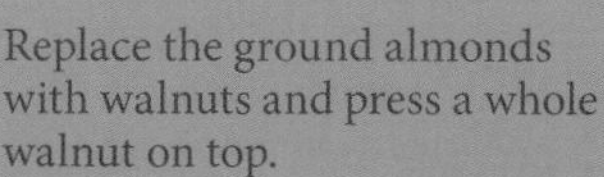

Walnut Cupcakes

197

Replace the ground almonds with walnuts and press a whole walnut on top.

PREPARATION TIME: 20 MINUTES

COOKING TIME: 20 MINUTES

INGREDIENTS

55 g / 2 oz / ½ cup self-raising flour, sifted
2 tsp baking powder
55 g / 2 oz / ½ cup ground almonds
110 g / 4 oz / ½ cup caster (superfine) sugar
110 g / 4 oz / ½ cup butter, softened
2 large eggs
1 tsp almond essence
12 blanched almonds

- Preheat the oven to 190°C (170° fan) / 375 F / gas 5 and line a 12-hole cupcake tin with paper cases.
- Combine the flour, baking powder, ground almonds, sugar, butter, eggs and almond essence in a bowl and whisk together for 2 minutes.
- Divide the mixture between the paper cases and press a blanched almond into the top of each, then transfer to the oven and bake for 15 – 20 minutes.
- Test with a wooden toothpick, if it comes out clean, the cakes are done.
- Transfer the cakes to a wire rack and leave to cool.

198

MAKES 12

Chocolate Star Cupcakes

Chocolate Caramel Cupcakes

199

Replace the chocolate stars with 110g / 4 oz / ½ cup chocolate caramel sweets.

Chocolate Star Coconut Cupcakes

200

Add 3 tbsp of desiccated coconut to the cupcake batter, before baking.

Chocolate Star and Fruit Cupcakes

201

Add 75 g / 3 oz of dried fruit to the cupcake batter, before baking.

PREPARATION TIME: 25 MINUTES

COOKING TIME: 25 MINUTES

INGREDIENTS

1 large egg
120 ml / 4 fl. oz / ½ cup sunflower oil
120 ml / 4 fl. oz / ½ cup milk
375 g / 12 ½ oz / 2 ½ cups self-raising flour, sifted
1 tsp baking powder
200 g / 7 oz / ¾ cup caster (superfine) sugar
110 g / 4 oz milk chocolate stars

- Preheat the oven to 180°C (160° fan) / 350 F / gas 4 and line a 12-hole muffin tin with paper cases.
- Beat the egg in a jug with the oil and milk until well mixed.
- Mix the flour, baking powder, sugar and ¾ of the chocolate stars in a bowl, then pour in the egg mixture and stir just enough to combine.
- Divide the mixture between the paper cases and stud the tops with the rest of the chocolate stars, then bake in the oven for 20 – 25 minutes.
- Test with a wooden toothpick, if it comes out clean, the cakes are done.
- Transfer the cakes to a wire rack and leave to cool.

202

MAKES 12

Wholemeal Chocolate Cupcakes

- Preheat the oven to 180°C (160° fan) / 350 F / gas 4 and line a 12-hole muffin tin with paper cases.
- Beat the egg in a jug with the oil and oat milk until well mixed.
- Mix the flour, cocoa, baking powder, sugar and chocolate in a bowl, then pour in the egg mixture and stir just enough to combine.
- Divide the mixture between the paper cases, then bake in the oven for 20 – 25 minutes.
- Test with a wooden toothpick, if it comes out clean, the cakes are done.
- Transfer the cakes to a wire rack and leave to cool.

PREPARATION TIME: 25 MINUTES

COOKING TIME: 25 MINUTES

INGREDIENTS

1 large egg
120 ml / 4 fl. oz / ½ cup sunflower oil
120 ml / 4 fl. oz / ½ cup oat milk
375 g / 12 ½ oz / 2 ½ cups wholemeal flour, sifted
55 g / 2 oz / ½ cup unsweetened cocoa powder, sifted
2 tsp baking powder
200 g / 7 oz / ¾ cup caster (superfine) sugar
110 g / 4 oz / ½ cup dark chocolate, chopped

Apple and Chocolate Cupcakes

203

Add 1 grated apple to the mixture to make them extra moist.

204

MAKES 12

Chocolate Chip Cupcakes

- Preheat the oven to 190°C (170° fan) / 375 F / gas 5 and oil a 12-hole silicone cupcake mould.
- Combine the flour, sugar, butter and eggs in a bowl and whisk together for 2 minutes.
- Fold in ¾ of the chocolate chips then divide the mixture between the paper cases.
- Sprinkle the rest of the chocolate chips on top then transfer to the oven and bake for 15 – 20 minutes.
- Test with a wooden toothpick, if it comes out clean, the cakes are done.
- Transfer the cakes to a wire rack and leave to cool.

PREPARATION TIME: 20 MINUTES

COOKING TIME: 20 MINUTES

INGREDIENTS

110 g / 4 oz / ½ cup self-raising flour, sifted
110 g / 4 oz / ½ cup caster (superfine) sugar
110 g / 4 oz / ½ cup butter, softened
2 large eggs
1 tsp vanilla extract
150 g / 5 oz / 1 cup chocolate chips

White and Dark Chocolate Cupcakes

205

Try using a mixture of white and dark chocolate chips.

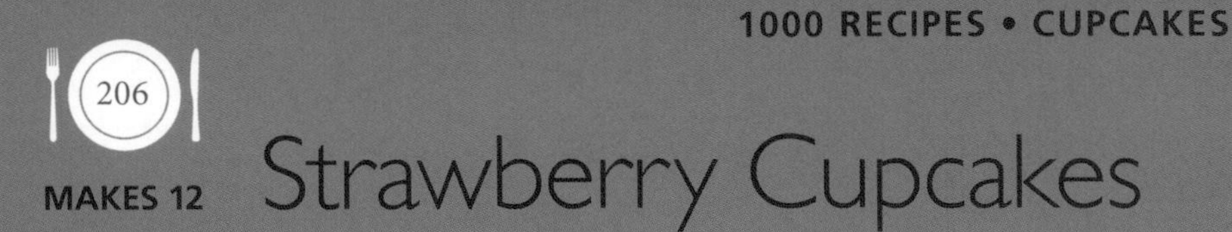

206

MAKES 12

Strawberry Cupcakes

PREPARATION TIME: 25 MINUTES

COOKING TIME: 25 MINUTES

INGREDIENTS

1 large egg
120 ml / 4 fl. oz / ½ cup sunflower oil
120 ml / 4 fl. oz / ½ cup milk
225 g / 7 ½ oz / 1 ½ cups self-raising flour, sifted
1 tsp baking powder
200 g / 7 oz / ¾ cup caster (superfine) sugar
150 g / 5 oz / 1 cup strawberries, chopped

- Preheat the oven to 180°C (160° fan) / 350 F / gas 4 and line a 12-hole muffin tin with paper cases.
- Beat the egg in a jug with the oil and milk until well mixed.
- Mix the flour, baking powder, sugar and chopped strawberries in a bowl, then pour in the egg mixture and stir just enough to combine.
- Divide the mixture between the paper cases and bake in the oven for 20 – 25 minutes.
- Test with a wooden toothpick, if it comes out clean, the cakes are done.
- Transfer the cakes to a wire rack and leave to cool.

Strawberry and Orange Cupcakes

207

Try adding the grated zest of 1 orange to the muffin mixture.

208

MAKES 12

Honey and Calendula Cupcakes

PREPARATION TIME: 25 MINUTES

COOKING TIME: 20 MINUTES

INGREDIENTS

110 g / 4 oz / ½ cup self-raising flour, sifted
55 g / 2 oz / ¼ cup caster (superfine) sugar
110 g / 4 oz / ½ cup honey
110 g / 4 oz / ½ cup butter, softened
2 large eggs
1 tbsp dried calendula petals

TO DECORATE
1 tbsp cater (superfine) sugar
1 tbsp dried calendula petals

- Preheat the oven to 190°C (170° fan) / 375 F / gas 5 and oil a 12-hole silicone flower cupcake mould.
- Combine the flour, sugar, honey, butter, eggs and calendula petals in a bowl and whisk together for 2 minutes.
- Divide the mixture between the moulds, then transfer to the oven and bake for 15 – 20 minutes.
- Test with a wooden toothpick, if it comes out clean, the cakes are done.
- Transfer the cakes to a wire rack to cool, then turn out to reveal the flower impressions.
- Sprinkle the cakes with a little caster sugar and scatter with dried calendula petals.

Honey and Lavender Cupcakes

209

These cakes work really well with dried lavender flowers too, but reduce the quantity to 2 tsp in the cake mixture.

210

MAKES 12

Orange and Cinnamon Cupcakes

- Preheat the oven to 190°C (170° fan) / 375 F / gas 5 and line a 12-hole cupcake tin with paper cases.
- Combine the flour, sugar, butter, eggs, orange zest and cinnamon in a bowl and whisk together for 2 minutes, then fold in ¾ of the chocolate chips.
- Divide the mixture between the paper cases and sprinkle the rest of the chocolate chips on top, then transfer to the oven and bake for 15 – 20 minutes.
- Test with a wooden toothpick, if it comes out clean, the cakes are done.
- Transfer the cakes to a wire rack and leave to cool.
- To make the glaze, combine the ingredients in a small saucepan and boil for 2 minutes or until syrupy.
- Remove the cinnamon stick and leave to cool then spoon on top of the cakes.

PREPARATION TIME: 20 MINUTES

COOKING TIME: 20 MINUTES

INGREDIENTS

110 g / 4 oz / 1 cup self-raising flour, sifted
110 g / 4 oz / ½ cup caster (superfine) sugar
110 g / 4 oz / ½ cup butter, softened
2 large eggs
1 orange, zest finely grated
2 tsp ground cinnamon
150 g / 5 oz / 1 cup chocolate chips

FOR THE GLAZE
½ orange, juiced
60 ml / 2 fl. oz / ¼ cup honey
1 cinnamon stick

Orange, Cinnamon and Fruit Cupcakes

211

Replace the chocolate chips with 110g / 4 oz / ½ cup raisins that have been soaked in the juice of 1 orange for 1 hour.

212

MAKES 12

Coconut and Orange Cupcakes

- Preheat the oven to 190°C (170° fan) / 375 F / gas 5 and line a 12-hole cupcake tin with paper cases.
- Pour the orange juice over the coconut and leave to soak for 10 minutes.
- Combine the flour, sugar, butter, eggs and coconut mixture in a bowl and whisk together for 2 minutes.
- Divide the mixture between the paper cases, then transfer to the oven and bake for 15 – 20 minutes.
- Transfer the cakes to a wire rack and leave to cool.
- To make the topping, whisk the cream with the icing sugar until it forms soft peaks.
- Spoon the whipped cream into a piping bag fitted with a large star nozzle and pipe a swirl on top of each cake.
- Sprinkle each cake with shredded coconut and orange zest.

PREPARATION TIME: 30 MINUTES

COOKING TIME: 20 MINUTES

INGREDIENTS

1 orange, juiced
28 g / 1 oz / ⅛ cup desiccated coconut
110 g / 4 oz / ½ cup self-raising flour, sifted
110 g / 4 oz / ½ cup caster (superfine) sugar
110 g / 4 oz / ½ cup butter, softened
2 large eggs

TO DECORATE
225 ml / 8 fl. oz / 1 cup double (heavy) cream
2 tbsp icing (confectioners') sugar
2 tbsp sweetened shredded coconut
1 orange, zest finely pared

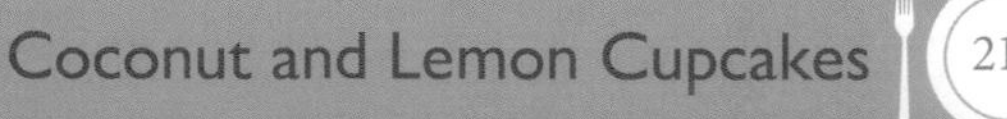

Coconut and Lemon Cupcakes

213

Replace the orange juice with lemon juice and decorate the cakes with finely pared lemon and lime zest for a bright combination.

214

MAKES 12

St. Clements Cupcakes

PREPARATION TIME: 1 HOUR

COOKING TIME: 20 MINUTES

INGREDIENTS

110 g / 4 oz / ½ cup self-raising flour, sifted
110 g / 4 oz / ½ cup caster (superfine) sugar
110 g / 4 oz / ½ cup butter, softened
2 large eggs
1 orange, zest finely grated
1 lemon, zest finely grated

TO DECORATE

110 g / 4 oz / ½ cup butter, softened
225 g / 8 oz / 2 cups icing (confectioners') sugar
2 tbsp lemon juice
110 g / 4 oz / ½ cup marmalade

- Preheat the oven to 190°C (170° fan) / 375 F / gas 5 and line a 12-hole cupcake tin with paper cases.
- Combine the flour, sugar, butter, eggs, orange and lemon zest in a bowl and whisk together for 2 minutes.
- Divide the mixture between the paper cases, then transfer to the oven and bake for 15 – 20 minutes.
- Transfer the cakes to a wire rack and leave to cool.
- To make the buttercream, beat the butter with a wooden spoon until light and fluffy then beat in the icing sugar a quarter at a time.
- Use a whisk to incorporate the lemon juice, then whisk for 2 minutes.
- Use a palate knife to spread each cake generously with the icing.
- Top each cake with a spoonful of marmalade.

Grapefruit Cupcakes

215

Replace the orange and lemon zest with the finely grated zest of a grapefruit and replace the lemon juice in the icing with grapefruit juice. Top the cakes with grapefruit marmalade.

216

MAKES 12

Chocolate Flower Cupcakes

PREPARATION TIME: 30 MINUTES

COOKING TIME: 20 MINUTES

INGREDIENTS

110 g / 4 oz / ½ cup self-raising flour, sifted
28 g / 1 oz / ¼ cup unsweetened cocoa powder, sifted
110 g / 4 oz / ½ cup caster (superfine) sugar
110 g / 4 oz / ½ cup butter, softened
2 large eggs
1 tsp vanilla extract

TO DECORATE

225 ml / 8 fl. oz / 1 cup double (heavy) cream
225 g / 8 oz / 1 cup dark chocolate, minimum 60% cocoa solids, chopped
pink ready to roll fondant icing
12 silver balls
edible glitter

- Preheat the oven to 190°C (170° fan) / 375 F / gas 5 and line a 12-hole cupcake tin with paper cases.
- Combine the flour, cocoa, sugar, butter, eggs and vanilla extract in a bowl and whisk for 2 minutes.
- Divide the mixture between the paper cases then transfer to the oven and bake for 15 – 20 minutes.
- Transfer the cakes to a wire rack and leave to cool.
- Heat the cream until it starts to simmer, then pour it over the chopped chocolate.
- Stir the ganache until the mixture has cooled and thickened, then refrigerate until thick enough to pipe.
- Spoon the ganache into a piping bag fitted with a large star nozzle and pipe a spiral on top of each cake.
- Roll out the fondant icing and cut out 12 flower shapes.
- Top each cake with a fondant flower and fix a silver ball in the middle of each one with a dab of water.
- Sprinkle with edible glitter.

White Chocolate Flower Cupcakes

Replace the dark chocolate in the ganache with chopped white chocolate.

218

MAKES 12

White Chocolate Cupcakes

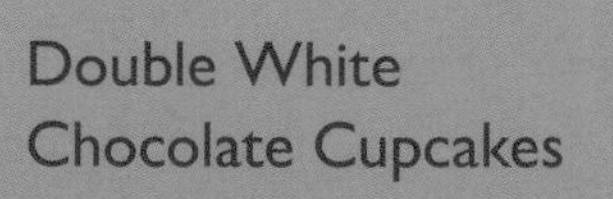

Double White Chocolate Cupcakes

219

Stir 110 g of melted white chocolate through the muffin mixture before baking. Top the cakes with whipped cream and white chocolate curls.

Dark Chocolate Cupcakes

220

Stir 110 g of melted dark chocolate through the cupcake mixture before baking. Top the cakes with whipped cream and dark chocolate curls.

PREPARATION TIME: 25 MINUTES

COOKING TIME:
20 – 25 MINUTES

INGREDIENTS

1 large egg
120 ml / 4 fl. oz / ½ cup sunflower oil
120 ml / 4 fl. oz / ½ cup milk
375 g / 12 ½ oz / 2 ½ cups self-raising flour, sifted
1 tsp baking powder
200 g / 7 oz / ¾ cup caster (superfine) sugar
110 g / 4 oz white chocolate, chopped

TO DECORATE
110 g / 4 oz white chocolate, chopped
mixed sweets

- Preheat the oven to 180°°C (160° fan) / 350 F / gas 4 and oil 12 silicone muffin moulds.
- Beat the egg in a jug with the oil and milk until well mixed.
- Mix the flour, baking powder, sugar and chocolate in a bowl, then pour in the egg mixture and stir just enough to combine.
- Divide the mixture between the moulds, then bake in the oven for 20 – 25 minutes.
- Test with a wooden toothpick, if it comes out clean, the cakes are done.
- Transfer the cakes to a wire rack and leave to cool.
- Melt the chocolate in a microwave or bain marie and spoon on top of the cakes.
- Top with a selection of multicoloured sweets.

221

MAKES 12

Christmas Cupcakes

PREPARATION TIME: 45 MINUTES

COOKING TIME: 25 MINUTES

INGREDIENTS

75 g / 2 ½ oz / ½ cup raisins
3 tbsp rum
1 large egg
120 ml / 4 fl. oz / ½ cup sunflower oil
120 ml / 4 fl. oz / ½ cup milk
375 g / 12 ½ oz / 2 ½ cups self-raising flour, sifted
1 tsp baking powder
200 g / 7 oz / ¾ cup caster (superfine) sugar

TO DECORATE
55 g / 2 oz milk chocolate, chopped
sugar strands
icing sugar to dust
sugar Christmas decorations

- Soak the raisins in the rum overnight.
- Preheat the oven to 180°C (160° fan) / 350 F / gas 4 and oil a 12-hole silicone muffin tin.
- Beat the egg in a jug with the oil and milk until well mixed.
- Mix the flour, baking powder, sugar and rum-soaked raisins in a bowl, then pour in the egg mixture and stir just enough to combine.
- Divide the mixture between the moulds, then bake in the oven for 20 – 25 minutes.
- Test with a wooden toothpick, if it comes out clean, the cakes are done.
- Transfer the cakes to a wire rack and leave to cool.
- Melt the chocolate in a microwave or bain marie and drizzle a line across each cake.
- Sprinkle the chocolate with sugar strands and dust the top of the cakes with icing sugar.
- Arrange the sugar Santa heads, stockings and bells on top of the cakes.

222

Brandy Butter Christmas cupcakes

Whisk together 110g / 4 oz / ½ cup of butter, 110g / 4 oz / ½ cup light brown sugar and 3 tbsp of brandy until smooth. Top the cakes with a sprig of holly.

223

Christmas Almond Cupcakes

Add 2 tsp of almond essence to the cupcake batter before cooking.

224

Christmas Cherry Cupcakes

Replace the raisins with 75 g / 2 ½ oz of finely chopped candied cherries.

225

MAKES 12

Sun-dried Tomato and Garlic Cupcakes

- Mix the butter with the garlic and oregano and spoon onto a piece of greaseproof paper.
- Roll up and twist the ends to make a tube of garlic butter, then chill in the fridge for 30 minutes or until firm, then cut into 12 pieces.
- Preheat the oven to 180°C (160° fan) / 350 F / gas 4 and line a 12-hole muffin tin with paper cases.
- Beat the egg in a jug with the oil, yoghurt and cheese until well mixed.
- Mix the sun-dried tomatoes, flour, raising agents and salt in a bowl, then pour in the egg mixture and stir just enough to combine.
- Divide half the mixture between the paper cases and top with a piece of garlic butter.
- Top with the rest of the muffin mixture, then bake in the oven for 20 – 25 minutes. Serve warm.

PREPARATION TIME: 25 MINUTES

COOKING TIME: 25 MINUTES

INGREDIENTS

110 g / 4 oz / ½ cup butter, softened
2 cloves garlic, crushed
2 tbsp fresh oregano, chopped
2 large eggs
120 ml / 4 fl. oz / ½ cup sunflower oil
180 ml / 6 fl. oz / ¾ cup Greek yogurt
110 g / 4 oz / 1 cup Parmesan, grated
75 g / 2 ½ oz / ½ cup sun-dried tomatoes, chopped
225 g / 8 oz / 1 ½ cups plain (all purpose) flour
2 tsp baking powder
½ tsp bicarbonate of (baking) soda
½ tsp salt

Tomato, Garlic and Pesto Cupcakes

226

Try mixing 2 tbsp of pesto in with the wet ingredients before stirring in the egg mixture.

227

MAKES 12

Apricot and Almond Cupcakes

- Preheat the oven to 190°C (170° fan) / 375 F / gas 5 and line a 12-hole cupcake tin with paper cases.
- Combine the flour, ground almonds, sugar, butter, eggs and almond essence in a bowl and whisk together for 2 minutes.
- Fold in the dried apricots then divide the mixture between the paper cases.
- Transfer the tin to the oven and bake for 15 – 20 minutes.
- Transfer the cakes to a wire rack to cool.
- To make the butterscotch icing, put the butter, cream, golden syrup and brown sugar in a small saucepan and boil for 2 minutes, stirring to dissolve the sugar.
- Leave to cool completely, then drizzle over the cakes.
- Decorate with the toasted almonds and apricot slices.

PREPARATION TIME: 20 MINUTES

COOKING TIME: 20 MINUTES

INGREDIENTS

55 g / 2 oz / ½ cup self-raising flour, sifted
55 g / 2 oz / ½ cup ground almonds
110 g / 4 oz / ½ cup caster (superfine) sugar
110 g / 4 oz / ½ cup butter, softened
2 large eggs
1 tsp almond essence
75 g / 2 ½ oz / ½ cup dried apricots, chopped

TO DECORATE
85 g / 3 oz / ½ cup butter
85 ml / 3 fl. oz / ⅓ cup double (heavy) cream
85 g / 3 oz / ¼ cup golden syrup
85 g / 3 oz / ½ cup dark brown sugar
2 tbsp flaked (slivered) almonds, toasted
4 dried apricots, sliced

Pear and Almond Cupcakes

228

This recipe works really well with dried pears instead of the apricots.

229

MAKES 12

Chocolate and Pistachio Cupcakes

PREPARATION TIME: 30 MINUTES

COOKING TIME: 20 MINUTES

INGREDIENTS

55 g / 2 oz / ½ cup self-raising flour
55 g / 2 oz / ½ cup ground pistachios
28 g / 1 oz / ¼ cup cocoa powder
110 g / 4 oz / ½ cup caster sugar
110 g / 4 oz / ½ cup butter, softened
2 large eggs
75 g / 2 ½ oz / ½ cup pistachio nuts, chopped
110 g / 4 oz / ½ cup dark chocolate, chopped

TO DECORATE
110 g / 4 oz / ½ cup butter, softened
225 g / 8 oz / 2 cups icing sugar
2 tbsp milk
1 tsp almond essence
2 tbsp ground pistachios
75 g / 2 ½ oz / ½ cup pistachio nuts, finely chopped

- Preheat the oven to 190°C (170° fan) / 375 F / gas 5 and line a 12-hole cupcake tin with paper cases.
- Combine the flour, ground pistachios, cocoa, sugar, butter and eggs in a bowl and whisk together for 2 minutes.
- Fold in the chopped pistachios and chocolate and divide the mixture between the paper cases. Transfer the tin to the oven and bake for 15 – 20 minutes.
- Transfer the cakes to a wire rack and leave to cool.
- To make the topping, beat the butter with a wooden spoon until light and fluffy then beat in the icing sugar a quarter at a time.
- Use a whisk to incorporate the milk, almond essence and ground pistachios then whisk for 2 minutes.
- Spread each cake with the buttercream and sprinkle liberally with the chopped pistachios.
- Top with woodland animal figurines.

Pistachio Cupcakes with Pistachio Ice Cream

230

Serve these cakes warm from the oven, un-iced, with a scoop of pistachio ice cream.

231

MAKES 12

Chocolate and Peppermint Cupcakes

PREPARATION TIME: 45 MINUTES

COOKING TIME: 20 MINUTES

INGREDIENTS

110 g / 4 oz / ½ cup self-raising flour, sifted
28 g / 1 oz / ¼ cup unsweetened cocoa powder, sifted
110 g / 4 oz / ½ cup caster (superfine) sugar
110 g / 4 oz / ½ cup butter, softened
2 large eggs
5 drops peppermint essence

TO DECORATE
55 g / 2 oz / ¼ cup butter, softened
110 g / 4 oz / 1 cup icing (confectioners') sugar
1 tbsp milk
5 drops peppermint essence
7 drops blue food colouring
blue edible glitter

- Preheat the oven to 190°C (170° fan) / 375 F / gas 5 and line a 12-hole cupcake tin with paper cases.
- Combine the flour, cocoa, sugar, butter, eggs and peppermint essence in a bowl and whisk for 2 minutes.
- Divide the mixture between the paper cases, then transfer to the oven and bake for 15 – 20 minutes.
- Transfer the cakes to a wire rack and leave to cool.
- To make the peppermint buttercream, beat the butter with a wooden spoon until light and fluffy then beat in the icing sugar a quarter at a time.
- Use a whisk to incorporate the milk, peppermint essence and food colouring, then whisk for 2 minutes.
- Use a palette knife to apply the icing, then sprinkle with edible glitter.

Coconut and Peppermint Cupcakes

232

Instead of the glitter, top the cakes with desiccated coconut.

233

MAKES 12

Chocolate and Coconut Cupcakes

- Preheat the oven to 190°C (170° fan) / 375 F / gas 5 and line a 12-hole cupcake tin with paper cases.
- Combine the flour, cocoa, sugar, butter, eggs and coconut in a bowl and whisk together for 2 minutes.
- Divide the mixture between the paper cases, then transfer to the oven and bake for 15 – 20 minutes.
- Test with a wooden toothpick, if it comes out clean, the cakes are done.
- Transfer the cakes to a wire rack and leave to cool.
- Beat the butter with a wooden spoon until light and fluffy then beat in the icing sugar a quarter at a time.
- Use a whisk to incorporate the coconut cream, then whisk for 2 minutes.
- Pile the buttercream on top of the cakes with a spoon and sprinkle with desiccated coconut.

PREPARATION TIME: 1 HOUR

COOKING TIME: 30 MINUTES

INGREDIENTS

110 g / 4 oz / ½ cup self-raising flour
28 g / 1 oz / ¼ cup cocoa powder
110 g / 4 oz / ½ cup caster sugar
110 g / 4 oz / ½ cup butter, softened
2 large eggs
28 g / 1 oz / ⅛ cup desiccated coconut

TO DECORATE

110 g / 4 oz / ½ cup butter, softened
225 g / 8 oz / 2 cups icing sugar
2 – 4 tbsp coconut cream
28 g / 1 oz / ⅛ cup desiccated coconut

Milk Chocolate Cupcakes

234

MAKES 12

PREPARATION TIME: 15 MINUTES

COOKING TIME: 20 MINUTES

INGREDIENTS

110 g / 4 oz / ½ cup self-raising flour, sifted
28 g / 1 oz / ¼ cup unsweetened cocoa powder, sifted
110 g / 4 oz / ½ cup caster (superfine) sugar
110 g / 4 oz / ½ cup butter, softened
110 g / 4 oz milk chocolate, chopped
2 large eggs

TO DECORATE

225 g / 8 oz / 1 cup milk chocolate
225 ml / 8 fl. oz / 1 cup double (heavy) cream

- Preheat the oven to 190°C (170° fan) / 375 F / gas 5 and line a 12-hole cupcake tin with paper cases.
- Combine the flour, cocoa, sugar, butter and eggs in a bowl and whisk together for 2 minutes.
- Fold in the chopped chocolate and divide the mixture between the paper cases.
- Transfer the tin to the oven and bake for 15 – 20 minutes.
- Test with a wooden toothpick, if it comes out clean, the cakes are done.
- Transfer the cakes to a wire rack and leave to cool.
- To make the milk chocolate ganache, chop the chocolate and transfer to a mixing bowl.
- Heat the cream until it starts to simmer, then pour over the chopped chocolate and stir until the mixture has cooled and thickened.
- Pile the ganache on top of the cakes with a spoon.

Valentine Cupcakes

235

MAKES 12

PREPARATION TIME: 1 HOUR

COOKING TIME: 20 MINUTES

INGREDIENTS

110 g / 4 oz / ½ cup self-raising flour
28 g / 1 oz / ¼ cup cocoa powde,
110 g / 4 oz / ½ cup caster sugar
110 g / 4 oz / ½ cup butter, softened
2 large eggs

TO DECORATE

110 g / 4 oz / ½ cup butter, softened
225 g / 8 oz / 2 cups icing (confectioners') sugar
28 g / 1 oz / ¼ cup unsweetened cocoa powder, sifted
2 tbsp milk
12 fruit jelly hearts

- Preheat the oven to 190°C (170° fan) / 375 F / gas 5 and line a 12-hole cupcake tin with paper cases.
- Combine the flour, cocoa, sugar, butter and eggs in a bowl and whisk together for 2 minutes.
- Divide the mixture between the paper cases, then transfer to the oven and bake for 15 – 20 minutes.
- Transfer the cakes to a wire rack and leave to cool.
- To make the buttercream, beat the butter with a wooden spoon until light and fluffy then beat in the icing sugar and cocoa a quarter at a time.
- Use a whisk to incorporate the milk, then whisk for 2 minutes.
- Spoon the buttercream into a piping bag fitted with a large plain nozzle and pipe a generous swirl on top of each cake.
- Top with a fruit jelly heart.

236

MAKES 12

Pink Party Cupcakes

PREPARATION TIME: 45 MINUTES

COOKING TIME: 20 MINUTES

INGREDIENTS

110 g / 4 oz / ½ cup self-raising flour, sifted
110 g / 4 oz / ½ cup caster (superfine) sugar
110 g / 4 oz / ½ cup butter, softened
2 large eggs
1 tbsp strawberry syrup
5 drops pink food colouring

TO DECORATE

225 g / 8 oz / 2 cups icing (confectioners') sugar
boiling water, to mix
6 drops pink food colouring
hundreds and thousands

- Preheat the oven to 190°C (170° fan) / 375F / gas 5 and line a 12-hole cupcake tin with pink paper cases.
- Combine the flour, sugar, butter, eggs, strawberry syrup and food colouring in a bowl and whisk together for 2 minutes.
- Divide the mixture between the paper cases, then transfer to the oven and bake for 15 – 20 minutes.
- Test with a wooden toothpick, if it comes out clean, the cakes are done.
- Transfer the cakes to a wire rack and leave to cool.
- Sift the icing sugar into a bowl, then slowly stir in the boiling water and food colouring a few drops at a time until you have a runny icing.
- Dip the top of each cupcake in the icing, then sprinkle with hundreds and thousands.

Raspberry Party Cupcakes

237

Try flavouring these cakes with raspberry syrup and topping with pink sweets instead.

238

MAKES 12

Cranberry and White Chocolate Cupcakes

PREPARATION TIME 40 MINUTES

COOKING TIME 20 MINUTES

INGREDIENTS

110 g / 4 oz / ½ cup self-raising flour, sifted
110 g / 4 oz / ½ cup caster (superfine) sugar
110 g / 4 oz / ½ cup butter, softened
2 large eggs
75 g / 2 ½ oz / ½ cup dried cranberries
110 g / 4 oz white chocolate, chopped

TO DECORATE

225 g / 8 oz / 1 cup white chocolate
225 ml / 8 fl. oz / 1 cup double (heavy) cream
sweets and cake sprinkles to decorate

- Preheat the oven to 190°C (170° fan) / 375 F / gas 5 and line a 12-hole cupcake tin with paper cases.
- Combine the flour, sugar, butter and eggs in a bowl and whisk together for 2 minutes.
- Fold in the cranberries and chopped white chocolate and divide the mixture between the paper cases.
- Transfer the tin to the oven and bake for 15 – 20 minutes.
- Transfer the cakes to a wire rack and leave to cool.
- To make the topping, chop the white chocolate and transfer to a mixing bowl.
- Heat the cream until it starts to simmer, then pour over the chopped chocolate and stir until the mixture has cooled and thickened.
- Spread each cake with the white chocolate ganache and decorate with sweets.

Double White Chocolate and Cranberry Cupcakes

239

Sprinkle the iced cakes with dried cranberries and white chocolate curls instead.

MAKES 12

Cherry and Vanilla Cupcakes

PREPARATION TIME: 25 MINUTES

COOKING TIME: 20 MINUTES

INGREDIENTS

110 g / 4 oz / ½ cup self-raising flour, sifted
110 g / 4 oz / ½ cup caster (superfine) sugar
110 g / 4 oz / ½ cup butter, softened
2 large eggs
1 tsp vanilla extract

TO DECORATE
225 g / 8 oz / 2 cups icing (confectioners') sugar
boiling water, to mix
6 glace cherries, halved

- Preheat the oven to 190°C (170° fan) / 375 F / gas 5 and line a 12-hole cupcake tin with paper cases.
- Combine the flour, sugar, butter, eggs and vanilla extract in a bowl and whisk together for 2 minutes.
- Divide the mixture between the paper cases, then transfer to the oven and bake for 15 – 20 minutes.
- Test with a wooden toothpick, if it comes out clean, the cakes are done.
- Transfer the cakes to a wire rack and leave to cool.
- Sieve the icing sugar into a bowl, then slowly stir in the boiling water a few drops at a time until you have a thick icing.
- Spoon the icing onto the cakes and top each one with half a glace cherry.

241

Angelica and Vanilla Cupcakes

Replace the cherry on top of the cupcakes with a piece of candied angelica and add 75g / 3 oz / ⅓ cup chopped angelica to the cake mixture.

242

Chocolate and Vanilla Cupcakes

Replace the cherry on top of the cupcakes with a chocolate ball and add 75 g / 3 oz of chocolate chips to the mixture.

Cherry, Coconut and Vanilla Cupcakes

Add 3 tbsp of desiccated coconut to the cupcake mixture.

244

MAKES 12

Butterfly Cupcakes

Lemon Butterfly Cupcakes

245

Add the finely grated zest of 1 lemon to the cake mixture and replace the strawberry jam with lemon curd.

Blackberry Butterfly Cupcakes

246

Replace the strawberry jam with blackberry jam.

Strawberry and Lime Butterfly Cupcakes

247

Replace the milk in the buttercream with lime juice.

PREPARATION TIME: 40 MINUTES

COOKING TIME: 20 MINUTES

INGREDIENTS

110 g / 4 oz / ½ cup self-raising flour, sifted
110 g / 4 oz / ½ cup caster (superfine) sugar
110 g / 4 oz / ½ cup butter, softened
2 large eggs
1 tsp vanilla extract

TO DECORATE
110 g / 4 oz / ½ cup butter, softened
225 g / 8 oz / 2 cups icing (confectioners') sugar
2 tbsp milk
1 tsp vanilla extract
110 g / 4 oz / ½ cup strawberry jam (jelly)

- Preheat the oven to 190°C (170° fan) / 375 F / gas 5 and line a 12-hole cupcake tin with paper cases.
- Combine the flour, sugar, butter, eggs and vanilla extract in a bowl and whisk together for 2 minutes.
- Divide the mixture between the cake cases then transfer to the oven and bake for 15 – 20 minutes.
- Test with a wooden toothpick, if it comes out clean, the cakes are done.
- Transfer the cakes to a wire rack and leave to cool.
- To make the buttercream, beat the butter with a wooden spoon until light and fluffy then beat in the icing sugar a quarter at a time.
- Use a whisk to incorporate the milk and vanilla extract, then whisk for 2 minutes.
- Spoon the icing into a piping bag fitted with a large star nozzle.
- Using a sharp knife, cut a shallow cone out of the centre of each cake and reserve.
- Pipe a swirl of buttercream into the centre of each cake.
- Take the reserved cake pieces and cut each one in half to make the butterfly wings.
- Press the wings into the icing then spoon on a line of jam to form the bodies.

248

MAKES 12

Chocolate, Pistachio and Cherry Cupcakes

- Preheat the oven to 190°C (170° fan) / 375 F / gas 5 and line a 12-hole cupcake tin with paper cases.
- Combine the flour, ground pistachios, sugar, butter and eggs in a bowl and whisk together for 2 minutes.
- Fold in the chopped chocolate, pistachios and cherries and divide the mixture between the paper cases.
- Transfer the tin to the oven and bake for 15 – 20 minutes.
- Transfer the cakes to a wire rack and leave to cool.
- To make the topping, beat the butter with a wooden spoon until light and fluffy then beat in the icing sugar a quarter at a time.
- Add the milk and whisk for 2 minutes.
- Spread each cake with the buttercream and sprinkle liberally with chopped pistachios and chocolate curls.
- Top each cake with a cocktail cherry.

PREPARATION TIME: 30 MINUTES

COOKING TIME: 20 MINUTES

INGREDIENTS

55 g / 2 oz / ½ cup self-raising flour
55 g / 2 oz / ½ cup ground pistachios
110 g / 4 oz / ½ cup caster sugar
110 g / 4 oz / ½ cup butter, softened
2 large eggs
110 g / 4 oz white chocolate, chopped
75 g / 2 ½ oz / ½ cup pistachio nuts, chopped
75 g / 2 ½ oz / ½ cup cocktail cherries, drained and quartered

TO DECORATE

110 g / 4 oz / ½ cup butter, softened
225 g / 8 oz / 2 cups icing (confectioners') sugar
2 tbsp milk
75 g / 2 ½ oz / ½ cup pistachio nuts, finely chopped
white chocolate curls
12 cocktail cherries

Fresh Cherry Cupcakes

249

Replace the cocktail cherries in the mixture with fresh cherries and top the cakes with a fresh cherry with the stalk attached.

250

MAKES 24

Bacon and Prune Mini Cupcakes

- Preheat the oven to 180°°C (160° fan) / 350 F / gas 4 and line a 24-hole muffin tin with paper cases.
- Fry the bacon in the olive oil until crisp.
- Beat the egg in a jug with the oil, yoghurt, cheese and crispy bacon until well mixed.
- Mix the flour, raising agents and salt in a bowl, then pour in the egg mixture and stir just enough to combine.
- Divide the mixture between the paper cases and top each one with half a prune, then bake in the oven for 10 – 15 minutes.
- Test with a wooden toothpick, if it comes out clean, the cupcakes are done.
- Serve warm.

PREPARATION TIME: 25 MINUTES

COOKING TIME: 10 – 15 MINUTES

INGREDIENTS

2 rashers of bacon, chopped
1 tbsp olive oil
2 large eggs
120 ml / 4 fl. oz / ½ cup sunflower oil
180 ml / 6 fl. oz / ¾ cup Greek yoghurt
110 g / 4 oz / 1 cup parmesan, grated
225 g / 8 oz / 1 ½ cups plain flour
2 tsp baking powder
½ tsp bicarbonate of (baking) soda
½ tsp salt
12 prunes, halved and stoned

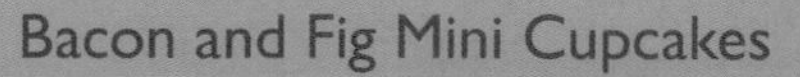

Bacon and Fig Mini Cupcakes

251

Replace the prune halves with quarters of fresh fig.

252

MAKES 12

Chestnut Flour Cupcakes

PREPARATION TIME: 20 MINUTES

COOKING TIME: 20 MINUTES

INGREDIENTS

55 g / 2 oz / ½ cup self-raising flour, sifted
55 g / 2 oz / ½ cup chestnut flour, sifted
110 g / 4 oz / ½ cup caster (superfine) sugar
110 g / 4 oz / ½ cup butter, softened
2 large eggs

- Preheat the oven to 190°C (170° fan) / 375 F / gas 5 and line a 12-hole cupcake tin with paper cases.
- Combine the flours, sugar, butter and eggs in a bowl and whisk together for 2 minutes.
- Divide the mixture between the paper cases, then transfer to the oven and bake for 15 – 20 minutes.
- Test with a wooden toothpick, if it comes out clean, the cakes are done.
- Transfer the cakes to a wire rack and leave to cool.

Chestnut Cupcakes with Chestnut Cream

253

For a chestnut cream topping, fold together equal quantities of whipped cream and sweetened chestnut puree.

254

MAKES 12

Bullseye Cupcakes

PREPARATION TIME: 45 MINUTES

COOKING TIME: 20 MINUTES

INGREDIENTS

110 g / 4 oz / ½ cup self-raising flour, sifted
110 g / 4 oz / ½ cup caster (superfine) sugar
110 g / 4 oz / ½ cup butter, softened
2 large eggs
1 tsp vanilla extract

TO DECORATE

225 g / 8 oz / 2 cups icing (confectioners') sugar
Boiling water, to mix
55 g / 2 oz / ¼ cup dark chocolate, chopped
12 small red sweets

- Preheat the oven to 190°C (170° fan) / 375 F / gas 5 and line a 12-hole cupcake tin with paper cases.
- Combine the flour, sugar, butter, eggs and vanilla extract in a bowl and whisk together for 2 minutes.
- Divide the mixture between the paper cases, then transfer to the oven and bake for 15 – 20 minutes.
- Transfer the cakes to a wire rack and leave to cool.
- Sift the icing sugar into a bowl, then slowly stir in the boiling water a few drops at a time until you have a very thick icing.
- Spread the icing onto the cakes with a palette knife.
- Melt the chocolate in a microwave or bain marie and use a piping bag with a small plain nozzle to pipe a circle of chocolate on top of each cake.
- Finish the cakes by putting a small red sweet in the centre of each 'target'.

Archery Target Cupcakes

255

Try mixing up red, blue and yellow icing and piping a full archery target on top of each cake.

256

MAKES 22

Pink Iced Cinnamon Cupcakes

Pink Cinnamon and Cocoa Cupcakes

257

Add 1 tbsp of unsweetened cocoa powder to the cake mixture and sprinkle the cakes with cocoa powder to finish.

Pink Cinnamon and Coconut Cupcakes

258

Add 2 tbsp of desiccated coconut to the cake mixture.

Pink Cinnamon and Almond Cupcakes

259

Add 2 tbsp of almond extract and top with flaked almonds.

PREPARATION TIME: 25 MINUTES

COOKING TIME: 20 MINUTES

INGREDIENTS

110 g / 4 oz / ½ cup self-raising flour, sifted
110 g / 4 oz / ½ cup caster (superfine) sugar
110 g / 4 oz / ½ cup butter, softened
2 large eggs
2 tsp ground cinnamon

TO DECORATE
225 g / 8 oz / 2 cups icing (confectioners') sugar
boiling water, to mix
pink food colouring
1 tsp ground cinnamon

- Preheat the oven to 190°C (170° fan) / 375 F / gas 5 and line a 12-hole cupcake tin with paper cases.
- Combine the flour, sugar, butter, eggs and cinnamon in a bowl and whisk together for 2 minutes.
- Divide the mixture between the paper cases, then transfer to the oven and bake for 15 – 20 minutes.
- Test with a wooden toothpick, if it comes out clean, the cakes are done.
- Transfer the cakes to a wire rack and leave to cool.
- Sieve the icing sugar into a bowl, then slowly stir in the boiling water a few drops at a time until you have a spoonable icing.
- Stir in the food colouring a drop at a time until you reach your desired colour.
- Spoon the icing onto the cakes and sprinkle over the ground cinnamon.

260

MAKES 24

Chocolate and Cherry Mini Cupcakes

Chocolate and Cherry Jam Cupcakes

261

Layer 1 tsp of cherry jam inside each cupcake before baking. Dip 24 fresh cherries in melted dark chocolate and put one on top of each cake.

Chocolate and Date Cupcakes

262

Replace the glace cherries with dates.

PREPARATION TIME: 25 MINUTES

COOKING TIME: 20 MINUTES

INGREDIENTS

1 large egg
120 ml / 4 fl. oz / ½ cup sunflower oil
120 ml / 4 fl. oz / ½ cup milk
375 g / 12 ½ oz / 2 ½ cups self-raising flour, sifted
55 g / 2 oz / ½ cup unsweetened cocoa powder, sifted
1 tsp baking powder
200 g / 7 oz / ¾ cup caster (superfine) sugar
110 g / 4 oz / ½ cup dark chocolate, minimum 60% cocoa solids, chopped

TO DECORATE

225 g / 8 oz / 1 cup dark chocolate
24 glace cherries

- Preheat the oven to 180°C (160° fan) / 350 F / gas 4 and line a 24-hole muffin tin with paper cases.
- Beat the egg in a jug with the oil and milk until well mixed.
- Mix the flour, cocoa, baking powder, sugar and chocolate in a bowl, then pour in the egg mixture and stir just enough to combine.
- Divide the mixture between the paper cases, then bake in the oven for 15 – 20 minutes.
- Test with a wooden toothpick, if it comes out clean, the cakes are done.
- Transfer the cakes to a wire rack and leave to cool.
- Melt the chocolate in a microwave or bain marie and leave to cool a little.
- Spread the cooled chocolate on top of the cupcakes and top each one with a glace cherry.

263

MAKES 12

Blueberry and Chocolate Cupcakes

- Preheat the oven to 190°C (170° fan) / 375 F / gas 5 and line a 12-hole cupcake tin with paper cases.
- Combine the flour, cocoa, sugar, butter and eggs in a bowl and whisk together for 2 minutes.
- Fold in the blueberries and divide the mixture between the paper cases. Transfer the tin to the oven and bake for 15 – 20 minutes.
- Transfer the cakes to a wire rack and leave to cool.
- To make the topping, beat the butter with a wooden spoon until light and fluffy then beat in the icing sugar and cocoa a quarter at a time.
- Add the milk then whisk for 2 minutes. Spread each cake with the buttercream and top with the blueberries.
- Dust the cakes with a little icing sugar and finish with a scattering of hundreds and thousands.

PREPARATION TIME:
1 HOUR 30 MINUTES

COOKING TIME: 20 MINUTES

INGREDIENTS

110 g / 4 oz / ½ cup self-raising flour, sifted
28 g / 1 oz / ¼ cup unsweetened cocoa powder, sifted
110 g / 4 oz / ½ cup caster sugar
110 g / 4 oz / ½ cup butter, softened
2 large eggs
75 g / 2 ½ oz / ½ cup blueberries

TO DECORATE
110 g / 4 oz / ½ cup butter, softened
225 g / 8 oz / 2 cups icing sugar
28 g / 1 oz / ¼ cup unsweetened cocoa powder, sifted
2 tbsp milk
75 g / 2 ½ oz / ½ cup blueberries
icing sugar, for dusting
hundreds and thousands

Blueberry Jam Cupcakes

264

Top them with a dollop of whipped cream and a spoonful of blueberry jam before piling on the blurberries.

265

MAKES 12

Mini Shallot and Basil Cupcakes

- Preheat the oven to 180°°C (160° fan) / 350 F / gas 4 and oil a 12-hole silicone cupcake mould.
- Fry the shallots in the olive oil for 5 minutes until soft and translucent.
- Beat the eggs in a jug and stir in the fried shallots and basil leaves.
- Season well with salt and black pepper.
- Pour the mixture into the prepared moulds then bake in the oven for 5 – 10 minutes or until set.
- Remove from the oven and transfer to a wire rack to cool. Unmould from the cupcake mould and serve.

PREPARATION TIME: 35 MINUTES

COOKING TIME: 5 – 10 MINUTES

INGREDIENTS

2 shallots, sliced
2 tbsp olive oil
4 large eggs
15 g / ½ oz basil leaves

Mini Cheese and Onion Cupcakes

266

Replace the basil with 50 g of grated cheese.

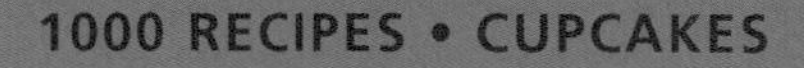

267

MAKES 12

Matcha Mini Loaf Cakes

PREPARATION TIME: 25 MINUTES

COOKING TIME: 25 MINUTES

INGREDIENTS

1 large egg
120 ml / 4 fl. oz / ½ cup sunflower oil
120 ml / 4 fl. oz / ½ cup milk
375 g / 12 ½ oz / 2 ½ cups wholemeal flour
2 tsp baking powder
200 g / 7 oz / ¾ cup caster (superfine) sugar
1 tbsp matcha green tea powder

- Preheat the oven to 180°C (160° fan) / 350 F / gas 4 and oil a 12-hole silicone mini loaf cake mould.
- Beat the egg in a jug with the oil and milk until well mixed.
- Mix the flour, baking powder, sugar and matcha in a bowl, then pour in the egg mixture and stir just enough to combine.
- Divide the mixture between the paper cases, then bake in the oven for 20 – 25 minutes.
- Test with a wooden toothpick, if it comes out clean, the cakes are done.
- Transfer the cakes to a wire rack and leave to cool.

Rose Petal Tea Flavour Loaf Cake

Substitute the matcha powder for 1 tbsp dried rose petals.

269

MAKES 12

Pink Iced Strawberry Cupcakes

PREPARATION TIME: 25 MINUTES

COOKING TIME: 25 MINUTES

INGREDIENTS

1 large egg
120 ml / 4 fl. oz / ½ cup sunflower oil
120 ml / 4 fl. oz / ½ cup milk
225 g / 7 ½ oz / 1 ½ cups self-raising flour, sifted
1 tsp baking powder
200 g / 7 oz / ¾ cup caster (superfine) sugar
150 g / 5 oz / 1 cup strawberries, chopped

TO DECORATE

110 g / 4 oz / ½ cup butter, softened
225 g / 8 oz / 2 cups icing (confectioners') sugar
2 tbsp strawberry syrup
2 tbsp hundreds and thousands
2 tbsp heart-shaped cake sprinkles

- Preheat the oven to 180°C (160° fan) / 350 F / gas 4 and line a 12-hole muffin tin with paper cases.
- Beat the egg in a jug with the oil and milk until well mixed.
- Mix the flour, baking powder, sugar and chopped strawberries in a bowl, then pour in the egg mixture and stir just enough to combine.
- Divide the mixture between the paper cases and bake in the oven for 20 – 25 minutes.
- Transfer the cakes to a wire rack and leave to cool.
- Beat the butter with a wooden spoon until light and fluffy then beat in the icing sugar a quarter at a time.
- Use a whisk to incorporate the strawberry syrup, then whisk for 2 minutes. Use a palette knife to cover the top of the cupcakes in icing.
- Mix the hundreds and thousands and cake sprinkles in a bowl and dip the top of the cupcakes in to coat.

Purple Iced Blueberry Cupcakes

270

Replace the strawberries with blueberries and replace the strawberry syrup in the buttercream with blueberry syrup.

271

MAKES 36

Chocolate Iced Mini Cupcakes

- Preheat the oven to 190°C (170° fan) / 375 F / gas 5 and line a 36 hole mini cupcake tin with paper cases.
- Combine the flour, cocoa, sugar, butter and eggs in a bowl and whisk together for 2 minutes.
- Divide the mixture between the paper cases, then transfer to the oven and bake for 10 – 15 minutes.
- Transfer the cakes to a wire rack and leave to cool.
- Beat the butter with a wooden spoon until light and fluffy then beat in the icing sugar and cocoa a quarter at a time.
- Use a whisk to incorporate the milk, then whisk for 2 minutes.
- Use a palette knife to apply the icing then sprinkle the cakes with sugar strands.

PREPARATION TIME: 1 HOUR

COOKING TIME: 15 MINUTES

INGREDIENTS

110 g / 4 oz / ½ cup self-raising flour, sifted
28 g / 1 oz / ¼ cup unsweetened cocoa powder, sifted
110 g / 4 oz / ½ cup caster (superfine) sugar
110 g / 4 oz / ½ cup butter, softened
2 large eggs

TO DECORATE
110 g / 4 oz / ½ cup butter, softened
225 g / 8 oz / 2 cups icing (confectioners') sugar
28 g / 1 oz / ¼ cup unsweetened cocoa powder, sifted
2 tbsp milk
4 tbsp sugar strands

Double Chocolate Iced Mini Cupcakes

272

Add white chocolate chips to the cake mixture and top the cake with white and dark chocolate chips instead of the sugar strands.

273

MAKES 12

Mint Chocolate Cupcakes

- Preheat the oven to 180°C (160° fan) / 350 F / gas 4 and line a 12-hole muffin tin with paper cases.
- Beat the egg in a jug with the oil and milk until well mixed.
- Mix the flour, cocoa, baking powder, sugar, chocolate and peppermint essence in a bowl, then pour in the egg mixture and stir just enough to combine.
- Divide the mixture between the paper cases, then bake in the oven for 20 – 25 minutes.
- Test with a wooden toothpick, if it comes out clean, the cakes are done.
- Transfer the cakes to a wire rack and leave to cool before dusting with icing sugar.

PREPARATION TIME: 25 MINUTES

COOKING TIME: 25 MINUTES

INGREDIENTS

1 large egg
120 ml / 4 fl. oz / ½ cup sunflower oil
120 ml / 4 fl. oz / ½ cup milk
375 g / 12 ½ oz / 2 ½ cups self-raising flour, sifted
55 g / 2 oz / ½ cup unsweetened cocoa powder, sifted
1 tsp baking powder
200 g / 7 oz / ¾ cup caster (superfine) sugar
110 g / 4 oz / ½ cup dark chocolate, minimum 60% cocoa solids, chopped
1 tsp peppermint essence
icing (confectioners') sugar to dust

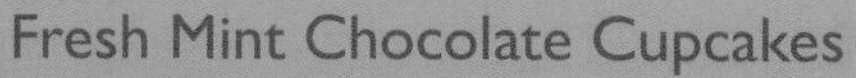

Fresh Mint Chocolate Cupcakes

274

Replace the peppermint essence with 1 tbsp chopped fresh mint leaves. Top the cupcakes with whipped cream and a fresh mint leaf.

275

MAKES 12

Cherry Bakewell cupcakes

PREPARATION TIME: 45 MINUTES

COOKING TIME: 20 MINUTES

INGREDIENTS

55 g / 2 oz / ½ cup self-raising flour, sifted
2 tsp baking powder
55 g / 2 oz / ½ cup ground almonds
110 g / 4 oz / ½ cup caster (superfine) sugar
110 g / 4 oz / ½ cup butter, softened
2 large eggs
1 tsp almond essence

TO DECORATE
225 g / 8 oz / 2 cups icing (confectioners') sugar
Boiling water, to mix
6 glace cherries, halved

- Preheat the oven to 190°C (170° fan) / 375 F / gas 5 and line a 12-hole cupcake tin with paper cases.
- Combine the flour, baking powder, ground almonds, sugar, butter, eggs and almond essence in a bowl and whisk together for 2 minutes.
- Divide the mixture between the paper cases then transfer to the oven and bake for 15 – 20 minutes.
- Test with a wooden toothpick, if it comes out clean, the cakes are done.
- Transfer the cakes to a wire rack and leave to cool.
- Sieve the icing sugar into a bowl, then slowly stir in the boiling water a few drops at a time until you have a thick icing.
- Spoon the icing onto the cakes and top each one with half a glace cherry.

Bakewell Cupcakes with Jam

276

Hide a tsp of raspberry jam (jelly) inside each cake as you fill the cases with cake mixture.

Apple Bakewell Cupcakes

277

Place a spoonful of apple compote in the centre of the cake and top with a slice of apple.

Chocolate Bakewell

278

Replace the cherry with a chocolate ball and drizzle the icing with melted dark chocolate.

279

MAKES 12

Chocolate and Coffee Cupcakes

- Preheat the oven to 190°C (170° fan) / 375 F / gas 5 and line a 12-hole cupcake tin with paper cases.
- Combine the flour, cocoa, sugar, butter, eggs and coffee powder in a bowl and whisk together for 2 minutes.
- Divide the mixture between the paper cases, then transfer to the oven and bake for 15 – 20 minutes.
- Transfer the cakes to a wire rack and leave to cool.
- To make the buttercream, beat the butter with a wooden spoon until light and fluffy then beat in the icing sugar, cocoa and coffee a quarter at a time.
- Use a whisk to incorporate the milk, then whisk for 2 minutes.
- Spoon the buttercream into a piping bag fitted with a large plain nozzle and pipe a generous swirl on top of each cake.

PREPARATION TIME: 15 MINUTES

COOKING TIME: 20 MINUTES

INGREDIENTS

110 g / 4 oz / ½ cup self-raising flour, sifted
28 g / 1 oz / ¼ cup unsweetened cocoa powder, sifted
110 g / 4 oz / ½ cup caster (superfine) sugar
110 g / 4 oz / ½ cup butter, softened
2 large eggs
2 tsp instant espresso powder

TO DECORATE

110 g / 4 oz / ½ cup butter, softened
225 g / 8 oz / 2 cups icing (confectioners') sugar
28 g / 1 oz / ¼ cup unsweetened cocoa powder, sifted
1 tsp instant espresso powder
2 tbsp milk

Coffee Bean-topped Cupcake

280

These cakes look great topped with chocolate-coated coffee beans.

281

MAKES 12

Wholemeal and Vanilla Cupcakes

- Preheat the oven to 190°C (170° fan) / 375 F / gas 5 and line a 12-hole cupcake tin with paper cases.
- Combine the flours, sugar, butter, eggs and vanilla extract in a bowl and whisk together for 2 minutes.
- Divide the mixture between the paper cases, then transfer to the oven and bake for 15 – 20 minutes.
- Test with a wooden toothpick, if it comes out clean, the cakes are done.
- Transfer the cakes to a wire rack and leave to cool Sprinkle with desiccated coconut and serve.

PREPARATION TIME: 25 MINUTES

COOKING TIME: 20 MINUTES

INGREDIENTS

55 g / 2 oz / ¼ cup self-raising flour, sifted
55 g / 2 oz / ¼ cup wholemeal flour
1 tsp bicarbonate of (baking) soda
110 g / 4 oz / ½ cup caster (superfine) sugar
110 g / 4 oz / ½ cup butter, softened
2 large eggs
1 tsp vanilla extract
1 tbsp desiccated coconut

Spiced Wholemeal Cupcakes

Try adding 1 tsp of mixed spice and 1 tsp of ground ginger to the cake mixture.

283

MAKES 12

Cashew and Maple Syrup Cupcakes

PREPARATION TIME: 1 HOUR

COOKING TIME: 20 MINUTES

INGREDIENTS

110 g / 4 oz / ½ cup self-raising flour, sifted
110 g / 4 oz / ½ cup caster (superfine) sugar
110 g / 4 oz / ½ cup butter, softened
2 large eggs
75 g / 2 ½ oz / ½ cup cashew nuts, chopped
120 ml / 4 fl. oz / ½ cup maple syrup

- Preheat the oven to 190°C (170° fan) / 375 F / gas 5 and line a 12-hole cupcake tin with paper cases.
- Combine the flour, sugar, butter, eggs and cashew nuts in a bowl and whisk together for 2 minutes.
- Divide the mixture between the paper cases, then transfer to the oven and bake for 15 – 20 minutes.
- Test with a wooden toothpick, if it comes out clean, the cakes are done.
- As soon as the cakes have come out of the oven, spoon over the maple syrup and let it soak in as they cool.

Pecan and Bourbon Cupcakes

284

Try this recipe with chopped pecans instead of the cashews and drizzle a tsp of bourbon over each cake after the maple syrup.

285

MAKES 12

Blackcurrant Buttercream Cupcakes

PREPARATION TIME: 1 HOUR

COOKING TIME: 20 MINUTES

INGREDIENTS

110 g / 4 oz / ½ cup self-raising flour, sifted
110 g / 4 oz / ½ cup caster (superfine) sugar
110 g / 4 oz / ½ cup butter, softened
2 large eggs
75 g / 2 ½ oz / ½ cup blackcurrants

TO DECORATE
110 g / 4 oz / ½ cup butter, softened
225 g / 8 oz / 2 cups icing (confectioners') sugar
2 tbsp blackcurrant syrup
white cake sprinkles

- Preheat the oven to 190°C (170° fan) / 375 F / gas 5 and line a 12-hole cupcake tin with paper cases.
- Combine the flour, sugar, butter and eggs in a bowl and whisk together for 2 minutes.
- Fold in the blackcurrants and divide the mixture between the paper cases. Transfer the tin to the oven and bake for 15 – 20 minutes.
- Transfer the cakes to a wire rack and leave to cool.
- To make the buttercream, beat the butter with a wooden spoon until light and fluffy then beat in the icing sugar a quarter at a time.
- Use a whisk to incorporate the blackcurrant syrup, then whisk for 2 minutes.
- Spoon the buttercream into a piping bag fitted with a large star nozzle and pipe a generous rosette on top of each cake.
- Finish with a scattering of cake sprinkles.

Fresh Blackcurrant Cupcakes

Try topping the finished cakes with a handful of fresh blackcurrants.

287

MAKES 12

Pineapple Cupcakes

Pineapple and Chilli Cupcakes

288

Add 1 small finely chopped red chilli to the muffin mixture.

Spiced Pineapple Muffins

289

Add ½ teaspoon of cinnamon and ½ teaspoon of ground nutmeg to the mixture.

Pina Colada Muffins

290

Add 1 tsp of coconut rum to the cake mixture. Decorate with coconut frosting, made with butter, icing sugar and coconut cream.

PREPARATION TIME: 25 MINUTES

COOKING TIME: 25 MINUTES

INGREDIENTS

1 large egg
120ml / 4 fl. oz / ½ cup sunflower oil
120ml / 4 fl. oz / ½ cup milk
375 g / 12 ½ oz / 2 ½ cups self-raising flour, sifted
1 tsp baking powder
200 g / 7 oz / ¾ cup caster (superfine) sugar
150 g / 5 oz / 1 cup canned pineapple pieces, drained

- Preheat the oven to 180°C (160° fan) / 350 F / gas 4 and line a 12-hole muffin tin with paper cases.
- Beat the egg in a jug with the oil and milk until well mixed.
- Mix the flour, baking powder, sugar and pineapple in a bowl, then pour in the egg mixture and stir just enough to combine.
- Divide the mixture between the paper cases, then bake in the oven for 20 – 25 minutes.
- Test with a wooden toothpick, if it comes out clean, the cakes are done.
- Transfer the cakes to a wire rack and leave to cool.

298

MAKES 12

Strawberry and Pistachio Cupcakes

PREPARATION TIME: 35 MINUTES

COOKING TIME: 20 MINUTES

INGREDIENTS

55 g / 2 oz / ½ cup self-raising flour, sifted
55 g / 2 oz / ½ cup ground pistachios
110 g / 4 oz / ½ cup caster (superfine) sugar
110 g / 4 oz / ½ cup butter, softened
2 large eggs
75 g / 2 ½ oz / ½ cup strawberries, chopped
36 whole pistachios

- Preheat the oven to 190°C (170° fan) / 375 F / gas 5 and line a 12-hole cupcake tin with paper cases.
- Combine the flour, ground pistachios, sugar, butter and eggs in a bowl and whisk together for 2 minutes.
- Fold in the chopped strawberries and divide the mixture between the paper cases, then press 3 whole pistachios into the top of each cake.
- Transfer the tin to the oven and bake for 15 – 20 minutes.
- Test with a wooden toothpick, if it comes out clean, the cakes are done.
- Transfer the cakes to a wire rack and leave to cool.

Raspberry and Pistachio Cupcakes

299

You can make these cakes with fresh raspberries in the cake mixture too.

300

MAKES 12

Wholemeal Hazelnut Cupcakes

PREPARATION TIME: 25 MINUTES

COOKING TIME: 20 MINUTES

INGREDIENTS

55 g / 2 oz / ¼ cup wholemeal flour
55 g / 2 oz / ¼ cup ground hazelnuts
1 tsp bicarbonate of (baking) soda
110 g / 4 oz / ½ cup caster (superfine) sugar
110 g / 4 oz / ½ cup butter, softened
2 large eggs
1 tsp vanilla extract

- Preheat the oven to 190°C (170° fan) / 375 F / gas 5 and line a 12-hole cupcake tin with paper cases.
- Combine the flour, ground hazelnuts (cob nuts), sugar, butter, eggs and vanilla extract in a bowl and whisk together for 2 minutes.
- Divide the mixture between the paper cases, then transfer to the oven and bake for 15 – 20 minutes.
- Test with a wooden toothpick, if it comes out clean, the cakes are done.
- Transfer the cakes to a wire rack and leave to cool.

Wholemeal hazelnut and Nutmeg Cupcakes

Add 1 tsp of freshly grated nutmeg to the cupcake mixture.

302

MAKES 12

Vanilla and Chocolate Heart Cupcakes

Lavender and Chocolate Heart Cupcakes

303

Replace the vanilla extract with 1 tbsp dried lavender flowers. Add a few drops of purple food colouring to the icing.

Vanilla and Mint Chocolate Heart Cupcakes

304

Add a few drops of peppermint oil to the mixture.

Chocolate Heart Cupcakes

305

Add 75g of cocoa powder to the cake mixture for extra decadence.

PREPARATION TIME: 25 MINUTES

COOKING TIME: 25 MINUTES

INGREDIENTS

1 large egg
120 ml / 4 fl. oz / ½ cup sunflower oil
120 ml / 4 fl. oz / ½ cup milk
375 g / 12 ½ oz / 2 ½ cups self-raising flour, sifted
1 tsp baking powder
200 g / 7 oz / ¾ cup caster (superfine) sugar
1 tsp vanilla extract

TO DECORATE

225 g / 8 oz / 2 cups icing (confectioners') sugar
boiling water, to mix
6 white chocolate hearts
6 dark chocolate hearts

- Preheat the oven to 180°C (160° fan) / 350 F / gas 4 and line a 12-hole muffin tin with paper cases.
- Beat the egg in a jug with the oil and milk until well mixed.
- Mix the flour, baking powder, sugar and vanilla in a bowl, then pour in the egg mixture and stir just enough to combine.
- Divide the mixture between the paper cases and bake in the oven for 20 – 25 minutes.
- Test with a wooden toothpick, if it comes out clean, the cakes are done.
- Transfer the cakes to a wire rack and leave to cool.
- Sieve the icing sugar into a bowl, then slowly stir in the boiling water a few drops at a time until you have a thick icing.
- Spoon onto the cakes and top each one with a chocolate heart.

322

MAKES 12

Lemon Porridge Breakfast Cupcakes

PREPARATION TIME: 25 MINUTES

COOKING TIME: 25 MINUTES

INGREDIENTS

1 large egg
120 ml / 4 fl. oz / ½ cup sunflower oil
120 ml / 4 fl. oz / ½ cup milk
1 lemon, juiced
375 g / 12 ½ oz / 2 ½ cups self-raising flour, sifted
1 tsp baking powder
200 g / 7 oz / ¾ cup caster (superfine) sugar
1 tbsp lemon zest, finely grated
75 g / 2 ½ oz / ½ cup porridge oats

- Preheat the oven to 180°C (160° fan) / 350 F / gas 4 and oil a 12-hole silicone muffin tin.
- Beat the egg in a jug with the oil, milk and lemon juice until well mixed.
- Mix the flour, baking powder, sugar, lemon zest and oats in a bowl, then pour in the egg mixture and stir just enough to combine.
- Divide the mixture between the moulds, then bake in the oven for 20 – 25 minutes.
- Test with a wooden toothpick, if it comes out clean, the cakes are done.
- Transfer the cakes to a wire rack and leave to cool.

Lemon Marmalade Breakfast Cupcakes

323

Glaze these cupcakes with warm lemon marmalade when they come out of the oven.

Fruit and Porridge Muffins

324

Add a handful of raisins and sultanas to the mixture before baking.

Orange Porridge Breakfast Muffins

325

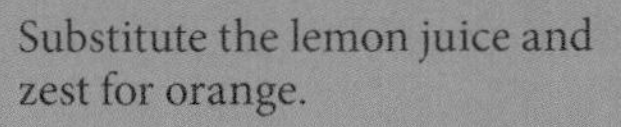

Substitute the lemon juice and zest for orange.

326

MAKES 12

Chocolate Caramac cupcakes

- Preheat the oven to 190°C (170° fan) / 375 F / gas 5 and line a 12-hole cupcake tin with paper cases.
- Combine the flour, cocoa, sugar, butter, eggs and vanilla extract in a bowl and whisk together for 2 minutes.
- Fold in the chopped Caramac then divide the mixture between the paper cases and bake for 15 – 20 minutes.
- Transfer the cakes to a wire rack and leave to cool.
- Heat the cream until it starts to simmer, then pour it over the chopped chocolate.
- Stir the ganache until the mixture has cooled and thickened, then refrigerate until thick enough to pipe.
- Spoon the ganache into a piping bag fitted with a large star nozzle and pipe a spiral on top of each cake.
- Use a vegetable peeler to make small curls of Caramac and scatter over the cakes.
- Sprinkle with edible glitter.

PREPARATION TIME 10 MINUTES

COOKING TIME 45 MINUTES

INGREDIENTS

110 g / 4 oz / ½ cup self-raising flour, sifted
28 g / 1 oz / ¼ cup unsweetened cocoa powder, sifted
110 g / 4 oz / ½ cup caster (superfine) sugar
110 g / 4 oz / ½ cup butter, softened
2 large eggs
1 tsp vanilla extract
110 g / 4 oz Caramac

TO DECORATE

225 ml / 8 fl. oz / 1 cup double (heavy) cream
225 g / 8 oz / 1 cup dark chocolate, minimum 60% cocoa solids, chopped
55 g / 2 oz Caramac
edible glitter

Caramac Cupcakes

327

Leave the cocoa powder out of the cake mixture and top the cakes with melted Caramac instead of the dark chocolate ganache.

328

MAKES 24

Goat's Cheese and Thyme Mini Cupcakes

- Preheat the oven to 180°C (160° fan) / 350 F / gas 4 and line a 24-hole muffin tin with paper cases.
- Beat the egg in a jug with the oil, yoghurt and cheese until well mixed.
- Mix the flour, raising agents, salt and thyme in a bowl, then pour in the egg mixture and stir just enough to combine.
- Divide the mixture between the paper cases, then bake in the oven for 10 – 15 minutes.
- Test with a wooden toothpick, if it comes out clean, the cupcakes are done.
- Serve warm.

PREPARATION TIME: 25 MINUTES

COOKING TIME: 15 MINUTES

INGREDIENTS

2 large eggs
120 ml / 4 fl. oz / ½ cup sunflower oil
180 ml / 6 fl. oz / ¾ cup Greek yogurt
110 g / 4 oz / 1 cup goat's cheese, cubed
225 g / 8 oz / 1 ½ cups plain (all purpose) flour
2 tsp baking powder
½ tsp bicarbonate of (baking) soda
½ tsp salt
2 tbsp fresh thyme leaves

Cheese, Onion and Thyme Mini Cupcakes

329

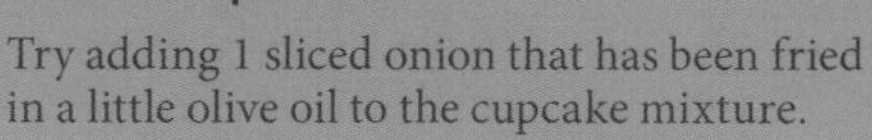

Try adding 1 sliced onion that has been fried in a little olive oil to the cupcake mixture.

330

MAKES 12

Iced Almond Cupcakes

PREPARATION TIME: 35 MINUTES

COOKING TIME: 20 MINUTES

INGREDIENTS

55 g / 2 oz / ½ cup self-raising flour, sifted
55 g / 2 oz / ½ cup ground almonds
110 g / 4 oz / ½ cup caster (superfine) sugar
110 g / 4 oz / ½ cup butter, softened
2 large eggs
1 tsp almond essence

TO DECORATE
225 g / 8 oz / 2 cups icing (confectioners') sugar
3 drops of almond essence
boiling water, to mix
12 small pink sweets

- Preheat the oven to 190°C (170° fan) / 375 F / gas 5 and line a 12-hole cupcake tin with paper cases.
- Combine the flour, ground almonds, sugar, butter, eggs and almond essence in a bowl and whisk together for 2 minutes.
- Divide the cake mixture between the paper cases, then transfer to the oven and bake for 15 – 20 minutes.
- Test with a wooden toothpick, if it comes out clean, the cakes are done.
- Transfer the cakes to a wire rack to cool completely.
- Sift the icing sugar into a bowl and add the almond essence, then slowly stir in the boiling water a few drops at a time until you have a thick icing.
- Spoon the icing on top of the cakes and decorate with the sweets.

Double Almond Cupcakes

331

These little cakes look great scattered with flaked (slivered) almonds instead of the sweets too.

332

MAKES 12

Apple, Almond and Cinnamon Cupcakes

PREPARATION TIME: 25 MINUTES

COOKING TIME: 25 MINUTES

INGREDIENTS

1 large egg
120 ml / 4 fl. oz / ½ cup sunflower oil
120 ml / 4 fl. oz / ½ cup milk
225 g / 7 ½ oz / 1 ½ cups self-raising flour, sifted
1 tsp baking powder
150 g / 5 oz / 1 ¼ cups ground almonds
200 g / 7 oz / ¾ cup caster (superfine) sugar
1 tsp ground cinnamon
1 apple, peeled, cored and sliced

- Preheat the oven to 180°C (160° fan) / 350 F / gas 4 and line a 12-hole muffin tin with paper cases.
- Beat the egg in a jug with the oil and milk until well mixed.
- Mix the flour, baking powder, ground almonds, sugar, cinnamon and apple slices in a bowl, then pour in the egg mixture and stir just enough to combine.
- Divide the mixture between the paper cases and bake in the oven for 20 – 25 minutes.
- Test with a wooden toothpick, if it comes out clean, the cakes are done.
- Transfer the cakes to a wire rack and leave to cool.

Pear, Almond and Cinnamon Cupcakes

333

This recipe is lovely with sliced pears instead of the apple.

334

MAKES 12

White and Dark Chocolate Cupcakes

- Preheat the oven to 190°C (170° fan) / 375 F / gas 5 and line a 12-hole cupcake tin with paper cases.
- Combine the flour, sugar, butter, eggs and vanilla extract in a bowl and whisk together for 2 minutes.
- Use half of the mixture to fill 6 of the paper cases.
- Mix the cocoa with the milk then fold it into the rest of the mixture and use it to fill the remaining cake cases.
- Bake for 15 – 20 minutes. Transfer the cakes to a wire rack and leave to cool.
- Chop the 2 chocolates and transfer to 2 separate mixing bowls. Heat the cream until it starts to simmer, then divide between the 2 chocolate bowls.
- Stir the ganache until the mixture has cooled and thickened. Use the white chocolate ganache to top the chocolate cupcakes and the dark chocolate ganache to top the vanilla cupcakes.

PREPARATION TIME: 1 HOUR 15 MINUTES

COOKING TIME: 20 MINUTES

INGREDIENTS

110 g / 4 oz / 1 cup self-raising flour, sifted
110 g / 4 oz / ½ cup caster (superfine) sugar
110 g / 4 oz / ½ cup butter, softened
2 large eggs
1 tsp vanilla extract
28 g / 1 oz / ¼ cup unsweetened cocoa powder, sifted
1 tbsp milk

TO DECORATE

110 g / 4 oz / ½ cup white chocolate
110 g / 4 oz / ½ cup dark chocolate, minimum 60% cocoa solids
225 ml / 8 fl. oz / 1 cup double (heavy) cream

Mix and Match Cupcakes

335

Stir 5 tbsp white chocolate chips into the chocolate cake mixture and stir 5 tbsp dark chocolate chips into the vanilla cake mixture.

336

MAKES 12

Wholemeal Cranberry Cupcakes

- Preheat the oven to 180°C (160° fan) / 350 F / gas 4 and oil a 12-hole silicone muffin tin.
- Beat the egg in a jug with the oil and milk until well mixed.
- Mix the flour, baking powder, sugar and cranberries in a bowl, then pour in the egg mixture and stir just enough to combine.
- Divide the mixture between the moulds, then bake in the oven for 20 – 25 minutes.
- Test with a wooden toothpick, if it comes out clean, the cakes are done.
- Transfer the cakes to a wire rack and leave to cool.

PREPARATION TIME: 25 MINUTES

COOKING TIME: 25 MINUTES

INGREDIENTS

1 large egg
120 ml / 4 fl. oz / ½ cup sunflower oil
120 ml / 4 fl. oz / ½ cup milk
375 g / 12 ½ oz / 2 ½ cups wholemeal flour
2 tsp baking powder
200 g / 7 oz / ¾ cup caster (superfine) sugar
150 g / 5 oz / 1 cup cranberries

Cranberry Cupcakes with Orange Butter

337

Mix 110g / 4 oz softened butter with the finely grated zest of 1 orange then refrigerate until firm. Form into small pats and serve with the cupcakes.

338

MAKES 12

Banana Cupcakes with Chocolate Ganache

PREPARATION TIME: 25 MINUTES

COOKING TIME: 25 MINUTES

INGREDIENTS

3 very ripe bananas
110 g / 4 oz / ⅔ cup soft light brown sugar
2 large eggs
120 ml / 4 fl. oz / ½ cup sunflower oil
225 g / 8 oz / 1 ½ cups plain (all purpose) flour
1 tsp bicarbonate of (baking) soda

TO DECORATE
225 g / 8 oz / ½ cup dark chocolate, minimum 60% cocoa solids
225 ml / 8 fl. oz / 1 cup double (heavy) cream
2 tbsp flaked (slivered) almonds

- Preheat the oven to 200°C (180° fan) / 400 F / gas 6 and line a 12-hole cupcake tin with paper cases.
- Mash the bananas with a fork then whisk in the sugar, eggs and oil.
- Sieve the flour and bicarbonate of soda into the bowl and stir to evenly mix all the ingredients together.
- Divide the mixture between the paper cases, then transfer to the oven and bake for 15 – 20 minutes.
- Transfer the cakes to a wire rack and leave to cool.
- To make the ganache, chop the chocolate and transfer to a mixing bowl.
- Heat the cream until it starts to simmer, then pour over the chopped chocolate and stir until the mixture has cooled and thickened.
- Apply the ganache with a palette knife and sprinkle the cakes with flaked almonds.

Chocolate and Banana Cupcakes

339

Try adding 110g / 4oz / ½ cup chopped dark chocolate to the cake mixture for chocolate and banana cupcakes.

340

MAKES 12

Fairy Ring Cupcakes

PREPARATION TIME: 1 HOUR

COOKING TIME: 20 MINUTES

INGREDIENTS

110 g / 4 oz / ½ cup self-raising flour, sifted
110 g / 4 oz / ½ cup caster (superfine) sugar
110 g / 4 oz / ½ cup butter, softened
2 large eggs
75 g / 2 ½ oz / ½ cup mixed forest fruits, chopped if large

TO DECORATE
110 g / 4 oz / ½ cup butter, softened
225 g / 8 oz / 2 cups icing (confectioners') sugar
2 tbsp milk
5 drops of blue, green and red food colouring
55 g / 2 oz ready to roll fondant icing

- Preheat the oven to 190°C (170° fan) / 375 F / gas 5 and line a 12-hole cupcake tin with foil cases.
- Combine the flour, sugar, butter and eggs in a bowl and whisk together for 2 minutes.
- Fold in the forest fruits and divide the mixture between the paper cases. Bake for 15 – 20 minutes.
- Transfer the cakes to a wire rack and leave to cool.
- Beat the butter with a wooden spoon until light and fluffy then beat in the icing sugar. Add the milk, then whisk for 2 minutes.
- Spoon 1 tbsp of the buttercream into a small piping bag fitted with a small plain nozzle and set aside.
- Stir the green food colouring into the rest of the buttercream until evenly coloured, then stir the blue food colouring in just enough to create a marbled effect.
- Spoon the buttercream into a piping bag fitted with a large star nozzle and pipe a swirl on top of each cake.
- Divide the fondant icing in 2 and colour one half red. Use the white icing to make the toadstool stalks and the red to make the caps and attach with a drop of water.
- Assemble the toadstools on top of the cakes and pipe the spots on with the reserved white buttercream.

341

MAKES 12

Orange and Ginger Cupcakes

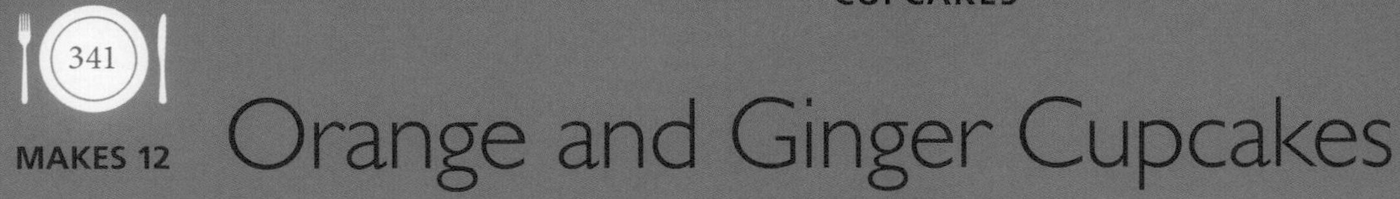
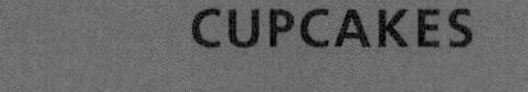

Orange and Nutmeg Cupcakes

342

Replace the ground ginger with 1 tsp of freshly grated nutmeg.

Orange and Cinnamon Cupcakes

343

Replace the ground ginger with 1 tsp of cinnamon.

Lemon and Ginger Cupcakes

344

Replace the orange with a lemon.

PREPARATION TIME: 25 MINUTES

COOKING TIME: 20 MINUTES

INGREDIENTS

110 g / 4 oz / ½ cup self-raising flour, sifted
110 g / 4 oz / ½ cup caster (superfine) sugar
110 g / 4 oz / ½ cup butter, softened
2 large eggs
2 tsp ground ginger
1 orange, zest finely grated
Icing (confectioners') sugar to dust

- Preheat the oven to 190°C (170° fan) / 375 F / gas 5 and line a 12-hole cupcake tin with paper cases.
- Combine the flour, sugar, butter, eggs, ground ginger and orange zest in a bowl and whisk together for 2 minutes.
- Divide the mixture between the paper cases, then transfer to the oven and bake for 15 – 20 minutes.
- Test with a wooden toothpick, if it comes out clean, the cakes are done.
- Transfer the cakes to a wire rack and leave to cool completely before dusting with icing sugar.

MAKES 12

Banana, Almond and Rum Cupcakes

Rum and Raisin Cupcakes

Try soaking 2 tbsp sultanas in 2 tbsp of rum overnight and adding them to the cake mixture.

Rum, Raisin and Cinnamon Cupcakes

347

Ass 1 tsp of cinnamon to the cake mixture before cooking.

PREPARATION TIME: 20 MINUTES

COOKING TIME: 20 MINUTES

INGREDIENTS

55 g / 2 oz / ½ cup self-raising flour, sifted
2 tsp baking powder
55 g / 2 oz / ½ cup ground almonds
110 g / 4 oz / ½ cup caster (superfine) sugar
110 g / 4 oz / ½ cup butter, softened
2 large eggs
1 tsp almond essence
2 medium bananas, sliced
60 ml / 2 fl. oz / ¼ cup dark rum

- Preheat the oven to 190°C (170° fan) / 375 F / gas 5 and line a 12-hole cupcake tin with paper cases.
- Combine the flour, baking powder, ground almonds, sugar, butter, eggs and almond essence in a bowl and whisk together for 2 minutes.
- Divide the mixture between the paper cases and press a banana slice into the top of each, then transfer to the oven and bake for 15 – 20 minutes.
- Test with a wooden toothpick, if it comes out clean, the cakes are done.
- As soon as the cakes come out of the oven, spoon 1 tsp of rum over each one.
- Transfer the cakes to a wire rack and leave to cool.

348

MAKES 36

Chocolate Maraschino Mini Cupcakes

- Preheat the oven to 190°C (170° fan) / 375 F / gas 5 and line a 36 mini cupcake tin with paper cases.
- Combine the flour, cocoa, sugar, butter and eggs in a bowl and whisk together for 2 minutes.
- Divide the mixture between the paper cases. Press a square of chocolate into the top of each one and top with a cherry.
- Transfer the tin to the oven and bake for 10 – 15 minutes.
- Serve immediately while the chocolate is still molten inside.

PREPARATION TIME: 45 MINUTES

COOKING TIME: 15 MINUTES

INGREDIENTS

110 g / 4 oz / ½ cup self-raising flour, sifted
28 g / 1 oz / ¼ cup unsweetened cocoa powder, sifted
110 g / 4 oz / ½ cup caster (superfine) sugar
110 g / 4 oz / ½ cup butter, softened
2 large eggs
150 g / 5 oz / ⅔ cup dark chocolate, minimum 60% cocoa solids
36 maraschino cherries with stems

Double Cherry Cupcakes

349

Try adding a spoonful of cherry jam (jelly) before topping with the chocolate and cherries for an extra layer of cherry flavour.

350

MAKES 12

Coconut Cream Cupcakes

- Preheat the oven to 190°C (170° fan) / 375 F / gas 5 and line a 12-hole cupcake tin with paper cases.
- Combine the flour, sugar, butter, eggs and coconut in a bowl and whisk together for 2 minutes.
- Divide the mixture between the paper cases, then transfer to the oven and bake for 15 – 20 minutes.
- Transfer the cakes to a wire rack and leave to cool.
- Sprinkle the desiccated coconut onto a baking tray and lightly toast under a hot grill for 2 minutes. Leave to cool.
- Sieve the icing sugar into a bowl and stir in the coconut cream a little at a time until it forms a thick, spreadable icing.
- Use a palate knife to apply a thick layer of icing to each cake, then dip the tops in the toasted coconut.

PREPARATION TIME: 1 HOUR 15 MINUTES

COOKING TIME: 20 MINUTES

INGREDIENTS

28 g / 1 oz / ⅛ cup desiccated coconut
110 g / 4 oz / 1 cup self-raising flour, sifted
110 g / 4 oz / ½ cup caster (superfine) sugar
110 g / 4 oz / ½ cup butter, softened
2 large eggs
28 g / 1 oz / ⅛ cup desiccated coconut

TO DECORATE

225 g / 8 oz / 2 cups icing (confectioners') sugar
2 – 4 tbsp coconut cream

Coconut and Rum Cupcakes

351

Drizzle a tablespoon of white rum over each cupcake as they come out of the oven before cooling and icing.

352

MAKES 12

Chocolate and Almond Cupcakes

- Preheat the oven to 180°C (160° fan) / 350 F / gas 4 and line a 12-hole muffin tin with paper cases.
- Beat the egg in a jug with the oil and milk until well mixed.
- Mix the flour, baking powder, ground almonds and sugar in a bowl, then pour in the egg mixture and chopped chocolate and stir just enough to combine.
- Divide the mixture between the paper cases and sprinkle with flaked almonds, then bake in the oven for 20 – 25 minutes.
- Test with a wooden toothpick, if it comes out clean, the cakes are done.
- Transfer the cakes to a wire rack and leave to cool.

PREPARATION TIME: 25 MINUTES

COOKING TIME: 25 MINUTES

INGREDIENTS

1 large egg
120ml / 4 fl. oz / ½ cup sunflower oil
120ml / 4 fl. oz / ½ cup milk
375 g / 12 ½ oz / 2 ½ cups self-raising flour, sifted
1 tsp baking powder
55 g / 2 oz / ½ cup ground almonds
200 g / 7 oz / ¾ cup caster sugar
110 g / 4 oz / ½ cup dark chocolate, chopped
75 g / 2 ½ oz / ½ cup flaked (slivered) almonds

Blackcurrant Cupcakes

353

MAKES 12

PREPARATION TIME: 25 MINUTES

COOKING TIME: 25 MINUTES

INGREDIENTS

1 large egg
120 ml / 4 fl. oz / ½ cup sunflower oil
120 ml / 4 fl. oz / ½ cup milk
375 g / 12 ½ oz / 2 ½ cups self-raising flour, sifted
1 tsp baking powder
200 g / 7 oz / ¾ cup caster (superfine) sugar
150 g / 5 oz / 1 cup blackcurrants

- Preheat the oven to 180°C (160° fan) / 350 F / gas 4 and oil a 12-hole silicone muffin mould.
- Beat the egg in a jug with the oil and milk until well mixed.
- Mix the flour, baking powder, sugar and blackcurrants in a bowl, then pour in the egg mixture and stir just enough to combine.
- Divide the mixture between the moulds, then bake in the oven for 20 – 25 minutes.
- Test with a wooden toothpick, if it comes out clean, the cakes are done.
- Transfer the cakes to a wire rack and leave to cool.

Fruit Gum Cupcakes

354

MAKES 12

PREPARATION TIME: 1 HOUR

COOKING TIME: 20 MINUTES

INGREDIENTS

110 g / 4 oz / ½ cup self-raising flour
110 g / 4 oz / ½ cup caster sugar
110 g / 4 oz / ½ cup butter, softened
2 large eggs
75 g / 2 ½ oz / ½ cup small fruit gums

TO DECORATE

110 g / 4 oz / ½ cup butter, softened
225 g / 8 oz / 2 cups icing (confectioners') sugar
2 tbsp milk
75 g / 2 ½ oz / ½ cup small fruit gums

- Preheat the oven to 190°C (170° fan) / 375 F / gas 5 and line a 12-hole cupcake tin with paper cases.
- Combine the flour, sugar, butter and eggs in a bowl and whisk together for 2 minutes.
- Fold in the fruit gums and divide the mixture between the paper cases. Transfer the tin to the oven and bake for 15 – 20 minutes. Transfer the cakes to a wire rack and leave to cool.
- To make the buttercream, beat the butter with a wooden spoon until light and fluffy then beat in the icing sugar a quarter at a time.
- Use a whisk to incorporate the milk, then whisk for 2 minutes.
- Spoon the buttercream into a piping bag fitted with a large star nozzle and pipe a generous rosette on top of each cake.
- Finish with a scattering of fruit gums.

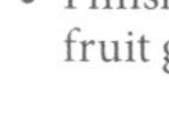

355

MAKES 12

Raspberry and Ginger Cupcakes

- Preheat the oven to 180°C (160° fan) / 350 F / gas 4 and line a 12-hole muffin tin with paper cases.
- Beat the egg in a jug with the oil and milk until well mixed.
- Mix the flour, baking powder, sugar, raspberries and ginger in a bowl, then pour in the egg mixture and stir just enough to combine.
- Divide the mixture between the moulds, then bake in the oven for 20 – 25 minutes.
- Test with a wooden toothpick, if it comes out clean, the cakes are done.
- Transfer the cakes to a wire rack and leave to cool.

PREPARATION TIME: 25 MINUTES

COOKING TIME: 25 MINUTES

INGREDIENTS

1 large egg
120 ml / 4 fl. oz / ½ cup sunflower oil
120 ml / 4 fl. oz / ½ cup milk
375 g / 12 ½ oz / 2 ½ cups self-raising flour, sifted
1 tsp baking powder
200 g / 7 oz / ¾ cup caster (superfine) sugar
150 g / 5 oz / 1 cup raspberries
75 g / 2 ½ oz / ½ cup crystallised ginger, chopped

Extra Ginger Cupcakes

356

For extra ginger flavour, add 2 tsp ground ginger to the dry ingredients before mixing.

357

MAKES 24

Wholemeal Apple and Cheddar Mini Cupcakes

- Preheat the oven to 180°C (160° fan) / 350 F / gas 4 and oil a 24-hole silicone muffin mould.
- Beat the egg in a jug with the oil, yoghurt, cheese and apple until well mixed.
- Mix the flour, raising agents and salt in a bowl, then pour in the egg mixture and stir just enough to combine.
- Divide the mixture between the paper cases, then bake in the oven for 10 – 15 minutes.
- Test with a wooden toothpick, if it comes out clean, the cupcakes are done.
- Serve warm.

PREPARATION TIME: 25 MINUTES

COOKING TIME: 15 MINUTES

INGREDIENTS

2 large eggs
120 ml / 4 fl. oz / ½ cup sunflower oil
180 ml / 6 fl. oz / ¾ cup Greek yogurt
110 g / 4 oz / 1 cup Cheddar, grated
1 apple, peeled, cored and grated
225 g / 8 oz / 1 ½ cups wholemeal flour
2 tsp baking powder
½ tsp bicarbonate of (baking) soda
½ tsp salt

Pear and Cheddar Mini Cupcakes

358

Replace the apple with a pear.

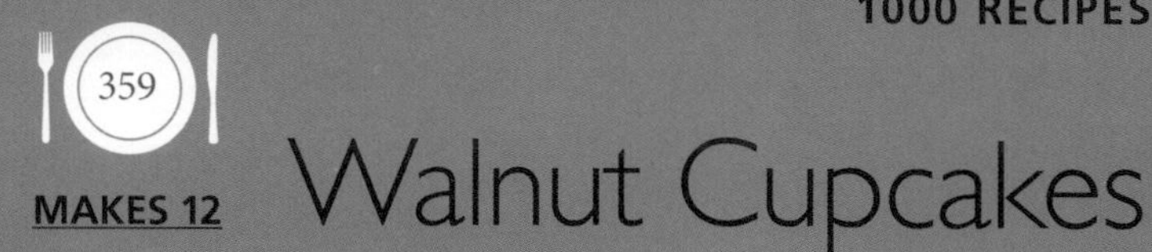

359

MAKES 12

Walnut Cupcakes

PREPARATION TIME: 20 MINUTES

COOKING TIME: 20 MINUTES

INGREDIENTS

55 g / 2 oz / ¼ cup self-raising flour, sifted
2 tsp baking powder
55 g / 2 oz / ¼ cup ground walnuts
110 g / 4 oz / ½ cup caster (superfine) sugar
110 g / 4 oz / ½ cup butter, softened
2 large eggs
75 g / 2 ½ oz / ½ cup walnuts, chopped

- Preheat the oven to 190°C (170° fan) / 375 F / gas 5 and line a 12-hole cupcake tin with paper cases.
- Combine the flour, baking powder, ground walnuts, sugar, butter, eggs and chopped walnuts in a bowl and whisk together for 2 minutes.
- Divide the mixture between the paper cases, then transfer to the oven and bake for 15 – 20 minutes.
- Test with a wooden toothpick, if it comes out clean, the cakes are done.
- Transfer the cakes to a wire rack and leave to cool.

Walnut and Honey Cupcakes

360

Try drizzling these cakes with honey when they come out of the oven and serve warm with honeycomb ice cream.

Almond and Honey Cupcakes

361

Replace the walnuts with almonds and drizzle with honey when they come out of the oven.

362

MAKES 12

Pink Flower Cupcakes

Purple Flower Cupcakes

363

Replace the rose water with a few drops of lavender oil and use purple food colouring to colour the icing. Top the cakes with purple sugar flowers.

Yellow Flower Cupcakes

364

Replace the rose water with a few drops of lemon juice and use yellow food colouring to colour the icing. Top the cakes with yellow sugar flowers.

PREPARATION TIME: 25 MINUTES

COOKING TIME: 20 MINUTES

INGREDIENTS

110 g / 4 oz / ½ cup self-raising flour, sifted
110 g / 4 oz / ½ cup caster (superfine) sugar
110 g / 4 oz / ½ cup butter, softened
2 large eggs
1 tbsp rose water

TO DECORATE

225 g / 8 oz / 2 cups icing (confectioners') sugar
boiling water ,to mix
pink food colouring
pink and yellow sugar flowers

- Preheat the oven to 190°C (170° fan) / 375 F / gas 5 and line a 12-hole cupcake tin with paper cases.
- Combine the flour, sugar, butter, eggs and rose water in a bowl and whisk together for 2 minutes.
- Divide the mixture between the paper cases, then transfer to the oven and bake for 15 – 20 minutes.
- Test with a wooden toothpick, if it comes out clean, the cakes are done.
- Transfer the cakes to a wire rack and leave to cool.
- Sieve the icing sugar into a bowl, then slowly stir in the boiling water a few drops at a time until you have a thick icing.
- Stir in the food colouring a drop at a time until you reach your desired colour.
- Spread the icing onto the cakes with the back of a spoon.
- Top the cakes with sugar flowers.

MAKES 12

Chocolate and Strawberry Cupcakes

Mint and Chocolate Cupcakes

366

Add 1 tbsp of chopped fresh mint to the cupcake mixture.

Chocolate and Sultana Cupcakes

367

Add 75 g / 3 oz of sultanas to the cupcake mixture.

Chocolate and Raisin Cupcakes

Add 75 g / 3 oz of raisin to the cupcake mixture.

PREPARATION TIME: 25 MINUTES

COOKING TIME:
20 – 25 MINUTES

INGREDIENTS

1 large egg
120 ml / 4 fl. oz / ½ cup sunflower oil
120 ml / 4 fl. oz / ½ cup milk
375 g / 12 ½ oz / 2 ½ cups self-raising flour, sifted
1 tsp baking powder
200 g / 7 oz / ¾ cup caster (superfine) sugar
110 g / 4 oz dark chocolate, minimum 60% cocoa solids, chopped
150 g / 5 oz / 1 cup strawberries, chopped

TO DECORATE
6 strawberries, halved
12 sprigs of mint

- Preheat the oven to 180°°C (160° fan) / 350 F / gas 4 and line a 12-hole muffin tin with paper cases.
- Beat the egg in a jug with the oil and milk until well mixed.
- Mix the flour, baking powder and sugar in a bowl, then pour in the egg mixture, chocolate and strawberries and stir just enough to combine.
- Divide the mixture between the paper cases, then bake in the oven for 20 – 25 minutes.
- Test with a wooden toothpick, if it comes out clean, the cakes are done.
- Transfer the cakes to a wire rack and leave to cool before decorating each cake with half a strawberry and a sprig of mint.

369

Spicy Wholemeal Mini Cupcakes

MAKES 24

- Preheat the oven to 190°C (170° fan) / 375 F / gas 5 and oil a 24-hole silicone mini cupcake mould.
- Combine the flours, sugar, butter, eggs, spices and orange zest in a bowl and whisk together for 2 minutes.
- Divide the mixture between the moulds, then bake in the oven for 10 – 15 minutes.
- Test with a wooden toothpick, if it comes out clean, the cakes are done.
- Transfer the cakes to a wire rack and leave to cool.

PREPARATION TIME: 25 MINUTES

COOKING TIME: 15 MINUTES

INGREDIENTS

55 g / 2 oz / ¼ cup self-raising flour, sifted
55 g / 2 oz / ¼ cup wholemeal flour
1 tsp bicarbonate of (baking) soda
110 g / 4 oz / ½ cup caster (superfine) sugar
110 g / 4 oz / ½ cup butter, softened
2 large eggs
1 tsp ground mixed spice
½ tsp freshly grated nutmeg
1 orange, zest finely grated

370

Crunchy Nut Cupcakes

Add 5 tbsp chopped walnuts to the cake mixture for extra texture.

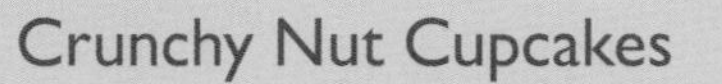

371

Chocolate Honeycomb Cupcakes

MAKES 12

- Preheat the oven to 190°C (170° fan) / 375 F / gas 5 and line a 12-hole cupcake tin with paper cases.
- Combine the flour, sugar, butter and eggs in a bowl and whisk together for 2 minutes.
- Fold in the honeycomb balls and divide the mixture between the paper cases.
- Transfer the tin to the oven and bake for 15 – 20 minutes.
- Transfer the cakes to a wire rack and leave to cool.
- To make the icing, sift the icing sugar into a bowl, then slowly stir in the boiling water a few drops at a time until you have a thick icing.
- Stir in the food colouring until it is evenly coloured, then spoon the icing on top of the cakes.
- Top each cake with a chocolate honeycomb ball.

PREPARATION TIME: 45 MINUTES

COOKING TIME: 20 MINUTES

INGREDIENTS

110 g / 4 oz / ½ cup self-raising flour, sifted
110 g / 4 oz / ½ cup caster (superfine) sugar
110 g / 4 oz / ½ cup butter, softened
2 large eggs
75 g / 2 ½ oz / ½ cup chocolate honeycomb balls

TO DECORATE

225 g / 8 oz / 2 cups icing (confectioners') sugar
boiling water, to mix
5 drops blue food colouring
12 chocolate honeycomb balls

372

Buttercream and Honeycomb Cupcakes

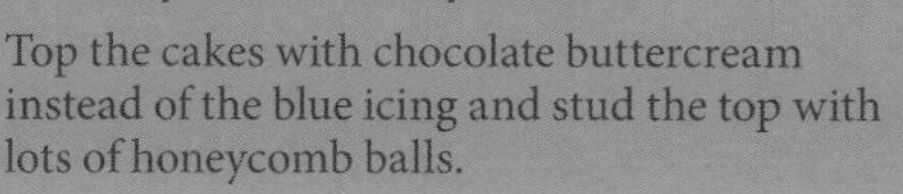

Top the cakes with chocolate buttercream instead of the blue icing and stud the top with lots of honeycomb balls.

373

MAKES 12

Coconut Cupcakes

PREPARATION TIME: 1 HOUR

COOKING TIME: 20 MINUTES

INGREDIENTS

110 g / 4 oz / 1 cup self-raising flour, sifted
110 g / 4 oz / ½ cup caster (superfine) sugar
110 g / 4 oz / ½ cup butter, softened
2 large eggs
28 g / 1 oz / ⅛ cup desiccated coconut

TO DECORATE
28 g / 1 oz / ⅛ cup desiccated coconut

- Preheat the oven to 190°C (170° fan) / 375 F / gas 5 and line a 12-hole cupcake tin or 36 hole mini cupcake tin with paper cases.
- Combine the flour, sugar, butter, eggs and coconut in a bowl and whisk together for 2 minutes.
- Divide the mixture between the paper cases, then transfer to the oven and bake for 15 – 20 minutes for the normal sized cakes or 10 – 15 minutes for the mini ones.
- Test with a wooden toothpick, if it comes out clean, the cakes are done.
- Sprinkle the desiccated coconut onto a small plate and press the top of each cake in it whilst still warm.
- Transfer the cakes to a wire rack and leave to cool.

Sweet Chocolate Coconut Cupcakes

374

Spread the top of the cakes with melted chocolate before dipping in the coconut.

375

MAKES 12

Lemon Cupcakes

PREPARATION TIME: 20 MINUTES

COOKING TIME: 20 MINUTES

INGREDIENTS

110 g / 4 oz / 1 cup self-raising flour, sifted
110 g / 4 oz / ½ cup caster (superfine) sugar
110 g / 4 oz / ½ cup butter, softened
2 large eggs
1 lemon, zest finely grated

- Preheat the oven to 190°C (170° fan) / 375 F / gas 5 and line 12 dariole moulds with greaseproof paper.
- Combine the flour, sugar, butter, eggs and lemon zest in a bowl and whisk together for 2 minutes.
- Divide the mixture between the paper cases, then transfer to the oven and bake for 15 – 20 minutes.
- Test with a wooden toothpick, if it comes out clean, the cakes are done.
- Transfer the cakes to a wire rack and leave to cool.

Lemon Curd Cupcakes

376

Slice a circle out of the cupcake. Top each cupcake with a spoonful of lemon curd and replace the top.

377

MAKES 12

Walnut and Coffee Cupcakes

Cupcakes with Coffee Icing

378

Sieve 150g / 5 oz / ⅔ cup icing sugar and 2 tsp instant coffee powder into a bowl and add enough boiling water to make a pourable icing. Drizzle over the cakes before topping with the walnut halves.

Pistachio and Coffee Cupcakes

379

Replace the walnuts with pistachio nuts.

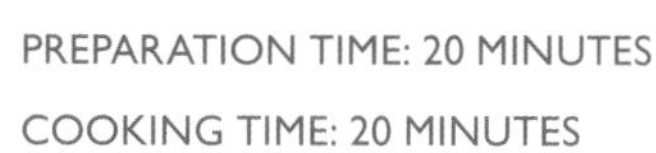

PREPARATION TIME: 20 MINUTES

COOKING TIME: 20 MINUTES

INGREDIENTS

110 g / 4 oz / 1 cup self-raising flour, sifted
110 g / 4 oz / ½ cup caster (superfine) sugar
110 g / 4 oz / ½ cup butter, softened
2 large eggs
2 tsp instant espresso powder
75 g / 2 ½ oz / ½ cup walnuts, chopped
12 walnut halves

- Preheat the oven to 190°C (170° fan) / 375 F / gas 5 and line a 12-hole cupcake tin with paper cases.
- Combine the flour, sugar, butter, eggs, espresso powder and chopped walnuts in a bowl and whisk together for 2 minutes.
- Divide the mixture between the paper cases, then transfer to the oven and bake for 15 – 20 minutes.
- Test with a wooden toothpick, if it comes out clean, the cakes are done.
- Transfer the cakes to a wire rack and leave to cool.
- Top each cake with a walnut half to finish.

380

MAKES 12

Chocolate and Marmalade Cupcakes

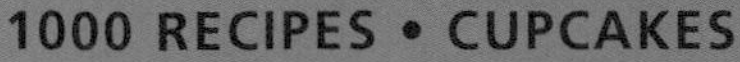

Matcha and Buttercream Cupcakes

381

Ice the cupcakes with buttercream flavoured with 1 tsp of matcha green tea powder and decorate with a sprinkling of chocolate chips.

Chocolate and Raspberry Jam Cupcakes

382

Replace the marmalade with raspberry jam.

PREPARATION TIME: 25 MINUTES

COOKING TIME: 20 MINUTES

INGREDIENTS

110 g / 4 oz / ½ cup self-raising flour, sifted
28 g / 1 oz / ¼ cup unsweetened cocoa powder, sifted
1 tbsp matcha green tea powder
110 g / 4 oz / ½ cup caster (superfine) sugar
110 g / 4 oz / ½ cup butter, softened
2 large eggs

TO DECORATE
2 tsp matcha green tea powder
110 g / 4 oz / ½ cup marmalade

- Preheat the oven to 190°C (170° fan) / 375 F / gas 5 and line a 12-hole cupcake tin with paper cases.
- Combine the flour, cocoa, matcha, sugar, butter and eggs in a bowl and whisk together for 2 minutes.
- Divide the mixture between the paper cases, then transfer to the oven and bake for 15 – 20 minutes.
- Test with a wooden toothpick, if it comes out clean, the cakes are done.
- Transfer the cakes to a wire rack and leave to cool completely before sprinkling with a little matcha powder.
- Sieve the marmalade into a small saucepan to remove any peel and heat gently until runny.
- Spoon the hot marmalade over the cakes.

383

MAKES 24

Szechuan Pepper Mini Cupcakes

- Preheat the oven to 180°C (160° fan) / 350 F / gas 4 and line a 24-hole mini muffin tin with paper cases.
- Beat the egg in a jug with the oil and milk until well mixed.
- Mix the flour, baking powder, sugar and pepper in a bowl, then pour in the egg mixture and stir just enough to combine.
- Divide the mixture between the moulds, then bake in the oven for 15 – 20 minutes.
- Test with a wooden toothpick, if it comes out clean, the cakes are done.
- Transfer the cakes to a wire rack and leave to cool.
- To decorate, melt the chocolates in 3 separate bowls and spoon into small piping bags.
- Pipe lines of the 3 chocolates across the top of the cupcakes and leave to set.

PREPARATION TIME: 25 MINUTES

COOKING TIME: 20 MINUTES

INGREDIENTS

1 large egg
120 ml / 4 fl. oz / ½ cup sunflower oil
120 ml / 4 fl. oz / ½ cup milk
375 g / 12 ½ oz / 2 ½ cups self-raising flour, sifted
1 tsp baking powder
200 g / 7 oz / ¾ cup caster (superfine) sugar
2 tsp ground Szechuan pepper

TO DECORATE
55 g / 2 oz dark / ¼ cup chocolate, minimum 60% cocoa solids, chopped
55 g / 2 oz / ¼ cup milk chocolate, chopped
55 g / 2 oz / ¼ cup white chocolate, chopped

Szechuan and Orange Mini Cupcakes

384

Szechuan pepper goes really well with orange, try adding the finely grated zest of 1 orange to the cupcake mixture.

385

MAKES 12

Fig and Caraway Cupcakes

- Preheat the oven to 190°C (170° fan) / 375 F / gas 5 and oil a 12-hole silicone cupcake mould.
- Sieve the flour and bicarbonate of soda together into a bowl.
- Put the golden syrup, butter and brown sugar in a small saucepan and boil gently for 2 minutes, stirring to dissolve the sugar.
- Pour the butter and sugar mixture onto the flour with the eggs, milk caraway seeds and chopped figs and fold it all together until smooth.
- Divide the mixture between the paper cases, then transfer to the oven and bake for 20 – 25 minutes.
- Test with a wooden toothpick, if it comes out clean, the cakes are done.
- Transfer the cakes to a wire rack and leave to cool.

PREPARATION TIME: 25 MINUTES

COOKING TIME: 25 MINUTES

INGREDIENTS

250 g / 9 oz / 1 ¾ cups self-raising flour
1 tsp bicarbonate of (baking) soda
200 g / 8 ½ oz / ½ cup golden syrup
125 g / 4 ½ oz / ½ cup butter
125 g / 4 ½ oz / ¾ cup dark brown sugar
2 large eggs, beaten
240 ml / 8 fl. oz / 1 cup milk
2 tsp caraway seeds
75 g / 2 ½ oz / ½ cup dried figs, chopped

Apricot and Caraway Cupcakes

386

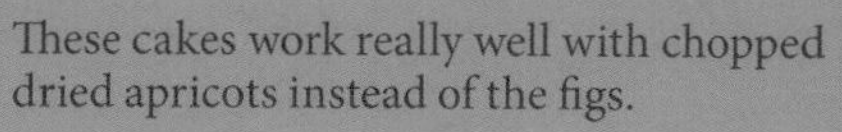
These cakes work really well with chopped dried apricots instead of the figs.

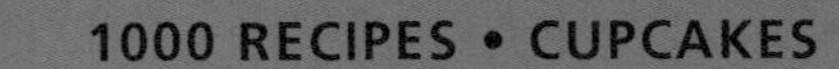

387

MAKES 12

Raspberry and Almond Cupcakes

PREPARATION TIME: 20 MINUTES

COOKING TIME: 20 MINUTES

INGREDIENTS

55 g / 2 oz / ½ cup self-raising flour, sifted
55 g / 2 oz / ½ cup ground almonds
110 g / 4 oz / ½ cup caster (superfine) sugar
110 g / 4 oz / ½ cup butter, softened
2 large eggs
1 tsp almond essence
150 g / 5 oz / 1 cup raspberries

- Preheat the oven to 190°C (170° fan) / 375 F / gas 5 and line a 12-hole cupcake tin with paper cases.
- Combine the flour, ground almonds, sugar, butter, eggs and almond essence in a bowl and whisk together for 2 minutes.
- Fold in the raspberries, divide the mixture between the paper cases and transfer the tin to the oven to bake for 15 – 20 minutes.
- Test with a wooden toothpick, if it comes out clean, the cakes are done.
- Transfer the cakes to a wire rack and leave to cool.

Cupcakes with Almond Drizzle

388

Mix 225g / 8 oz / 1 cup icing sugar with ½ tsp almond essence and just enough boiling water to make a runny glaze.

389

MAKES 12

Saffron and Honey Cupcakes

PREPARATION TIME: 1 HOUR

COOKING TIME: 20 MINUTES

INGREDIENTS

110 g / 4 oz / 1 cup self-raising flour, sifted
110 g / 4 oz / ½ cup caster (superfine) sugar
110 g / 4 oz / ½ cup butter, softened
2 large eggs

FOR THE SOAKING SYRUP
1 lemon, juiced
110 g / 4 oz / ½ cup honey
pinch saffron

- Preheat the oven to 190°C (170° fan) / 375 F / gas 5 and 12-hole silicone cake mould with oil.
- Combine the flour, sugar, butter and eggs in a bowl and whisk together for 2 minutes.
- Divide the mixture between the moulds, then transfer them to the oven and bake for 15 – 20 minutes.
- Test with a wooden toothpick, if it comes out clean, the cakes are done.
- While the cakes are cooking, make the soaking syrup. Put the lemon juice and honey in a small saucepan and boil for 2 minutes.
- Turn off the heat, stir in the saffron and leave to infuse for 10 minutes.
- Strain the syrup through a sieve to remove the saffron.
- When the cakes are ready, spoon over the soaking syrup and leave them to cool in their moulds.

Calendula Cupcakes

390

To add extra sunshine to these cheerful cakes, garnish with fresh calendula petals.

391

MAKES 12

Hot Cherry and Amaretto Cupcakes

- Preheat the oven to 180°C (160° fan) / 350 F / gas 4 and oil a 12 ramekin dishes.
- Beat the egg in a jug with the oil, milk and Amaretto until well mixed.
- Mix the flour, baking powder, sugar and cherries in a bowl, then pour in the egg mixture and stir just enough to combine.
- Divide the mixture between the moulds, then bake in the oven for 20 – 25 minutes.
- Test with a wooden toothpick, if it comes out clean, the cakes are done.
- Transfer the cakes to a wire rack and leave to cool.

PREPARATION TIME: 25 MINUTES

COOKING TIME: 25 MINUTES

INGREDIENTS

1 large egg
120 ml / 4 fl. oz / ½ cup sunflower oil
120 ml / 4 fl. oz / ½ cup milk
2 tbsp Amaretto
375 g / 12 ½ oz / 2 ½ cups self-raising flour, sifted
1 tsp baking powder
200 g / 7 oz / ¾ cup caster (superfine) sugar
150 g / 5 oz / 1 cup cherries, stoned

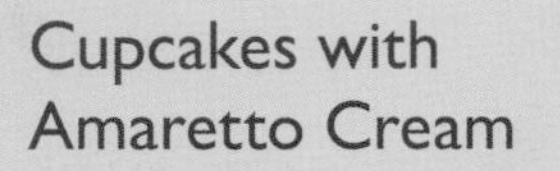

Cupcakes with Amaretto Cream

392

Whip together 300ml / 10 fl. oz / 1 ⅓ cups double (heavy) cream with 2 tbsp Amaretto and 2 tbsp icing sugar until thick.

393

MAKES 12

Chestnut and Orange Cupcakes

- Preheat the oven to 190°C (170° fan) / 375 F / gas 5 and line a 12-hole cupcake tin with paper cases.
- Combine the flours, sugar, butter, eggs and marmalade in a bowl and whisk together for 2 minutes.
- Divide the mixture between the paper cases, then transfer to the oven and bake for 15 – 20 minutes.
- Test with a wooden toothpick, if it comes out clean, the cakes are done.
- Transfer the cakes to a wire rack and leave to cool.

PREPARATION TIME: 20 MINUTES

COOKING TIME: 20 MINUTES

INGREDIENTS

55 g / 2 oz / ½ cup self-raising flour, sifted
55 g / 2 oz / ½ cup chestnut flour, sifted
110 g / 4 oz / ½ cup caster (superfine) sugar
110 g / 4 oz / ½ cup butter, softened
2 large eggs
55 g / 2 oz / ¼ cup thick cut marmalade

Double Chestnut Cupcakes

394

For extra texture, try adding 6 chopped cooked chestnuts to the cake mixture.

395

MAKES 12

Strawberry Mint Cupcakes

PREPARATION TIME: 35 MINUTES

COOKING TIME: 20 MINUTES

INGREDIENTS

110 g / 4 oz / ½ cup self-raising flour, sifted
110 g / 4 oz / ½ cup caster (superfine) sugar
110 g / 4 oz / ½ cup butter, softened
2 large eggs
6 strawberries, chopped
2 tbsp fresh mint, shredded

- Preheat the oven to 190°C (170° fan) / 375 F / gas 5 and oil a 12-hole silicone cupcake mould.
- Combine the flour, baking powder, sugar, butter and eggs in a bowl and whisk together for 2 minutes.
- Fold in the strawberries and shredded mint.
- Divide the mixture between the paper cases then transfer to the oven and bake for 15 – 20 minutes.
- Test with a wooden toothpick, if it comes out clean, the cakes are done.
- Transfer the cakes to a wire rack and leave to cool.

Strawberry and Black Pepper Cupcakes

396

Replace the mint with ½ tsp freshly ground black pepper for a spicy kick.

397

MAKES 12

Ginger and Cinnamon Cupcakes

PREPARATION TIME: 20 MINUTES

COOKING TIME: 20 MINUTES

INGREDIENTS

250 g / 9 oz / 1 ¾ cups self-raising flour
1 tsp bicarbonate of (baking) soda
2 tsp ground ginger
2 tsp ground cinnamon
200 g / 8 ½ oz / ½ cup golden syrup
125 g / 4 ½ oz / ½ cup butter
125 g / 4 ½ oz / ¾ cup light brown sugar
4 pieces stem ginger, chopped
2 large eggs, beaten
240 ml / 8 fl. oz / 1 cup milk

- Preheat the oven to 190°C (170° fan) / 375 F / gas 5 and line a 12-hole muffin tin with paper cases.
- Sieve the flour, bicarbonate of soda and spices into a bowl.
- Put the golden syrup, butter, brown sugar and stem ginger in a small saucepan and boil gently for 2 minutes, stirring to dissolve the sugar.
- Pour the butter and sugar mixture onto the flour with the eggs and milk and fold it all together until smooth.
- Divide the mixture between the cases and bake in the oven for 20 – 25 minutes.
- Test with a wooden toothpick, if it comes out clean, the cakes are done.
- Transfer the cakes to a wire rack and leave to cool.

Ginger and Nutmeg Cupcakes

Replace the ground cinnamon with 1 tsp freshly grated nutmeg. Mix 1 tsp of freshly grated nutmeg with 2 tbsp caster sugar and sprinkle over the cupcakes, once cooked.

399

MAKES 12

Marbled Cupcakes

Marbled Chocolate Chunk Cupcakes

400

Add 110g / 4 oz / ½ cup of chopped white chocolate to the cupcake mixture. Top with melted dark and white chocolate, marbled together.

Nutty Marbled Cupcakes

401

Add 75g / 3 oz of chopped walnuts to the cupcake mixture and sprinkle the tops with chopped hazelnuts.

PREPARATION TIME: 25 MINUTES

COOKING TIME: 25 MINUTES

INGREDIENTS

1 large egg
120 ml / 4 fl. oz / ½ cup sunflower oil
120 ml / 4 fl. oz / ½ cup milk
375 g / 12 ½ oz / 2 ½ cups self-raising flour, sifted
1 tsp baking powder
200 g / 7 oz / ¾ cup caster (superfine) sugar
110 g / 4 oz / ½ cup dark chocolate, chopped

TO DECORATE
110 g / 4 oz / ½ cup dark chocolate, minimum 60% cocoa solids, chopped
2 tbsp grape-nuts

- Preheat the oven to 180°C (160° fan) / 350 F / gas 4 and line a 12-hole muffin tin with paper cases.
- Beat the egg in a jug with the oil and milk until well mixed.
- Mix the flour, baking powder and sugar in a bowl, then pour in the egg mixture and stir just enough to combine.
- Melt the chocolate in a microwave or bain marie and fold through the muffin mixture until it looks marbled.
- Divide the mixture between the paper cases, then bake in the oven for 20 – 25 minutes.
- Test with a wooden toothpick, if it comes out clean, the cakes are done.
- Transfer the cakes to a wire rack and leave to cool.
- Melt the chocolate in a bain marie and leave to cool until thick.
- Spoon the chocolate onto the cakes and top with a sprinkle of grape-nuts.

MAKES 12

Coffee Cream and Chocolate Cupcakes

Chocolate Chunk and Coffee Cream Cupcakes

Add 100 g of chopped milk chocolate to the cake mixture and top the cupcakes with chocolate-coated coffee beans.

Coconut and Coffee Cream Cupcakes

404

Replace the double cream with coconut milk amd the chocolate sprinkles with desiccated coconut.

PREPARATION TIME:
1 HOUR 15 MINUTES

COOKING TIME:
15 – 20 MINUTES

INGREDIENTS

110 g / 4 oz / 1 cup self-raising flour, sifted
28 g / 1 oz / ¼ cup unsweetened cocoa powder, sifted
110 g / 4 oz / ½ cup caster (superfine) sugar
110 g / 4 oz / ½ cup butter, softened
2 large eggs
2 tsp instant espresso powder

TO DECORATE
2 tsp instant espresso powder
225 ml / 8 fl. oz / 1 cup double (heavy) cream
2 tbsp icing sugar
chocolate sprinkles

- Preheat the oven to 190°°C (170° fan) / 375 F / gas 5 and line a 12-hole cupcake tin with paper cases.
- Combine the flour, cocoa, sugar, butter, eggs and espresso powder in a bowl and whisk together for 2 minutes.
- Divide the mixture between the paper cases, then transfer to the oven and bake for 15 – 20 minutes.
- Test with a wooden toothpick, if it comes out clean, the cakes are done.
- Transfer the cakes to a wire rack and leave to cool.
- To make the coffee cream, stir the espresso powder into the cream, then whisk with the icing sugar until thick.
- Spoon the cream into a piping bag fitted with a large star nozzle and pipe a generous swirl on top of each cake.
- Top with chocolate sprinkles.

405

MAKES 12

Raspberry and Coconut Cupcakes

- Preheat the oven to 180°C (160° fan) / 350 F / gas 4 and oil a 12-hole silicone muffin tin.
- Beat the egg in a jug with the oil and milk until well mixed.
- Mix the flour, baking powder, sugar, coconut and raspberries in a bowl, then pour in the egg mixture and stir just enough to combine.
- Divide the mixture between the moulds, then bake in the oven for 20 – 25 minutes.
- Test with a wooden toothpick, if it comes out clean, the cakes are done.
- Transfer the cakes to a wire rack and leave to cool.
- Add a raspberry to the top of each cake before serving.

PREPARATION TIME: 25 MINUTES

COOKING TIME: 25 MINUTES

INGREDIENTS

1 large egg
120 ml / 4 fl. oz / ½ cup sunflower oil
120 ml / 4 fl. oz / ½ cup milk
375 g / 12 ½ oz / 2 ½ cups self-raising flour, sifted
1 tsp baking powder
200 g / 7 oz / ¾ cup caster (superfine) sugar
28 g / 1 oz / ⅛ cup desiccated coconut
150 g / 5 oz / 1 cup raspberries

Orange-soaked Coconut Cupcakes

406

To make the coconut more moist, soak it in the juice of 1 orange for 30 minutes before beginning the recipe.

407

MAKES 12

Ham, Pea and Cheese Cupcakes

- Preheat the oven to 180°C (160° fan) / 350 F / gas 4 and line a 12-hole muffin tin with paper cases.
- Beat the egg in a jug with the oil, yoghurt and cheese until well mixed.
- Mix the ham, peas, flour, raising agents and salt in a bowl, then pour in the egg mixture and stir just enough to combine.
- Divide the mixture between the paper cases, then bake in the oven for 20 – 25 minutes.
- Test with a wooden toothpick, if it comes out clean, the cupcakes are done.
- Transfer the cupcakes to a wire rack and leave to cool completely.

PREPARATION TIME: 25 MINUTES

COOKING TIME: 25 MINUTES

INGREDIENTS

2 large eggs
120 ml / 4 fl. oz / ½ cup sunflower oil
180 ml / 6 fl. oz / ¾ cup Greek yogurt
110 g / 4 oz / 1 cup Emmental, cubed
75 g / 2 ½ oz / ½ cup cooked ham, chopped
2 tbsp peas, cooked
225 g / 8 oz / 1 ½ cups plain (all purpose) flour
2 tsp baking powder
½ tsp bicarbonate of (baking) soda
½ tsp salt

Dill, Pea and Cheese Cupcakes

408

For a vegetarian alternative, leave out the ham and replace it with 2 tbsp chopped dill.

409

MAKES 12

Rhubarb and Vanilla Cupcakes

PREPARATION TIME: 35 MINUTES

COOKING TIME: 20 MINUTES

INGREDIENTS

1 stem of rhubarb
2 tbsp granulated sugar
110 g / 4 oz / 1 cup self-raising flour, sifted
110 g / 4 oz / ½ cup caster (superfine) sugar
110 g / 4 oz / ½ cup butter, softened
2 large eggs
1 vanilla pod, seeds only

- Preheat the oven to 190°C (170° fan) / 375 F / gas 5 and line a 12-hole cupcake tin with paper cases.
- Cut the rhubarb into small chunks and toss with the granulated sugar, then tip into a roasting tin and bake for 10 minutes.
- Combine the flour, sugar, butter, eggs and vanilla seeds in a bowl and whisk together for 2 minutes.
- Divide the mixture between the paper cases, and top with the cooked rhubarb pieces, then transfer to the oven and bake for 15 – 20 minutes.
- Test with a wooden toothpick, if it comes out clean, the cakes are done.
- Transfer the cakes to a wire rack and leave to cool.

Rhubarb and Ginger Cupcakes

410

Try replacing the vanilla seeds with 2 tbsp chopped stem ginger.

411

MAKES 12

Black Cherry and Marzipan Cupcakes

PREPARATION TIME: 25 MINUTES

COOKING TIME: 25 MINUTES

INGREDIENTS

1 large egg
120 ml / 4 fl. oz / ½ cup sunflower oil
120 ml / 4 fl. oz / ½ cup milk
375 g / 12 ½ oz / 2 ½ cups self-raising flour, sifted
1 tsp baking powder
200 g / 7 oz / ¾ cup caster (superfine) sugar
150 g / 5 oz / 1 cup black cherries in syrup, drained
150 g / 5 oz / 1 cup marzipan, cubed

- Preheat the oven to 180°C (160° fan) / 350 F / gas 4 and line a 12-hole muffin tin with paper cases.
- Beat the egg in a jug with the oil and milk until well mixed.
- Mix the flour, baking powder, sugar, cherries and marzipan in a bowl, then pour in the egg mixture and stir just enough to combine.
- Divide the mixture between the paper cases, then bake in the oven for 20 – 25 minutes.
- Test with a wooden toothpick, if it comes out clean, the cakes are done.
- Transfer the cakes to a wire rack and leave to cool.

Zesty Cherry and Marzipan Cupcakes

412

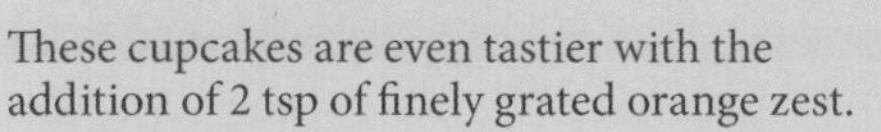

These cupcakes are even tastier with the addition of 2 tsp of finely grated orange zest.

413

MAKES 12

Pistachio and Black Cherry Cupcakes

- Preheat the oven to 190°C (170° fan) / 375 F / gas 5 and line a 12-hole cupcake tin with paper cases.
- Combine the flour, baking powder, ground pistachios, sugar, butter, eggs and almond essence in a bowl and whisk together for 2 minutes.
- Divide half the mixture between the paper cases and press 2 cherries into the top of each.
- Divide the rest of the mixture between the cases then transfer to the oven and bake for 15 – 20 minutes.
- Test with a wooden toothpick, if it comes out clean, the cakes are done.
- Transfer the cakes to a wire rack and leave to cool.
- Pull away the tops of the cupcakes to reveal the cherries within.

PREPARATION TIME: 20 MINUTES

COOKING TIME: 20 MINUTES

INGREDIENTS

55 g / 2 oz / ½ cup self-raising flour, sifted
2 tsp baking powder
55 g / 2 oz / ½ cup ground pistachios
110 g / 4 oz / ½ cup caster (superfine) sugar
110 g / 4 oz / ½ cup butter, softened
2 large eggs
1 tsp almond essence
24 black cherries in syrup, drained

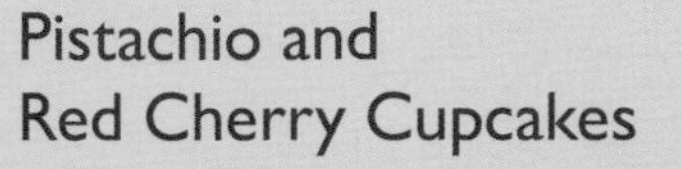

Pistachio and Red Cherry Cupcakes

414

Replace the black cherries with red cherries.

415

MAKES 12

Spicy Raisin Cupcakes

- Preheat the oven to 190°C (170° fan) / 375 F / gas 5 and line a 12-hole cupcake tin with paper cases.
- Combine the flour, ground pecans, sugar, butter, eggs, raisins and spices in a bowl and whisk together for 2 minutes.
- Divide the mixture between the paper cases, then transfer to the oven and bake for 15 – 20 minutes.
- Test with a wooden toothpick, if it comes out clean, the cakes are done.
- Transfer the cakes to a wire rack to cool.

PREPARATION TIME: 35 MINUTES

COOKING TIME: 20 MINUTES

INGREDIENTS

110 g / 4 oz / ½ cup self-raising flour, sifted
110 g / 4 oz / ½ cup caster (superfine) sugar
110 g / 4 oz / ½ cup butter, softened
2 large eggs
75 g / 2 ½ oz / ½ cup raisins
1 tsp mixed spice
½ tsp freshly grated nutmeg

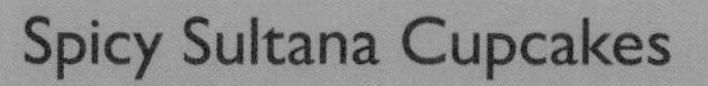

Spicy Sultana Cupcakes

416

Replace the raisins with sultanas.

417

MAKES 12

Chocolate Cupcakes

PREPARATION TIME: 25 MINUTES

COOKING TIME: 20 MINUTES

INGREDIENTS

110 g / 4 oz / 1 cup self-raising flour, sifted
28 g / 1 oz / ¼ cup unsweetened cocoa powder, sifted
110 g / 4 oz / ½ cup caster (superfine) sugar
110 g / 4 oz / ½ cup butter, softened
2 large eggs

TO DECORATE
icing (confectioners') sugar to dust

- Preheat the oven to 190°C (170° fan) / 375 F / gas 5 and line a 12-hole cupcake tin with paper cases.
- Combine the flour, cocoa, sugar, butter and eggs in a bowl and whisk together for 2 minutes.
- Divide the mixture between the paper cases, then transfer to the oven and bake for 15 – 20 minutes.
- Test with a wooden toothpick, if it comes out clean, the cakes are done.
- Transfer the cakes to a wire rack and leave to cool completely before dusting lightly with icing (confectioners') sugar.

Chocolate Lime Cupcakes

418

Top these cakes with a spoonful of lime marmalade for chocolate lime cupcakes.

419

MAKES 12

Almond and Pistachio Cupcakes

PREPARATION TIME: 25 MINUTES

COOKING TIME: 25 MINUTES

INGREDIENTS

250 g / 9 oz / 1 ¼ cups self-raising flour
1 tsp bicarbonate of (baking) soda
200 g / 8 ½ oz / ½ cup golden syrup
125 g / 4 ½ oz / ½ cup butter
125 g / 4 ½ oz / ¾ cup dark brown sugar
2 large eggs, beaten
240 ml / 8 fl. oz / 1 cup milk
1 tsp almond essence
75 g / 2 ½ oz / ½ cup flaked (slivered) almonds
75 g / 2 ½ oz / ½ cup pistachio nuts, shelled and chopped

- Preheat the oven to 190°C (170° fan) / 375 F / gas 5 and line a 12-hole mini loaf cake tin with paper cases.
- Sieve the flour and bicarbonate of soda together into a bowl.
- Put the golden syrup, butter and brown sugar in a small saucepan and boil gently for 2 minutes, stirring to dissolve the sugar.
- Pour the butter and sugar mixture onto the flour with the eggs, milk and almond essence and fold it all together until smooth.
- Divide the mixture between the paper cases, sprinkle with the flaked almonds and chopped pistachios, then transfer to the oven and bake for 20 – 25 minutes.
- Transfer the cakes to a wire rack and leave to cool.

Crunchy Cupcakes

420

For extra crunch, double the quantity of nuts and stir half of them through the cake mixture before spooning into the cases.

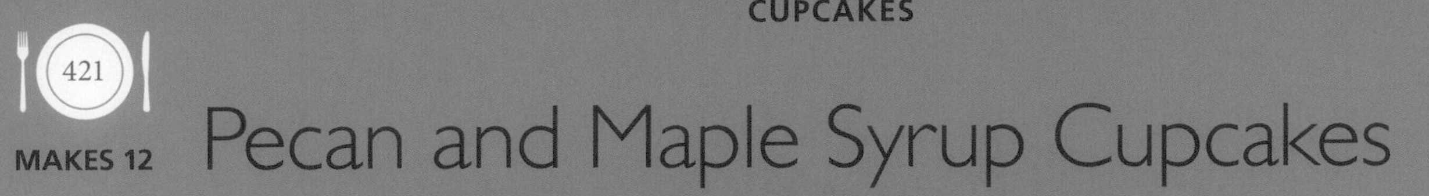

421

MAKES 12

Pecan and Maple Syrup Cupcakes

Pecan and Honey Cupcakes

422

For a sweeter taste, add 1 tsp of honey to the syrup micture.

Almond and Honey Cupcakes

423

Replace the pecans with almonds.

PREPARATION TIME: 35 MINUTES

COOKING TIME: 20 MINUTES

INGREDIENTS

55 g / 2 oz / ½ cup self-raising flour, sifted
55 g / 2 oz / ½ cup ground pecan nuts
110 g / 4 oz / ½ cup caster (superfine) sugar
110 g / 4 oz / ½ cup butter, softened
2 large eggs
75 g / 2 ½ oz / ½ cup pecan nuts, chopped
120 ml / 4 fl. oz / ½ cup maple syrup

- Preheat the oven to 190°C (170° fan) / 375 F / gas 5 and line a 12-hole cupcake tin with paper cases.
- Combine the flour, ground pecans, sugar, butter, eggs and chopped pecans in a bowl and whisk together for 2 minutes.
- Divide the mixture between the paper cases, then transfer to the oven and bake for 15 – 20 minutes.
- Test with a wooden toothpick, if it comes out clean, the cakes are done.
- Leave the cakes to cool completely, then pour over the maple syrup.

424

MAKES 24

Smoked Haddock Mini Cupcakes

Smoked Haddock and Garlic Cupcakes

425

Try adding 1 tsp of crushed garlic to the egg mixture before stirring into the dry ingredients.

Smoked Salmon Cupcakes

426

Replace the smoked haddock with smoked salmon.

PREPARATION TIME: 25 MINUTES

COOKING TIME: 15 MINUTES

INGREDIENTS

150 g / 5 oz smoked haddock fillet
2 large eggs
120 ml / 4 fl. oz / ½ cup sunflower oil
180 ml / 6 fl. oz / ¾ cup Greek yogurt
110 g / 4 oz / 1 cup Emmental, grated
225 g / 8 oz / 1 ½ cups plain (all purpose) flour
2 tsp baking powder
½ tsp bicarbonate of (baking) soda
½ tsp salt
2 tbsp flat leaf parsley, chopped

- Put the smoked haddock fillet in a bowl and pour over enough boiling water to cover.
- Cover the bowl and leave to stand for 10 minutes, then drain.
- Remove any skin and bones from the fish and break it into flakes with your fingers.
- Preheat the oven to 180°C (160° fan) / 350 F / gas 4 and line a 24-hole muffin tin with paper cases.
- Beat the egg in a jug with the oil, yoghurt and cheese until well mixed.
- Mix the flour, raising agents, salt, parsley and flaked haddock in a bowl, then pour in the egg mixture and stir just enough to combine.
- Divide the mixture between the paper cases, then bake in the oven for 10 – 15 minutes.
- Test with a wooden toothpick, if it comes out clean, the cupcakes are done.
- Serve warm.

427

MAKES 12

Marbled Chocolate Cupcakes

- Preheat the oven to 190°C (170° fan) / 375 F / gas 5 and line a 12-hole cupcake tin with paper cases.
- Combine the flour, sugar, butter and eggs in a bowl and whisk together for 2 minutes.
- Divide the mixture in half and stir the cocoa powder into one half.
- Fill the paper cases with alternate teaspoons of each cake mixture until they are both used up.
- Use a tooth pick to swirl the mixtures together to create a marbled effect.
- Transfer the tin to the oven and bake for 15 – 20 minutes.
- Test with a wooden toothpick, if it comes out clean, the cakes are done.
- Transfer the cakes to a wire rack and leave to cool completely before dusting lightly with icing sugar.

PREPARATION TIME: 25 MINUTES

COOKING TIME: 20 MINUTES

INGREDIENTS

110 g / 4 oz / ½ cup self-raising flour, sifted
110 g / 4 oz / ½ cup caster (superfine) sugar
110 g / 4 oz / ½ cup butter, softened
2 large eggs
28 g / 1 oz / ¼ cup unsweetened cocoa powder, sifted

Marbled Chocolate Chip Cupcakes

428

Add 75g / 3 oz / ⅓ cup white chocolate chips to the plain cake mixture and 75g / 3 oz / ⅓ cup dark chocolate chips to the chocolate cake mixture.

429

MAKES 24

Parmesan and Rosemary Mini Cupcakes

- Preheat the oven to 180°C (160° fan) / 350 F / gas 4 and line a 24-hole muffin tin with paper cases.
- Beat the egg in a jug with the oil, yoghurt and cheese until well mixed.
- Mix the flour, raising agents, salt and rosemary in a bowl, then pour in the egg mixture and stir just enough to combine.
- Divide the mixture between the paper cases, then bake in the oven for 10 – 15 minutes.
- Test with a wooden toothpick, if it comes out clean, the cupcakes are done.
- Serve warm.

PREPARATION TIME: 25 MINUTES

COOKING TIME: 15 MINUTES

INGREDIENTS

2 large eggs
120 ml / 4 fl. oz / ½ cup sunflower oil
180 ml / 6 fl. oz / ¾ cup Greek yogurt
110 g / 4 oz / 1 cup Parmesan, grated
225 g / 8 oz / 1 ½ cups plain (all purpose) flour
2 tsp baking powder
½ tsp bicarbonate of (baking) soda
½ tsp salt
2 tbsp fresh rosemary, chopped

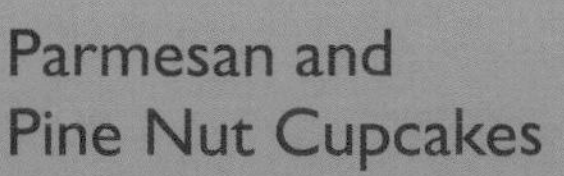

Parmesan and Pine Nut Cupcakes

430

Add 2 tbsp of pine nuts to the cupcake mixture.

431

MAKES 24

Mini Bakewell Tarts

PREPARATION TIME: 2 HOURS

COOKING TIME: 15 MINUTES

INGREDIENTS

225 g / 8 oz / 1 ½ cups plain (all purpose) flour
110 g / 4 oz / ½ cup butter, cubed and chilled

FOR THE FRANGIPANE
55 g / 2 oz / ½ cup ground almonds
55 g / 2 oz / ¼ cup caster (superfine) sugar
55 g / 2 oz / ¼ cup butter, softened
1 large egg
1 tsp almond essence

TO DECORATE
110 g / 4 oz / ½ cup raspberry jam
225 g / 8 oz / 2 cups icing (confectioners') sugar
boiling water to mix
12 glace cherries, halved

- Preheat the oven to 200°C (180° fan) / 400 F / gas 6.
- Sieve the flour into a mixing bowl then rub in the butter until the mixture resembles fine breadcrumbs.
- Stir in just enough cold water to bring the pastry together into a pliable dough.
- Roll out the pastry on a floured surface and cut out 24 circles then use them to line 24 mini tartlet tins and crimp around the edges.
- To make the frangipane, combine the ground almonds, sugar, butter, egg and almond essence in a bowl and whisk together for 2 minutes.
- Add a tsp of jam to each pastry case, then top with the frangipane mixture and bake for 15 – 20 minutes. Leave to cool completely.
- To make the icing, sieve the icing sugar into a bowl, then slowly stir in the boiling water a few drops at a time until you have a thick icing.
- Spoon the icing on top of the tarts and finish with half a cherry.

432

MAKES 12

Chocolate and Yeast Extract Cupcakes

PREPARATION TIME: 25 MINUTES

COOKING TIME: 20 MINUTES

INGREDIENTS

110 g / 4 oz / ½ cup self-raising flour, sifted
28 g / 1 oz / ¼ cup unsweetened cocoa powder, sifted
110 g / 4 oz / ½ cup caster (superfine) sugar
110 g / 4 oz / ½ cup butter, softened
2 large eggs
1 tbsp yeast extract

TO DECORATE
225 g / 8 oz / 2 cups icing (confectioners') sugar
28 g / 1 oz / ¼ cup unsweetened cocoa powder, sifted
Boiling water, to mix
1 tsp yeast extract

- Preheat the oven to 190°C (170° fan) / 375 F / gas 5 and line a 12-hole cupcake tin with paper cases.
- Combine the flour, cocoa, sugar, butter, eggs and yeast extract in a bowl and whisk together for 2 minutes.
- Divide the mixture between the paper cases, then transfer to the oven and bake for 15 – 20 minutes.
- Test with a wooden toothpick, if it comes out clean, the cakes are done.
- Transfer the cakes to a wire rack and leave to cool.
- Sift the icing sugar and cocoa into a bowl, then slowly stir in the boiling water a few drops at a time until you have a thick icing.
- Stir in the yeast extract until smooth then drizzle over the cupcakes.

Chocolate and Liquorice Cupcakes

Replace the yeast extract in the cake mixture and icing with liquorice syrup. Decorate the cakes with liquorice sweets.

434

MAKES 12

Gingerbread Man Cupcakes

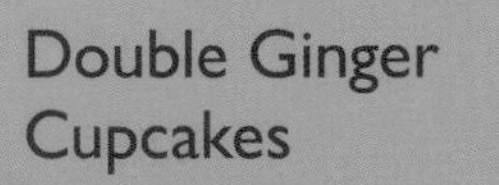

Double Ginger Cupcakes

435

For extra ginger flavour, add 2 tbsp chopped stem ginger to the cake mixture and sprinkle the finished cakes with crystallised ginger pieces instead of the gingerbread men.

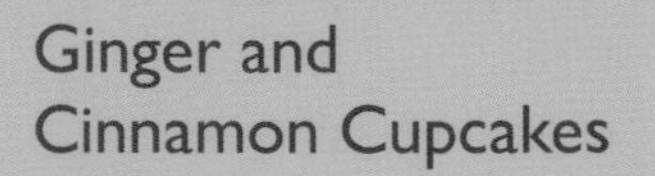

Ginger and Cinnamon Cupcakes

436

Add 1 tsp of cinnamon to the cupcake mixture.

PREPARATION TIME: 2 HOURS

COOKING TIME: 20 MINUTES

INGREDIENTS

110 g / 4 oz / 1 cup self-raising flour, sifted
110 g / 4 oz / ½ cup caster (superfine) sugar
110 g / 4 oz / ½ cup butter, softened
2 large eggs
1 tsp ground ginger
1 tsp ground mixed spice

TO DECORATE
225 g / 8 oz / 2 cups icing (confectioners') sugar
Boiling water, to mix
Black food colouring
225 g / 8 oz / 1 cup ready-to-roll fondant icing
Brown food colouring

- Preheat the oven to 190°C (170° fan) / 375 F / gas 5 and line a 12-hole cupcake tin with silver paper cases.
- Combine the flour, sugar, butter, eggs and spices in a bowl and whisk together for 2 minutes.
- Divide the mixture between the paper cases, then transfer to the oven and bake for 15 – 20 minutes.
- Transfer the cakes to a wire rack and leave to cool.
- To make the icing, sieve the icing sugar into a bowl and stir in the boiling water a few drops at a time until you have a smooth, thick icing.
- Put 2 tsp of the icing in a separate bowl and stir in a little black food colouring.
- Spoon the rest of the icing onto the cakes and leave to set while you make the gingerbread men.
- Knead the fondant icing with a little brown food colouring until pliable and evenly coloured.
- Dust your work surface with a little icing sugar and roll out the fondant icing.
- Use a small gingerbread man cutter to cut out 12 'men' and transfer them carefully to the cupcakes.
- Spoon the black icing into a small paper piping bag and snip off the end, then pipe on the eyes and the mouth.

MAKES 36

Valentine Mini Cupcakes

Strawberry Valentine Cupcakes

438

Scoop out the centre of the cakes and add ½ tsp of strawberry jam, before replacing the centres and icing as usual.

Chocolate Valentine Cupcakes

439

Aadd 2 tbsp cocoa powder to the cake mixture for chocolate valentine mini cupcakes.

PREPARATION TIME: 45 MINUTES

COOKING TIME: 15 MINUTES

INGREDIENTS

110 g / 4 oz / ½ cup self-raising flour, sifted
110 g / 4 oz / ½ cup caster (superfine) sugar
110 g / 4 oz / ½ cup butter, softened
2 large eggs
1 tsp vanilla extract

TO DECORATE

225 g / 8 oz / 2 cups icing (confectioners') sugar
Boiling water, to mix
36 red heart-shaped sweets

- Preheat the oven to 190°C (170° fan) / 375 F / gas 5 and line a 36 hole mini cupcake tin with paper cases.
- Combine the flour, sugar, butter, eggs and vanilla extract in a bowl and whisk together for 2 minutes.
- Divide the mixture between the paper cases then transfer to the oven and bake for 10 – 15 minutes.
- Test with a wooden toothpick, if it comes out clean, the cakes are done.
- Transfer the cakes to a wire rack and leave to cool.
- Sieve the icing sugar into a bowl, then slowly stir in the boiling water a few drops at a time until you have a thick icing.
- Spoon on top of the cakes and top with a heart-shaped sweet.

440

MAKES 24

Dark and White Chocolate Cupcakes

- Preheat the oven to 180°C (160° fan) / 350 F / gas 4 and line a 24-hole muffin tin with paper cases.
- Beat the egg in a jug with the oil and milk.
- Mix the flour, cocoa, baking powder, sugar and chocolate in a bowl, then pour in the egg mixture and stir just enough to combine.
- Divide the mixture between the paper cases, then bake in the oven for 15 – 20 minutes.
- Transfer the cakes to a wire rack and leave to cool.
- Chop the white chocolate and transfer to a mixing bowl.
- Heat the cream until it starts to simmer, then pour over the chopped chocolate and stir until the mixture has cooled and thickened.
- Refrigerate until thick enough to spread, then apply the ganache to the cupcakes with a palette knife and top each one with a chocolate button.

PREPARATION TIME 10 MINUTES

COOKING TIME 45 MINUTES

INGREDIENTS

1 large egg
120 ml / 4 fl. oz / ½ cup sunflower oil
120 ml / 4 fl. oz / ½ cup milk
375 g / 12 ½ oz / 2 ½ cups self-raising flour, sifted
55 g / 2 oz / ½ cup unsweetened cocoa powder, sifted
1 tsp baking powder
200 g / 7 oz / ¾ cup caster (superfine) sugar
110 g / 4 oz / ½ cup dark chocolate, minimum 60% cocoa solids, chopped

TO DECORATE
225 g / 8 oz white chocolate
225 ml / 8 fl. oz / 1 cup double (heavy) cream
24 dark chocolate buttons

Milk Chocolate Mini Cupcakes

441

Replace the dark chocolate chunks in the muffin mixture with milk chocolate chunks and replace the white chocolate in the ganache with milk chocolate.

442

MAKES 12

Lemon Cream Cheese Cupcakes

- Preheat the oven to 190°°C (170° fan) / 375 F / gas 5 and line a 12-hole cupcake tin with paper cases.
- Combine the flour, sugar, butter, eggs and lemon zest in a bowl and whisk together for 2 minutes.
- Divide the mixture between the paper cases, then transfer to the oven and bake for 15 – 20 minutes.
- Transfer the cakes to a wire rack and leave to cool.
- To make the icing, beat the cream cheese and butter together with a wooden spoon until light and fluffy then beat in the icing sugar a quarter at a time.
- Add the lemon juice then use a whisk to whip the mixture for 2 minutes until light.
- Spoon the icing onto the cakes and swirl with the back of the spoon.
- Sprinkle with the sugar sprinkles.

PREPARATION TIME: 1 HOUR

COOKING TIME:
15 – 20 MINUTES

INGREDIENTS

110 g / 4 oz / 1 cup self-raising flour, sifted
110 g / 4 oz / ½ cup caster (superfine) sugar
110 g / 4 oz / ½ cup butter, softened
2 large eggs
1 lemon, zest finely grated
To decorate
225 g / 8 oz / 1 cup cream cheese
110 g / 4 oz / ½ cup butter, softened
225 g / 8 oz / 2 cups icing (confectioners') sugar
1 tbsp lemon juice
yellow sugar sprinkles

Orange Cream Cheese Cupcakes

443

Replace the lemon zest in the cake mixture with orange zest and replace the lemon juice in the icing with orange juice. Sprinkle with orange sugar sprinkles to finish.

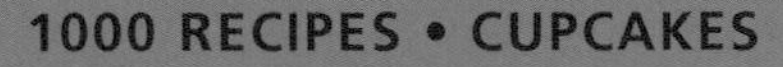

MAKES 12

Milk Chocolate Ganache Cupcakes

PREPARATION TIME: 30 MINUTES

COOKING TIME: 20 MINUTES

INGREDIENTS

110 g / 4 oz / ½ cup self-raising flour, sifted
28 g / 1 oz / ¼ cup unsweetened cocoa powder, sifted
110 g / 4 oz / ½ cup caster (superfine) sugar
110 g / 4 oz / ½ cup butter, softened
2 large eggs
1 tsp vanilla extract

TO DECORATE
225 ml / 8 fl. oz / 1 cup double (heavy) cream
225 g / 8 oz milk chocolate, chopped
2 tbsp unsweetened cocoa powder

- Preheat the oven to 190°C (170° fan) / 375 F / gas 5 and line a 12-hole cupcake tin with paper cases.
- Combine the flour, cocoa, sugar, butter, eggs and vanilla extract in a bowl and whisk together for 2 minutes.
- Divide the mixture between the paper cases then transfer to the oven and bake for 15 – 20 minutes.
- Transfer the cakes to a wire rack and leave to cool.
- Heat the cream until it starts to simmer, then pour it over the chopped chocolate.
- Stir the ganache until the mixture has cooled and thickened, then refrigerate until thick enough to pipe.
- Spoon the ganache into a piping bag and pipe a generous swirl on top of each cake.
- Dust the cakes with cocoa powder.

White Chocolate Ganache Cupcakes

Replace the milk chocolate in the ganache with chopped white chocolate and decorate the cakes with dark chocolate curls.

446

MAKES 12

Little Bear Cupcakes

PREPARATION TIME: 1 HOUR

COOKING TIME: 20 MINUTES

INGREDIENTS

110 g / 4 oz / ½ cup self-raising flour, sifted
110 g / 4 oz / ½ cup caster (superfine) sugar
110 g / 4 oz / ½ cup butter, softened
2 large eggs
1 tsp vanilla extract

TO DECORATE
110 g / 4 oz / ½ cup butter, softened
225 g / 8 oz / 2 cups icing (confectioners') sugar
2 tbsp milk
1 tsp vanilla extract
pink ready to roll fondant icing
2 tbsp dark chocolate, melted

- Preheat the oven to 190°C (170° fan) / 375 F / gas 5 and line a 12-hole cupcake tin with pink paper cases.
- Combine the flour, sugar, butter, eggs and vanilla extract in a bowl and whisk together for 2 minutes.
- Divide the mixture between the paper cases, then transfer to the oven and bake for 15 – 20 minutes.
- Transfer the cakes to a wire rack and leave to cool.
- Beat the butter with a wooden spoon until light and fluffy then beat in the icing sugar. Use a whisk to add the milk and vanilla extract, then whisk for 2 minutes.
- Reserve 1 tbsp of the buttercream and spoon the rest into a piping bag fitted with a star nozzle and pipe a swirl on top of each cake.
- Model the bears out of fondant icing. Spoon the melted chocolate into a small piping bag.
- Colour the reserved buttercream with a little blue food colouring and spoon into a small piping bag.
- Sit a bear on top of each cupcake and pipe on the eyes and noses with the chocolate.
- Finally, pipe on the blue bows with the buttercream.

447

MAKES 12

Chocolate and Strawberry Cupcakes

- Preheat the oven to 190°C (170° fan) / 375 F / gas 5 and line a 12-hole cupcake tin with paper cases.
- Combine the flour, cocoa, sugar, butter, eggs and strawberry syrup in a bowl and whisk together for 2 minutes.
- Divide the mixture between the paper cases, then transfer to the oven and bake for 15 – 20 minutes.
- Transfer the cakes to a wire rack and leave to cool.
- To make the strawberry cream, whisk the cream with the strawberry syrup until thick.
- Spoon the cream into a piping bag fitted with a large star nozzle and pipe a generous swirl on top of each cake.
- Sprinkle with heart-shaped cake sprinkles.

PREPARATION TIME: 35 MINUTES

COOKING TIME: 20 MINUTES

INGREDIENTS

110 g / 4 oz / ½ cup self-raising flour, sifted
28 g / 1 oz / ¼ cup unsweetened cocoa powder, sifted
110 g / 4 oz / ½ cup caster (superfine) sugar
110 g / 4 oz / ½ cup butter, softened
2 large eggs
2 tbsp strawberry syrup

TO DECORATE
225 ml / 8 fl. oz / 1 cup double (heavy) cream
2 tbsp strawberry syrup
Heart-shaped cake sprinkles

Chocolate and Orange Cream Cupcakes

448

Replace the strawberry syrup in the cake mixture and cream with 2 tsp of finely grated orange zest and decorate the cupcakes with candied peel.

449

MAKES 36

Chocolate and Sesame Cupcakes

- Preheat the oven to 170°C (150° fan) / 325 F / gas 3 and line a 36-hole mini cupcake tin with paper cases.
- Melt the chocolate, cocoa and butter together in a saucepan, then leave to cool a little.
- Whisk the sugar and eggs together with an electric whisk for 3 minutes or until very light and creamy.
- Pour in the chocolate mixture and sieve over the flour, then fold everything together with the sesame seeds until evenly mixed.
- Spoon into the cake cases and bake for 10 – 15 minutes or until the outside is set, but the centres are still quite soft, as they will continue to cook as they cool.

PREPARATION TIME: 25 MINUTES

COOKING TIME: 15 MINUTES

INGREDIENTS

110 g / 4 oz / ½ cup dark chocolate, minimum 60% cocoa solids, chopped
85 g / 3 oz / ¾ cup unsweetened cocoa powder, sifted
225 g / 8 oz / 1 cup butter
450 g / 15 oz / 2 ½ cups light brown sugar
4 large eggs
110 g / 4 oz / 1 cup self-raising flour
2 tbsp sesame seeds

Sesame and Coconut Cupcakes

450

Try adding 2 tbsp of desiccated coconut to the mixture with the sesame seeds.

451

MAKES 12

Banana Buttercream Cupcakes

PREPARATION TIME: 40 MINUTES

COOKING TIME: 20 MINUTES

INGREDIENTS

1 very ripe banana
110 g / 4 oz / ½ cup self-raising flour, sifted
110 g / 4 oz / ½ cup caster (superfine) sugar
110 g / 4 oz / ½ cup butter, softened
2 large eggs

TO DECORATE
1 very ripe banana
110 g / 4 oz / ½ cup butter, softened
225 g / 8 oz / 2 cups icing (confectioners') sugar
Pink food colouring
Pink heart-shaped cake sprinkles
Hundreds and thousands

- Preheat the oven to 190°C (170° fan) / 375F / gas 5 and line a 12-hole cupcake tin with paper cases.
- Blend the banana to a smooth puree in a food processor. Combine the flour, sugar, butter, eggs and banana puree in a bowl and whisk for 2 minutes.
- Divide the mixture between the paper cases.
- Bake for 15 – 20 minutes. Transfer the cakes to a wire rack and leave to cool.
- Mash the banana then beat into the butter with a wooden spoon until light and fluffy. Beat in the icing sugar and whisk for 2 minutes.
- Add a few drops of pink food colouring and swirl. Spoon the buttercream into a piping bag fitted with a large star nozzle and pipe a swirl on top of each cake.
- Scatter the sprinkles over the cakes.

Double Banana Buttercream Cupcakes

452

Press a slice of banana into the top of each cake before baking. Top the banana buttercream with dried banana chips instead of the cake sprinkles.

453

MAKES 12

Leek and Curry Cupcakes

PREPARATION TIME: 25 MINUTES

COOKING TIME: 25 MINUTES

INGREDIENTS

2 leeks, sliced
2 tbsp butter
2 large eggs
120 ml / 4 fl. oz / ½ cup sunflower oil
180 ml / 6 fl. oz / ¾ cup Greek yogurt
110 g / 4 oz / 1 cup Parmesan, grated
225 g / 8 oz / 1 ½ cups plain (all purpose) flour
2 tsp baking powder
½ tsp bicarbonate of (baking) soda
½ tsp salt
2 tsp curry powder

- Preheat the oven to 180°C (160° fan) / 350 F / gas 4 and oil a 12-hole silicone muffin mould.
- Fry the leeks in the butter for 5 minutes or until soft.
- Beat the egg in a jug with the oil, yoghurt, cheese and fried leeks until well mixed.
- Mix the flour, raising agents, salt and curry powder in a bowl, then pour in the egg mixture and stir just enough to combine.
- Divide the mixture between the moulds, then bake in the oven for 20 – 25 minutes.
- Test with a wooden toothpick, if it comes out clean, the cupcakes are done.
- Transfer the cupcakes to a wire rack and leave to cool.

Matar Paneer Cupcakes

Replace the Parmesan with 110g of cubed paneer cheese and add 110g / 4 oz / ½ cup cooked peas to the muffin mixture.

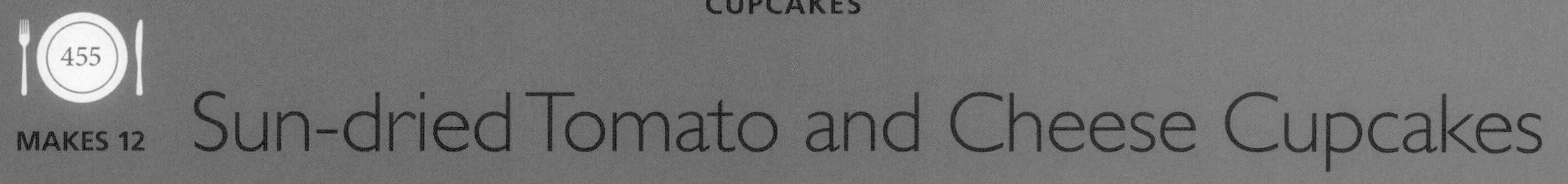

455

MAKES 12

Sun-dried Tomato and Cheese Cupcakes

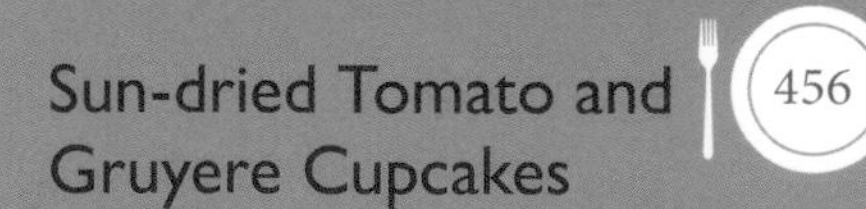

Sun-dried Tomato and Gruyere Cupcakes

456

Replace the sun-dried tomatoes with fried lardons and the goats' cheese with grated Gruyere.

PREPARATION TIME: 5 MINUTES

COOKING TIME: 10 MINUTES

INGREDIENTS

4 large eggs
75 g / 2 ½ oz / ½ cup sundried tomatoes, chopped
110 g / 4 oz / 1 cup goat's cheese, cubed

- Preheat the oven to 180°C (160° fan) / 350 F / gas 4 and line a 12-hole cupcake tin with paper cases.
- Beat the eggs in a jug and stir in the sun-dried tomatoes and goat's cheese.
- Season well with salt and black pepper.
- Pour the mixture into the paper cases then bake in the oven for 5 – 10 minutes or until set.

457

MAKES 24

Cheddar and Chive Mini Cupcakes

Sour Cream, Cheddar and Chive Cupcakes

458

Top the cupcakes with a spoonful of sour cream and a sprinkling of chopped chives.

PREPARATION TIME: 25 MINUTES

COOKING TIME:
10 – 15 MINUTES

INGREDIENTS

2 large eggs
120 ml / 4 fl. oz / ½ cup sunflower oil
180 ml / 6 fl. oz / ¾ cup Greek yoghurt
110 g / 4 oz / 1 cup cheddar, grated
225 g / 8 oz / 1 ½ cups plain flour
2 tsp baking powder
½ tsp bicarbonate of (baking) soda
½ tsp salt
2 tbsp fresh chives, chopped

- Preheat the oven to 180°°C (160° fan) / 350 F / gas 4 and oil a 24-hole muffin mould.
- Beat the egg in a jug with the oil, yoghurt and cheese until well mixed.
- Mix the flour, raising agents, salt and chives in a bowl, then pour in the egg mixture and stir just enough to combine.
- Divide the mixture between the paper cases, then bake in the oven for 10 – 15 minutes.
- Test with a wooden toothpick, if it comes out clean, the cupcakes are done.
- Serve warm.

459

MAKES 12

Sweet Potato Cupcakes

- Preheat the oven to 190C (170C fan) / 375F / gas 5 and line a 12-hole cupcake tin with paper cases.
- Combine the flour, sugar, butter, eggs and sweet potato puree in a bowl and whisk together for 2 minutes or until smooth.
- Divide the mixture between the paper cases, then transfer the tin to the oven and bake for 15 – 20 minutes.
- Test with a wooden toothpick, if it comes out clean, the cakes are done.
- Transfer the cakes to a wire rack and leave to cool completely.
- Melt the chocolate in a microwave or bain marie and spoon into a piping bag with a small star nozzle.
- Pipe the chocolate onto the cakes and finish with a couple of dried mango strips.

PREPARATION TIME 35 MINUTES

COOKING TIME 20 MINUTES

INGREDIENTS

110g / 4 oz / 1/2 cup self-raising flour, sifted
110g / 4 oz / ½ cup caster (superfine) sugar
110g / 4 oz / ½ cup butter, softened
2 large eggs
1 sweet potato (110g / 4oz / 1/2 cup) , peeled, cooked and pureed

TO DECORATE

110g / 4 oz / ½ cup milk chocolate, chopped
4 dried mango slices, cut into thin strips

460

MAKES 12

Pink Iced Wholemeal Cupcakes

- Preheat the oven to 190°C (170° fan) / 375 F / gas 5 and line a 12-hole cupcake tin with paper cases.
- Combine the flours, sugar, butter, eggs and vanilla extract in a bowl and whisk together for 2 minutes.
- Divide the mixture between the paper cases, then transfer to the oven and bake for 15 – 20 minutes.
- Test with a wooden toothpick, if it comes out clean, the cakes are done.
- Transfer the cakes to a wire rack and leave to cool completely before dusting with icing sugar.
- Beat the butter with a wooden spoon until light and fluffy then beat in the icing sugar a quarter at a time.
- Use a whisk to incorporate the milk and food colouring, then whisk for 2 minutes.
- Spoon the icing into a piping bag and pipe a small swirl on top of each cake.

PREPARATION TIME: 25 MINUTES

COOKING TIME: 20 MINUTES

INGREDIENTS

55 g / 2 oz / ½ cup self-raising flour, sifted
55 g / 2 oz / ½ cup wholemeal flour
1 tsp bicarbonate of (baking) soda
110 g / 4 oz / ½ cup caster (superfine) sugar
110 g / 4 oz / ½ cup butter, softened
2 large eggs
1 tsp vanilla extract
Icing (confectioners') sugar, to dust

TO DECORATE

110 g / 4 oz / ½ cup butter, softened
225 g / 8 oz / 2 cups icing (confectioners') sugar
2 tbsp milk
pink food colouring

Wholemeal Cupcakes with Orange Buttercream

461

Replace the milk in the buttercream with orange juice and replace the pink food colouring with 1 tsp finely grated orange zest.

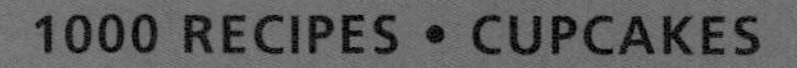

462

MAKES 12

Wholemeal Chocolate Cupcakes

- Preheat the oven to 190°C (170° fan) / 375 F / gas 5 and line a 12-hole cupcake tin with paper cases.
- Combine the flour, baking powder, cocoa, sugar, butter and eggs in a bowl and whisk together for 2 minutes.
- Divide the mixture between the paper cases, then transfer to the oven and bake for 15 – 20 minutes.
- Test with a wooden toothpick, if it comes out clean, the cakes are done.
- Transfer the cakes to a wire rack and leave to cool completely before dusting lightly with icing sugar.

PREPARATION TIME: 25 MINUTES

COOKING TIME: 20 MINUTES

INGREDIENTS

110 g / 4 oz / ½ cup wholemeal flour
1 tsp baking powder
28 g / 1 oz / ¼ cup unsweetened cocoa powder, sifted
110 g / 4 oz / ½ cup caster (superfine) sugar
110 g / 4 oz / ½ cup butter, softened
2 large eggs

TO DECORATE
1 tbsp icing (confectioners') sugar

463

MAKES 12

Rum and Orange Cupcakes

PREPARATION TIME: 35 MINUTES

COOKING TIME: 15 MINUTES

INGREDIENTS

150 g / 5 oz / 1 cup plain (all purpose) flour
2 tsp dried easy-blend yeast
1 tbsp caster (superfine) sugar
½ tsp salt
1 tbsp finely grated orange zest
3 large eggs, lightly beaten
75 g / 2 ½ oz / ⅓ cup butter, softened

FOR THE SOAKING SYRUP
450 g / 1 lb / 2 cups caster (superfine) sugar
2 oranges, juiced
240 ml / 8 fl. oz / 1 cup rum

- Oil a 12-hole heart-shaped silicone cupcake mould.
- Combine the flour, yeast, sugar, salt and orange zest in a bowl and gradually whisk in half of the beaten egg with an electric whisk.
- Continuing to whisk, incorporate half of the butter, followed by the rest of the egg.
- Beat the remaining butter in with a wooden spoon, then divide the mixture between the moulds.
- Leave the babas to prove in a warm, draught-free place for 1 hour or until they have doubled in size.
- Preheat the oven to 200°C (180° fan) / 400 F / gas 6.
- Bake the babas for 10 – 15 minutes or until golden brown and cooked through, then turn them out onto a wire rack.
- Put the sugar in a saucepan with the orange juice and 675ml / 1 ¼ pints / 3 cups water and stir over a medium heat to dissolve the sugar.
- Boil the sugar water for 5 minutes or until it starts to turn syrupy, then stir in the rum
- Transfer the babas to a mixing bowl, pour over the syrup and leave to soak for 10 minutes, turning occasionally.

464

MAKES 12

Plum and Almond Cupcakes

PREPARATION TIME: 20 MINUTES

COOKING TIME: 20 MINUTES

INGREDIENTS

55 g / 2 oz / ½ cup self-raising flour, sifted
55 g / 2 oz / ½ cup ground almonds
110 g / 4 oz / ½ cup caster (superfine) sugar
110 g / 4 oz / ½ cup butter, softened
2 large eggs
1 tsp almond essence
110 g / 4 oz / ½ cup plum jam (jelly)

- Preheat the oven to 190°C (170° fan) / 375 F / gas 5 and oil a 12-hole silicone cupcake mould.
- Combine the flour, ground almonds, sugar, butter, eggs and almond essence in a bowl and whisk together for 2 minutes.
- Divide half of the mixture between the paper cases then add 1 tsp of plum jam in the centre of each one.
- Top with the rest of the cake mixture then transfer the mould to the oven and bake for 15 – 20 minutes.
- Test with a wooden toothpick, if it comes out clean, the cakes are done.
- Transfer the cakes to a wire rack to cool.

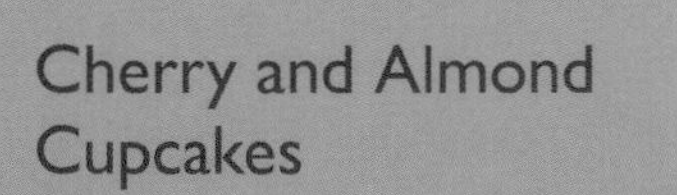

Cherry and Almond Cupcakes

465

Replace the plum jam with cherry jam.

468

MAKES 36

Elderflower Mini Cupcakes

PREPARATION TIME: 45 MINUTES

COOKING TIME: 15 MINUTES

INGREDIENTS

110 g / 4 oz / ½ cup self-raising flour, sifted
110 g / 4 oz / ½ cup caster (superfine) sugar
110 g / 4 oz / ½ cup butter, softened
2 large eggs
1 tbsp elderflower cordial

TO DECORATE
1 lemon, juiced
2 tbsp caster (superfine) sugar
2 tsp elderflower cordial
Handful fresh elderflowers

- Preheat the oven to 190°C (170 fan) / 375 F / gas 5 and line a 36 hole mini cupcake tin with paper cases.
- Combine the flour, sugar, butter, eggs and cordial in a bowl and whisk together for 2 minutes.
- Divide the mixture between the paper cases then transfer to the oven and bake for 10 – 15 minutes.
- Test with a wooden toothpick, if it comes out clean, the cakes are done.
- While the cakes are cooking, make the soaking syrup. Put the lemon juice and caster sugar in a small saucepan and boil for 2 minutes, then turn off the heat and stir in the elderflower cordial.
- When the cakes are ready, spoon over the soaking syrup and leave them to cool in their tin before topping with the fresh elderflowers.

Lemon Elderflower Cupcakes

469

For lemon and elderflower cupcakes, just add the grated zest of 1 lemon to the cake mixture and continue as above.

470

MAKES 12

Moist Cherry Frangipane Cupcakes

PREPARATION TIME: 20 MINUTES

COOKING TIME: 25 MINUTES

INGREDIENTS

55 g / 2 oz / ½ cup self-raising flour, sifted
55 g / 2 oz / ½ cup ground almonds
110 g / 4 oz / ½ cup caster (superfine) sugar
110 g / 4 oz / ½ cup butter, softened
2 large eggs
1 tsp almond essence
350 g / 12 oz fresh cherries
2 tbsp icing (confectioners') sugar

- Preheat the oven to 190°C (170° fan) / 375 F / gas 5 and oil a 6-hole silicone tartlet mould or 6 individual tartlet tins.
- Combine the flour, ground almonds, sugar, butter, eggs and almond essence in a bowl and whisk together for 2 minutes.
- Divide the mixture between the moulds.
- Stone the cherries with a cherry pitter and press 6 or 7 into the top of each cake.
- Transfer the cakes to the oven and bake for 20 – 25 minutes.
- Test with a wooden toothpick, if it comes out clean, the cakes are done.
- Transfer the cakes to a wire rack to cool.
- Dust the top of the cakes with icing sugar just before serving.

Mirabelle Plum Frangipane Cupcakes

471

For a seasonal change, try using small Mirabelle plums or greengages instead of the cherries.

472

MAKES 24

Courgette and Mint Mini Cupcakes

Courgette and Brie Cupcakes

473

Try adding 5 tbsp of chopped Brie to the mixture before baking.

Carrot and Parsley Mini Cupcakes

474

Replace the courgette with 2 grated carrots and the mint with fresh parsley.

PREPARATION TIME: 25 MINUTES

COOKING TIME: 15 MINUTES

INGREDIENTS

2 large eggs
120 ml / 4 fl. oz / ½ cup sunflower oil
180 ml / 6 fl. oz / ¾ cup Greek yogurt
2 courgettes (zucchini), coarsely grated
110 g / 4 oz / 1 cup Parmesan, grated
225 g / 8 oz / 1 ½ cups plain (all purpose) flour
2 tsp baking powder
½ tsp bicarbonate of (baking) soda
½ tsp salt
2 tbsp fresh mint, chopped

- Preheat the oven to 180°C (160° fan) / 350 F / gas 4 and line a 24-hole muffin tin with paper cases.
- Beat the egg in a jug with the oil, yoghurt, courgette and cheese until well mixed.
- Mix the flour, raising agents, salt and mint in a bowl, then pour in the egg mixture and stir just enough to combine.
- Divide the mixture between the paper cases, then bake in the oven for 10 – 15 minutes.
- Test with a wooden toothpick, if it comes out clean, the cupcakes are done.
- Serve warm.

MUFFINS AND MACAROONS

475

MAKES 12

Wholemeal Multi-seed Muffins

Wholemeal Crunch Muffins

476

For even more crunch, add 75g / 3oz chopped hazelnuts and 75g / 3 oz flaked almonds instead of the dried cranberries.

Crunchy Chocolate Muffins

477

Add 75g / 3oz chopped hazelnuts and 75g / 3 oz chocolate chips to the muffin mixture.

PREPARATION TIME: 25 MINUTES

COOKING TIME: 25 MINUTES

INGREDIENTS

1 large egg
120 ml / 4 fl. oz / ½ cup sunflower oil
120 ml / 4 fl. oz / ½ cup milk
375 g / 12 ½ oz / 2 ½ cups wholemeal flour
2 tsp baking powder
200 g / 7 oz / ¾ cup caster (superfine) sugar
75 g / 2 ½ oz / ½ cup dried cranberries
2 tbsp sesame seeds
2 tbsp sunflower seeds
2 tbsp hemp seeds
2 tbsp pumpkin seeds

- Preheat the oven to 180°C (160° fan) / 350 F / gas 4 and oil a 12-hole silicone muffin tin.
- Beat the egg in a jug with the oil and milk until well mixed.
- Mix the flour, baking powder, sugar, cranberries and ¾ of the mixed seeds in a bowl, then pour in the egg mixture and stir just enough to combine.
- Divide the mixture between the moulds and sprinkle over the rest of the seeds, then bake in the oven for 20 – 25 minutes.
- Test with a wooden toothpick, if it comes out clean, the muffins are done.
- Transfer the muffins to a wire rack and leave to cool.

478

MAKES 12

Spiced Blueberry Muffins

- Preheat the oven to 180°C (160° fan) / 350 F / gas 4 and oil a 12-hole silicone muffin tin.
- Beat the egg in a jug with the oil and milk until well mixed.
- Mix the flour, baking powder, sugar, blueberries and spices in a bowl, then pour in the egg mixture and stir just enough to combine.
- Divide the mixture between the moulds, then bake in the oven for 20 – 25 minutes.
- Test with a wooden toothpick, if it comes out clean, the muffins are done.
- Transfer the muffins to a wire rack and leave to cool before dusting with icing sugar.

PREPARATION TIME: 25 MINUTES

COOKING TIME: 25 MINUTES

INGREDIENTS

1 large egg
120 ml / 4 fl. oz / ½ cup sunflower oil
120 ml / 4 fl. oz / ½ cup milk
375 g / 12 ½ oz / 2 ½ cups self-raising flour, sifted
1 tsp baking powder
200 g / 7 oz / ¾ cup caster (superfine) sugar
150 g / 5 oz / 1 cup blueberries
1 tsp mixed spice
1 tsp ground cinnamon
½ tsp ground cloves
Icing (confectioners') sugar to dust

Spiced Blackberry Muffins

479

Replace the blueberries with 150g / 6 oz / ⅔ cup blackberries and replace the ground cinnamon with ½ tsp ground star anise.

480

MAKES 12

Wholemeal Orange and Chocolate Chip Muffins

- Preheat the oven to 190°°C (165° fan), 375F, gas 5 and Preheat the oven to 180°C (160° fan) / 350 F / gas 4 and line a 12-hole muffin tin with paper cases.
- Beat the egg in a jug with the oil and milk until well mixed.
- Mix the flour, baking powder, sugar, orange zest and chocolate chips in a bowl, then pour in the egg mixture and stir just enough to combine.
- Divide the mixture between the moulds, then bake in the oven for 20 – 25 minutes.
- Test with a wooden toothpick, if it comes out clean, the muffins are done.
- Transfer the muffins to a wire rack and leave to cool.
- Melt the chocolate in a microwave or bain marie and spoon it into a piping bag.
- Pipe the chocolate across the top of the muffins in a zigzag motion.

PREPARATION TIME: 35 MINUTES

COOKING TIME: 25 MINUTES

INGREDIENTS

1 large egg
120 ml / 4 fl. oz / ½ cup sunflower oil
120 ml / 4 fl. oz / ½ cup milk
375 g / 12 ½ oz / 2 ½ cups wholemeal flour
2 tsp baking powder
200 g / 7 oz / ¾ cup caster (superfine) sugar
1 orange, zest finely grated
75 g / 2 ½ oz / ½ cup chocolate chips

TO DECORATE

110 g / 4 oz / ½ cup dark chocolate, minimum 60% cocoa solids, chopped

Wholemeal Double Chocolate Muffins

481

Replace the orange zest with 4 tbsp unsweetened cocoa powder.

482

MAKES 12

Gremolata Muffins

PREPARATION TIME: 10 MINUTES

COOKING TIME: 25 MINUTES

INGREDIENTS

2 large eggs
120 ml / 4 fl. oz / ½ cup sunflower oil
180 ml / 6 fl. oz / ¾ cup Greek yogurt
110 g / 4 oz / 1 cup Parmesan, grated
225 g / 8 oz / 1 ½ cups plain (all purpose) flour
2 tsp baking powder
½ tsp bicarbonate of (baking) soda
½ tsp salt
½ tbsp chopped garlic
½ tbsp lemon zest, finely grated
2 tbsp flat leaf parsley, finely chopped

- Preheat the oven to 180°C (160° fan) / 350 F / gas 4 and oil a 12-hole silicone muffin tin.
- Beat the egg in a jug with the oil, yogurt and cheese until well mixed.
- Mix the flour, raising agents, salt garlic, lemon zest and parsley in a bowl, then pour in the egg mixture and stir just enough to combine.
- Divide the mixture between the moulds, then bake in the oven for 20 – 25 minutes.
- Test with a wooden toothpick, if it comes out clean, the muffins are done.
- Transfer the muffins to a wire rack and leave to cool.

Gremolata and Mozzarella Muffins

483

Add a cube of fresh mozzarella to the centre of each muffin before baking.

484

MAKES 12

Chocolate Orange Muffins

PREPARATION TIME: 25 MINUTES

COOKING TIME: 25 MINUTES

INGREDIENTS

1 large egg
120ml / 4 fl oz / ½ cup sunflower oil
120ml / 4 fl oz / ½ cup milk
375g / 12 ½ oz / 2 ½ cups self-raising flour, sifted
55g / 2 oz / ½ cup unsweetened cocoa powder, sifted
1 tsp baking powder
200g / 7 oz / ¾ cup caster (superfine) sugar
110g / 4 oz / ½ cup orange flavoured chocolate, chopped
1 orange, zest finely grated

- Preheat the oven to 180C (160C fan) / 350F / gas 4 and line a 12-hole muffin tin with paper cases.
- Beat the egg in a jug with the oil and milk until well mixed.
- Mix the flour, cocoa, baking powder, sugar, chocolate and orange zest in a bowl, then pour in the egg mixture and stir just enough to combine.
- Divide the mixture between the paper cases, then bake in the oven for 20 – 25 minutes.
- Test with a wooden toothpick, if it comes out clean, the muffins are done.
- Transfer the muffins to a wire rack and leave to cool completely.

Hot Orange Sauce

485

Make a hot chocolate orange sauce to accompany the muffins: heat 225ml / 8 fl. oz / 1 cup double cream until boiling then pour over 225g / 8 oz / 1 cup chopped orange flavoured chocolate and stir until smooth.

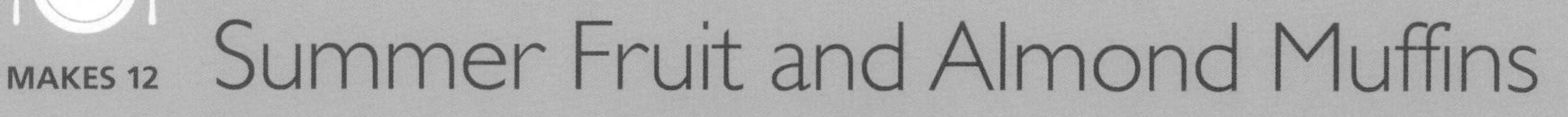

486

MAKES 12

Summer Fruit and Almond Muffins

Almond Drizzle Icing

487

Make an almond drizzle icing by mixing 225g / 8 oz icing sugar with ½ tsp almond essence and just enough boiling water to make a spoonable icing.

488

Summer Fruit and Walnut Muffins

Replace the almonds with walnuts.

PREPARATION TIME: 25 MINUTES

COOKING TIME:
20 – 25 MINUTES

INGREDIENTS

1 large egg
120 ml / 4 fl. oz / ½ cup sunflower oil
120 ml / 4 fl. oz / ½ cup milk
375 g / 12 ½ oz / 2 ½ cups self-raising flour, sifted
1 tsp baking powder
200 g / 7 oz / ¾ cup caster (superfine) sugar
150 g / 5 oz / 1 cup mixed summer fruits
75 g / 2 ½ oz / ½ cup flaked (slivered) almonds

- Preheat the oven to 180°C (160° fan) / 350 F / gas 4 and line a 12-hole muffin tin with paper cases.
- Beat the egg in a jug with the oil and milk until well mixed.
- Mix the flour, baking powder, sugar, fruit and almonds in a bowl, then pour in the egg mixture and stir just enough to combine.
- Divide the mixture between the paper cases, then bake in the oven for 20 – 25 minutes.
- Test with a wooden toothpick, if it comes out clean, the muffins are done.
- Transfer the muffins to a wire rack and leave to cool completely.

489

MAKES 12

Almond Muffins

Fruit and Nut Muffins

490

Use this as a base recipe and add your choice of dried fruit and nuts.

Marzipan Covered Muffins

491

Roll out 200 g / 7 oz of marzipan and cut out 12 circles. Lay a circle of marzipan on top of each muffin before baking for a golden bubbly crust.

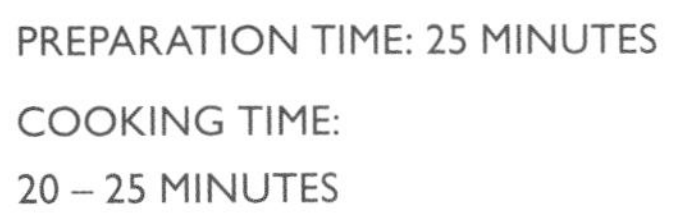

PREPARATION TIME: 25 MINUTES

COOKING TIME:
20 – 25 MINUTES

INGREDIENTS

1 large egg
120 ml / 4 fl. oz / ½ cup sunflower oil
120 ml / 4 fl. oz / ½ cup milk
375 g / 12 ½ oz / 2 ½ cups self-raising flour, sifted
1 tsp baking powder
200 g / 7 oz / ¾ cup caster (superfine) sugar
75 g / 2 ½ oz / ½ cup ground almonds
75 g / 2 ½ oz / ½ cup flaked (slivered) almonds

- Preheat the oven to 180°°C (160° fan) / 350 F / gas 4 and oil a 12-hole silicone muffin mould.
- Beat the egg in a jug with the oil and milk until well mixed.
- Mix the flour, baking powder, sugar and almonds in a bowl, then pour in the egg mixture and stir just enough to combine.
- Divide the mixture between the paper cases and sprinkle with flaked almonds, then bake in the oven for 20 – 25 minutes.
- Test with a wooden toothpick, if it comes out clean, the muffins are done.
- Transfer the muffins to a wire rack and leave to cool completely.

492

MAKES 12

Almond and Raspberry Muffins

- Preheat the oven to 180°C (160° fan) / 350 F / gas 4 and line a 12-hole muffin tin with paper cases.
- Beat the egg in a jug with the oil and milk until well mixed.
- Mix the flour, baking powder, sugar, ground almonds and raspberries in a bowl, then pour in the egg mixture and stir just enough to combine.
- Divide the mixture between the paper cases and bake in the oven for 20 – 25 minutes.
- Test with a wooden toothpick, if it comes out clean, the muffins are done.
- Transfer the muffins to a wire rack and leave to cool before dusting with icing sugar.

PREPARATION TIME: 25 MINUTES

COOKING TIME: 25 MINUTES

INGREDIENTS

1 large egg
120 ml / 4 fl. oz / ½ cup sunflower oil
120 ml / 4 fl. oz / ½ cup milk
375 g / 12 ½ oz / 2 ½ cups self-raising flour, sifted
1 tsp baking powder
200 g / 7 oz / ¾ cup caster (superfine) sugar
75 g / 2 ½ oz / ½ cup ground almonds
150 g / 5 oz / 1 cup raspberries
Icing (confectioners') sugar for dusting

Almond Muffins with Rosewater

493

Add 1 tbsp of rose water to the wet ingredients before mixing for an aromatic change.

494

MAKES 12

Spring Onion Muffins

- Preheat the oven to 180°C (160° fan) / 350 F / gas 4 and oil a 12-hole silicone muffin mould.
- Beat the egg in a jug with the oil, yogurt, cheese and spring onion until well mixed.
- Mix the flour, raising agents and salt in a bowl, then pour in the egg mixture and stir just enough to combine.
- Divide the mixture between the moulds, then bake in the oven for 20 – 25 minutes.
- Test with a wooden toothpick, if it comes out clean, the muffins are done.
- Serve warm.

PREPARATION TIME: 25 MINUTES

COOKING TIME: 25 MINUTES

INGREDIENTS

2 large eggs
120 ml / 4 fl. oz / ½ cup sunflower oil
180 ml / 6 fl. oz / ¾ cup Greek yogurt
110 g / 4 oz / 1 cup Comte cheese, grated
6 spring onions (scallions), chopped
225 g / 8 oz / 1 cup plain (all purpose) flour
2 tsp baking powder
½ tsp bicarbonate of (baking) soda
½ tsp salt

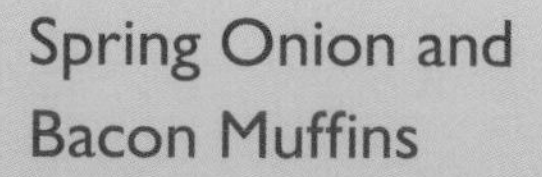

Spring Onion and Bacon Muffins

495

Add4 chopped rashers of smoked streaky bacon to the wet ingredients before folding everything together.

496

MAKES 12

Toffee and Chocolate Chunk Muffins

PREPARATION TIME: 25 MINUTES

COOKING TIME: 25 MINUTES

INGREDIENTS

1 large egg
120ml / 4 fl. oz / ½ cup sunflower oil
120ml / 4 fl. oz / ½ cup milk
375 g / 12 ½ oz / 2 ½ cups self-raising flour, sifted
1 tsp baking powder
200 g / 7 oz / ¾ cup caster (superfine) sugar
110 g / 4 oz chewy toffee, chopped
110 g / 4 oz / ½ cup dark chocolate, minimum 60% cocoa solids, chopped

- Preheat the oven to 180°C (160° fan) / 350 F / gas 4 and oil a 12-hole silicone muffin tin.
- Beat the egg in a jug with the oil and milk until well mixed.
- Mix the flour, baking powder, sugar, toffee and chocolate in a bowl, then pour in the egg mixture and stir just enough to combine.
- Divide the mixture between the moulds, then bake in the oven for 20 – 25 minutes.
- Test with a wooden toothpick, if it comes out clean, the muffins are done.
- Transfer the muffins to a wire rack and leave to cool completely.

Muffins with Toffee Sauce

497

Try icing the muffins with toffee sauce: melt equal quantities of butter, brown sugar, golden syrup and double cream in a saucepan and boil for 2 minutes then leave to cool and refrigerate until spreadable.

498

MAKES 12

Chocolate and Marshmallow Muffins

PREPARATION TIME: 25 MINUTES

COOKING TIME: 25 MINUTES

INGREDIENTS

1 large egg
120 ml / 4 fl. oz / ½ cup sunflower oil
120 ml / 4 fl. oz / ½ cup milk
375 g / 12 ½ oz / 2 ½ cups self-raising flour, sifted
55 g / 2 oz / ½ cup unsweetened cocoa powder, sifted
1 tsp baking powder
200 g / 7 oz / ¾ cup caster (superfine) sugar
110 g / 4 oz / ½ cup dark chocolate, minimum 60% cocoa solids, chopped
110 g / 4 oz / ½ cup mini marshmallows

- Preheat the oven to 180°C (160° fan) / 350 F / gas 4 and line a 12-hole muffin tin with paper cases.
- Beat the egg in a jug with the oil and milk until well mixed.
- Mix the flour, cocoa, baking powder, sugar, chocolate and marshmallows in a bowl, then pour in the egg mixture and stir just enough to combine.
- Divide the mixture between the paper cases, then bake in the oven for 20 – 25 minutes.
- Test with a wooden toothpick, if it comes out clean, the muffins are done.
- Transfer the muffins to a wire rack and leave to cool completely.

Marshmallow Muffins with Whipped Cream

499

For even more indulgence, top the muffins with a swirl of whipped cream and some extra marshmallows.

500

MAKES 12

Rainbow Muffins

White Chocolate Rainbow Muffins

501

Drizzle the muffins with melted white chocolate and top with extra coloured chocolates to decorate.

Milk Chocolate Rainbow Muffins

502

Alternatively, add 4 tbsp of unsweetened cocoa powder to the muffin mixture to make chocolate rainbow muffins.

PREPARATION TIME: 10 MINUTES

COOKING TIME: 25 MINUTES

INGREDIENTS

1 large egg
120 ml / 4 fl. oz / ½ cup sunflower oil
120 ml / 4 fl. oz / ½ cup milk
375 g / 12 ½ oz / 2 ½ cups self-raising flour, sifted
1 tsp baking powder
200 g / 7 oz / ¾ cup caster (superfine) sugar
110 g / 4 oz / ½ cup colourful shelled chocolates

- Preheat the oven to 180°C (160° fan) / 350 F / gas 4 and line a 12-hole muffin tin with paper cases.
- Beat the egg in a jug with the oil and milk until well mixed.
- Mix the flour, baking powder, sugar and Smarties in a bowl, then pour in the egg mixture and stir just enough to combine.
- Divide the mixture between the moulds, then bake in the oven for 20 – 25 minutes.
- Test with a wooden toothpick, if it comes out clean, the muffins are done.
- Transfer the muffins to a wire rack and leave to cool completely.

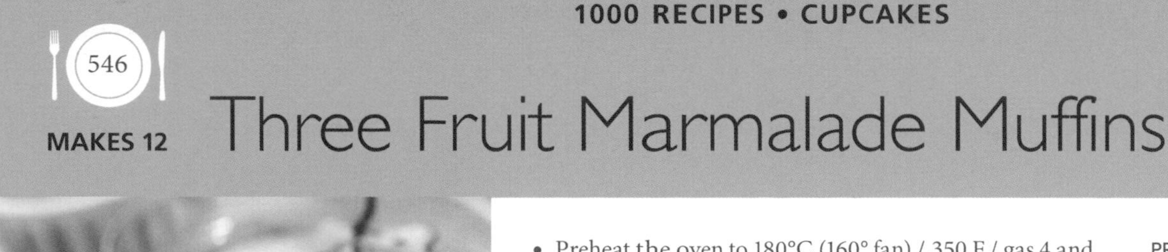

546

MAKES 12

Three Fruit Marmalade Muffins

- Preheat the oven to 180°C (160° fan) / 350 F / gas 4 and line a 12-hole muffin tin with paper cases.
- Beat the egg in a jug with the oil, milk and marmalade until well mixed.
- Mix the flour, baking powder and sugar in a bowl, then pour in the egg mixture and stir just enough to combine.
- Divide the mixture between the paper cases and bake in the oven for 20 – 25 minutes.
- Test with a wooden toothpick, if it comes out clean, the muffins are done.
- Transfer the muffins to a wire rack and leave to cool completely.

PREPARATION TIME: 25 MINUTES

COOKING TIME: 25 MINUTES

INGREDIENTS

1 large egg
120 ml / 4 fl. oz / ½ cup sunflower oil
120 ml / 4 fl. oz / ½ cup milk
110 g / 4 oz / ½ cup thick cut three fruit marmalade
375 g / 12 ½ oz / 2 ½ cups self-raising flour, sifted
1 tsp baking powder
200 g / 7 oz / ¾ cup caster (superfine) sugar

547

MAKES 12

Simple Carrot Muffins

PREPARATION TIME: 25 MINUTES

COOKING TIME: 25 MINUTES

INGREDIENTS

175 g / 6 oz / 1 cup soft brown sugar
2 large eggs
150 ml / 5 fl. oz / ¾ cup sunflower oil
175 g / 6 oz / 1 ¼ cups wholemeal flour
3 tsp baking powder
2 tsp ground cinnamon
1 orange, zest finely grated
200 g / 7 oz carrots, washed and coarsely grated

- Preheat the oven to 190°C (170° fan) / 375 F / gas 5 and line a 12-hole cupcake tin with paper cases.
- Whisk the sugar, eggs and oil together for 3 minutes until thick.
- Fold in the flour, baking powder and cinnamon, followed by the orange zest and carrots.
- Divide the mixture between the paper cases, then transfer the tin to the oven and bake for 20 - 25 minutes.
- Test with a wooden toothpick, if it comes out clean, the muffins are done.
- Transfer the muffins to a wire rack and leave to cool completely.

548

MAKES 12

Cinnamon Muffins

PREPARATION TIME: 30 MINUTES

COOKING TIME: 20 MINUTES

INGREDIENTS

110 g / 4 oz / ½ cup self-raising flour, sifted
110 g / 4 oz / ½ cup caster (superfine) sugar
110 g / 4 oz / ½ cup butter, softened
2 large eggs
2 tsp ground cinnamon
To decorate
225 ml / 8 fl. oz / 1 cup double (heavy) cream
2 tbsp icing (confectioners') sugar
1 tsp ground cinnamon

- Preheat the oven to 190°C (170° fan) / 375 F / gas 5 and line a 12-hole cupcake tin with paper cases.
- Combine the flour, sugar, butter, eggs and cinnamon in a bowl and whisk together for 2 minutes or until smooth.
- Divide the mixture between the paper cases, then transfer the tin to the oven and bake for 15 – 20 minutes.
- Test with a wooden toothpick, if it comes out clean, the muffins are done.
- Transfer the muffins to a wire rack and leave to cool completely.
- To make the topping, whisk the cream with the icing sugar until it forms soft peaks.
- Spoon the whipped cream into a piping bag fitted with a large star nozzle and pipe a swirl on top of each cake.
- Use a small sieve to dust each cake with cinnamon.

549

MAKES 12

Cranberry and Walnut Muffins

- Preheat the oven to 180°C (160° fan) / 350 F / gas 4 and oil a 12-hole silicone muffin tin.
- Beat the egg in a jug with the oil and milk until well mixed.
- Mix the flour, baking powder, sugar, cranberries and walnuts in a bowl, then pour in the egg mixture and stir just enough to combine.
- Divide the mixture between the paper cases, then bake in the oven for 20 – 25 minutes.
- Test with a wooden toothpick, if it comes out clean, the muffins are done.
- Transfer the muffins to a wire rack and leave to cool completely.

PREPARATION TIME: 25 MINUTES

COOKING TIME: 25 MINUTES

INGREDIENTS

1 large egg
120 ml / 4 fl. oz / ½ cup sunflower oil
120 ml / 4 fl. oz / ½ cup milk
375 g / 12 ½ oz / 2 ½ cups self-raising flour, sifted
1 tsp baking powder
200 g / 7 oz / ¾ cup caster (superfine) sugar
75 g / 2 ½ oz / ½ cup dried cranberries
75 g / 2 ½ oz / ½ cup walnuts, chopped

Cranberry, Walnut and Honey Muffins

550

Brush the muffins with honey as they come out of the oven for a delicious shiny glaze.

551

MAKES 12

Minted Pea Mini Muffins

- Preheat the oven to 180°C (160° fan) / 350 F / gas 4 and oil a 24-hole silicone muffin tin.
- Beat the egg in a jug with the oil, yoghrt, peas and cheese until well mixed.
- Mix the flour, raising agents, salt and mint in a bowl, then pour in the egg mixture and stir just enough to combine.
- Divide the mixture between the moulds, then bake in the oven for 10 – 15 minutes.
- Test with a wooden toothpick, if it comes out clean, the muffins are done.
- Serve warm.

PREPARATION TIME: 25 MINUTES

COOKING TIME: 15 MINUTES

INGREDIENTS

2 large eggs
120 ml / 4 fl. oz / ½ cup sunflower oil
180 ml / 6 fl. oz / ¾ cup Greek yogurt
150 g / 5 oz / 1 cup cooked peas
110 g / 4 oz / 1 cup Parmesan, grated
225 g / 8 oz / 1 ½ cups plain (all purpose) flour
2 tsp baking powder
½ tsp bicarbonate of (baking) soda
½ tsp salt
2 tbsp fresh mint, chopped

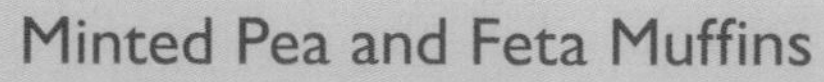

Minted Pea and Feta Muffins

552

Try adding 75g / 3 oz / ⅓ cup of cubed feta to the mixture before baking.

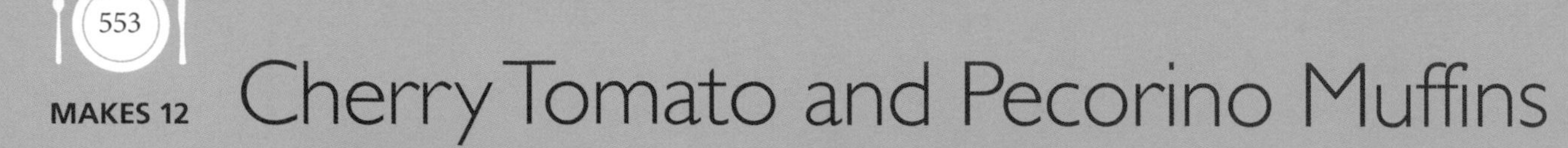

553

MAKES 12

Cherry Tomato and Pecorino Muffins

Cherry Tomato, Pesto and Mozzarella Muffins

554

Replace the Pecorino with cubed mozzarella and replace the basil with 100 g of pesto marbled through the mixture.

Sun-dried Tomato and Pecorino Muffins

555

Replace the cherry tomatoes with sun-dried tomatoes for a mediterranean twist.

PREPARATION TIME: 20 MINUTES

COOKING TIME: 20-25 MINUTES

INGREDIENTS

2 large eggs
120 ml / 4 fl. oz / ½ cup sunflower oil
180 ml / 6 fl. oz / ¾ cup Greek yoghurt
110 g / 4 oz / 1 cup Pecorino, cubed
150 g / 5 oz / 1 cup cherry tomatoes, halved
2 tbsp basil leaves, shredded
225 g / 8 oz / 1 ½ cups plain flour
2 tsp baking powder
½ tsp bicarbonate of (baking) soda
½ tsp salt

- Preheat the oven to 180°°C (160° fan) / 350 F / gas 4 and line a 12-hole muffin tin with paper cases.
- Beat the egg in a jug with the oil, yoghurt and cheese until well mixed.
- Mix the tomatoes, basil, flour, raising agents and salt in a bowl, then pour in the egg mixture and stir just enough to combine.
- Divide the mixture between the paper cases, then bake in the oven for 20 – 25 minutes.
- Test with a wooden toothpick, if it comes out clean, the muffins are done.
- Serve warm.

556

MAKES 12

Apple and Clove Muffins

- Preheat the oven to 180°C (160° fan) / 350 F / gas 4 and line a 12-hole muffin tin with paper cases.
- Beat the egg in a jug with the oil and milk until well mixed.
- Mix the flour, baking powder, sugar and cloves in a bowl, then pour in the egg mixture and stir just enough to combine.
- Divide the mixture between the paper cases and top with the sliced apple.
- Brush the apples with honey and bake in the oven for 20 – 25 minutes.
- Test with a wooden toothpick, if it comes out clean, the muffins are done.
- Transfer the muffins to a wire rack and leave to cool.

PREPARATION TIME: 25 MINUTES

COOKING TIME: 25 MINUTES

INGREDIENTS

1 large egg
120 ml / 4 fl. oz / ½ cup sunflower oil
120 ml / 4 fl. oz / ½ cup milk
225 g / 7 ½ oz / 1 ½ cups self-raising flour, sifted
1 tsp baking powder
200 g / 7 oz / ¾ cup caster (superfine) sugar
1 tsp ground cloves
2 apples, peeled, cored and sliced
2 tbsp honey

Spicy Apple and Clove Muffins

557

This recipe is lovely with sliced pears or plums instead of the apple. Alternatively, replace the ground cloves with ground allspice berries.

558

MAKES 12

Banana and Orange Muffins

- Preheat the oven to 190°C (170° fan) / 375 F / gas 5 and line a 12-hole cupcake tin with paper cases.
- Combine the flour, sugar, butter, eggs and orange zest in a bowl and whisk together for 2 minutes or until smooth.
- Divide the mixture between the paper cases.
- Cut each banana into 12 pieces and press 2 pieces of banana into the top of each cake.
- Transfer the tin to the oven and bake for 15 – 20 minutes.
- Test with a wooden toothpick, if it comes out clean, the muffins are done.
- Transfer the muffins to a wire rack and leave to cool completely.

PREPARATION TIME: 35 MINUTES

COOKING TIME: 20 MINUTES

INGREDIENTS

110 g / 4 oz / ½ cup self-raising flour, sifted
110 g / 4 oz / ½ cup caster (superfine) sugar
110 g / 4 oz / ½ cup butter, softened
2 large eggs
1 orange, zest finely grated
2 bananas
Icing (confectioners') sugar, to dust

Banana and Lime Muffins

559

Try making the muffins with lime zest instead of orange zest and make lime drizzle icing to go with them: sieve 110g / 4 oz / ½ cup icing sugar into a bowl and add just enough lime juice to make a runny icing.

560

MAKES 24

Mini Pesto Muffins

PREPARATION TIME: 25 MINUTES

COOKING TIME: 15 MINUTES

INGREDIENTS

2 large eggs
120 ml / 4 fl. oz / ½ cup sunflower oil
180 ml / 6 fl. oz / ¾ cup Greek yogurt
110 g / 4 oz / 1 cup pesto
225 g / 8 oz / 1 ½ cups plain (all purpose) flour
2 tsp baking powder
½ tsp bicarbonate of (baking) soda
½ tsp salt

- Preheat the oven to 180°C (160° fan) / 350 F / gas 4 and line a 24-hole muffin tin with paper cases.
- Beat the egg in a jug with the oil, yoghurt and pesto until well mixed.
- Mix the flour, raising agents and salt in a bowl, then pour in the egg mixture and stir just enough to combine.
- Divide the mixture between the paper cases, then bake in the oven for 10 – 15 minutes.
- Test with a wooden toothpick, if it comes out clean, the muffins are done.
- Serve warm.

Pesto and Parmesan Muffins

561

For extra texture, add 2 tbsp of pine nuts to the muffin mixture and sprinkle with grated Parmesan before baking.

562

MAKES 12

Courgette and Gruyere Muffins

PREPARATION TIME: 25 MINUTES

COOKING TIME: 25 MINUTES

INGREDIENTS

2 large eggs
120 ml / 4 fl. oz / ½ cup sunflower oil
180 ml / 6 fl. oz / ¾ cup Greek yogurt
110 g / 4 oz / 1 cup Gruyere cheese, cubed
1 medium courgette (zucchini), sliced
225 g / 8 oz / 1 cup plain (all purpose) flour
2 tsp baking powder
½ tsp bicarbonate of (baking) soda
½ tsp salt

- Preheat the oven to 180°C (160° fan) / 350 F / gas 4 and line a 12-hole muffin tin with paper cases.
- Beat the egg in a jug with the oil, yoghurt, cheese and courgette until well mixed.
- Mix the flour, raising agents and salt in a bowl, then pour in the egg mixture and stir just enough to combine.
- Divide the mixture between the paper cases, then bake in the oven for 20 – 25 minutes.
- Test with a wooden toothpick, if it comes out clean, the muffins are done.
- Serve warm.

Courgette and Pepper Muffins

563

Try swapping the courgette for 1 red pepper, deseeded and thinly sliced.

564

MAKES 12

Carrot and Ginger Muffins

- Preheat the oven to 190°C (170° fan) / 375 F / gas 5 and line a 12-hole muffin tin with paper cases.
- Whisk the sugar, eggs and oil together for 3 minutes until thick.
- Fold in the flour, baking powder and ground ginger, followed by the stem ginger and carrots.
- Divide the mixture between the paper cases, then transfer the tin to the oven and bake for 20 - 25 minutes.
- Test with a wooden toothpick, if it comes out clean, the muffins are done.
- Transfer the muffins to a wire rack and leave to cool.

PREPARATION TIME: 15 MINUTES

COOKING TIME: 25 MINUTES

INGREDIENTS

175 g / 6 oz / 1 cup soft brown sugar
2 large eggs
150 ml / 5 fl. oz / ¾ cup sunflower oil
175 g / 6 oz / 1 ¼ cups wholemeal flour
3 tsp baking powder
2 tsp ground ginger
6 pieces of stem ginger, chopped
200 g / 7 oz / 1 cup carrots, washed and coarsely grated

Parnsnip and Caraway Muffins

565

Try these muffins with grated parsnip instead of the carrots and add 2 tsp of caraway seeds to the mixture.

566

MAKES 12

Walnut and Butterscotch Muffins

- Preheat the oven to 180°°C (160° fan) / 350 F / gas 4 and oil a 12-hole silicone muffin tin.
- Beat the egg in a jug with the oil and milk until well mixed.
- Mix the flour, baking powder, sugar and walnuts in a bowl, then pour in the egg mixture and stir.
- Divide the mixture between the moulds and bake in the oven for 25 minutes.
- Test with a wooden toothpick, if it comes out clean, the muffins are done.
- Put the butter, cream, golden syrup and brown sugar in a small saucepan and boil for 2 minutes, stirring to dissolve the sugar.
- Stir in the walnuts and leave to cool.
- Make a hole in the top of each muffin with the back of a teaspoon and pour some of the butterscotch sauce inside.

PREPARATION TIME: 25 MINUTES

COOKING TIME: 20-25 MINUTES

INGREDIENTS

1 large egg
120 ml / 4 fl. oz / ½ cup sunflower oil
120 ml / 4 fl. oz / ½ cup milk
375 g / 12 ½ oz / 2 ½ cups self-raising flour, sifted
1 tsp baking powder
200 g / 7 oz / ¾ cup caster (superfine) sugar
75 g / 2 ½ oz / ½ cup walnuts, chopped

TO SERVE

85 g / 3 oz / ½ cup butter
85 ml / 3 fl. oz / ⅓ cup double cream
85 g / 3 oz / ¼ cup golden syrup
85 g / 3 oz / ½ cup dark brown sugar
75 g / 2 ½ oz / ½ cup walnuts, chopped

Walnut and Cinnamon Muffins

567

Add 1 tsp of ground cinnamon to the muffin mixture and cook the same.

MAKES 12

Apple and Cinnamon Cupcakes

Apple, Cinnamon and Clove Muffins

569

These simple muffins are delicious flavoured with cloves too – just replace the cinnamon with ½ tsp of ground cloves.

Apple Buttercream Muffins

570

Try icing them with cinnamon flavoured buttercream and top with an extra sprinkle of cinnamon.

PREPARATION TIME: 20 MINUTES

COOKING TIME: 20 MINUTES

INGREDIENTS

110 g / 4 oz / ½ cup self-raising flour, sifted
110 g / 4 oz / ½ cup caster (superfine) sugar
110 g / 4 oz / ½ cup butter, softened
2 large eggs
1 tsp ground cinnamon
1 apple, peeled, cored and grated

- Preheat the oven to 190°C (170° fan) / 375 F / gas 5 and line a 12-hole muffin tin with paper cases.
- Combine the flour, sugar, butter, eggs and cinnamon in a bowl and whisk together for 2 minutes or until smooth.
- Fold in the grated apple then divide the mixture between the muffin cases.
- Transfer the tin to the oven and bake for 15 – 20 minutes.
- Test with a wooden toothpick, if it comes out clean, the muffins are done.
- Transfer the muffins to a wire rack and leave to cool completely.

571

MAKES 12

Raisin and Coconut Muffins

- Preheat the oven to 180°°C (160° fan) / 350 F / gas 4 and oil a 12-hole silicone muffin tin.
- Beat the egg in a jug with the oil and milk until well mixed.
- Mix the flour, baking powder, sugar, raisins and coconut in a bowl, then pour in the egg mixture and stir just enough to combine.
- Divide the mixture between the paper cases, then bake in the oven for 20 – 25 minutes.
- Test with a wooden toothpick, if it comes out clean, the muffins are done.
- Transfer to a wire rack to cool and sprinkle with some more desiccated coconut.

PREPARATION TIME: 25 MINUTES

COOKING TIME: 20-25 MINUTES

INGREDIENTS

1 large egg
120 ml / 4 fl. oz / ½ cup sunflower oil
120 ml / 4 fl. oz / ½ cup milk
375 g / 12 ½ oz / 2 ½ cups self-raising flour, sifted
1 tsp baking powder
200 g / 7 oz / ¾ cup caster (superfine) sugar
75 g / 2 ½ oz / ½ cup raisins
75 g / 2 ½ oz / ½ cup desiccated coconut

TO DECORATE
2 tbsp desiccated coconut

Cherry and Coconut Muffins

572

Add 75 g / 2 ½ mixed candied peel and 75 g / ½ chopped glace cherries to the muffin mixture with the raisins.

573

MAKES 12

Blueberry, Lemon and Poppy Seed Muffins

- Preheat the oven to 180°C (160° fan) / 350 F / gas 4 and line a 12-hole muffin tin with paper cases.
- Beat the egg in a jug with the oil and milk until well mixed.
- Mix the flour, baking powder, sugar, blueberries, lemon zest and poppy seeds in a bowl, then pour in the egg mixture and stir just enough to combine.
- Divide the mixture between the moulds, then bake in the oven for 20 – 25 minutes.
- Test with a wooden toothpick, if it comes out clean, the muffins are done.
- Transfer the muffins to a wire rack and leave to cool completely.

PREPARATION TIME: 25 MINUTES

COOKING TIME: 25 MINUTES

INGREDIENTS

1 large egg
120 ml / 4 fl. oz / ½ cup sunflower oil
120 ml / 4 fl. oz / ½ cup milk
375 g / 12 ½ oz / 2 ½ cups self-raising flour, sifted
1 tsp baking powder
200 g / 7 oz / ¾ cup caster (superfine) sugar
150 g / 5 oz / 1 cup blueberries
1 lemon, zest finely grated
1 tbsp poppy seeds

Blueberry, Orange and Caraway Seeds Muffins

574

Try this recipe with orange zest instead of the lemon and swap the poppy seeds for caraway seeds.

575

MAKES 12

Courgette and Goat's Cheese Muffins

PREPARATION TIME: 25 MINUTES

COOKING TIME: 25 MINUTES

INGREDIENTS

2 large eggs
120 ml / 4 fl. oz / ½ cup sunflower oil
180 ml / 6 fl. oz / ¾ cup Greek yogurt
2 medium courgettes (zucchini), coarsely grated
110 g / 4 oz / 1 cup goats' cheese, cubed
225 g / 8 oz / 1 ½ cups plain (all purpose) flour
2 tsp baking powder
½ tsp bicarbonate of (baking) soda
½ tsp salt

- Preheat the oven to 180°C (160° fan) / 350 F / gas 4 and oil a 12-hole silicone muffin tin.
- Beat the egg in a jug with the oil, yogurt, cheese and courgette until well mixed.
- Mix the flour, raising agents and salt in a bowl, then pour in the egg mixture and stir just enough to combine.
- Divide the mixture between the paper cases, then bake in the oven for 20 – 25 minutes.
- Test with a wooden toothpick, if it comes out clean, the muffins are done.
- Serve warm.

Courgette and Cheddar Muffins

576

Replace the goat's cheese with Cheddar.

577

MAKES 12

Milk Chocolate Chunk Muffins

PREPARATION TIME: 25 MINUTES

COOKING TIME: 25 MINUTES

INGREDIENTS

1 large egg
120 ml / 4 fl. oz / ½ cup sunflower oil
120 ml / 4 fl. oz / ½ cup milk
375 g / 12 ½ oz / 2 ½ cups self-raising flour, sifted
1 tsp baking powder
200 g / 7 oz / ¾ cup caster (superfine) sugar
110 g / 4 oz / ½ cup milk chocolate, chopped

- Preheat the oven to 180°C (160° fan) / 350 F / gas 4 and oil a 12-hole silicone muffin tin.
- Beat the egg in a jug with the oil and milk until well mixed.
- Mix the flour, baking powder, sugar and chocolate in a bowl, then pour in the egg mixture and stir just enough to combine.
- Divide the mixture between the moulds, then bake in the oven for 20 – 25 minutes.
- Test with a wooden toothpick, if it comes out clean, the muffins are done.
- Transfer the muffins to a wire rack and leave to cool completely.

White Chocolate Chunk Muffins

578

Add 110g / 4oz / ½ cup white chocolate chunks to the muffin mixture too for extra sweetness.

579

MAKES 12

Wholemeal Raisin Muffins

Wholemeal Oat and Raisin Muffins

580

Add 75 g of porridge oats to the muffin mixture.

Wholemeal Candied Peel Muffins

581

Replace the raisins with 75 g of chopped mixed candied peel.

PREPARATION TIME: 25 MINUTES

COOKING TIME: 20 – 25 MINUTES

INGREDIENTS

1 large egg
120 ml / 4 fl. oz / ½ cup sunflower oil
120 ml / 4 fl. oz / ½ cup milk
375 g / 12 ½ oz / 2 ½ cups wholemeal flour
2 tsp baking powder
200 g / 7 oz / ¾ cup caster (superfine) sugar
75 g / 2 ½ oz / ½ cup raisins

- Preheat the oven to 180°°C (160° fan) / 350 F / gas 4 and line a 12-hole muffin tin with paper cases.
- Beat the egg in a jug with the oil and milk until well mixed.
- Mix the flour, baking powder, sugar and raisins in a bowl, then pour in the egg mixture and stir just enough to combine.
- Divide the mixture between the muffin papers, then bake in the oven for 20 – 25 minutes.
- Test with a wooden toothpick, if it comes out clean, the muffins are done.
- Transfer the muffins to a wire rack and leave to cool.

582

MAKES 12

Peach Muffins

PREPARATION TIME: 25 MINUTES

COOKING TIME: 25 MINUTES

INGREDIENTS

1 large egg
120 ml / 4 fl. oz / ½ cup sunflower oil
120 ml / 4 fl. oz / ½ cup milk
375 g / 12 ½ oz / 2 ½ cups self-raising flour, sifted
1 tsp baking powder
200 g / 7 oz / ¾ cup caster (superfine) sugar
2 peaches, stoned and chopped

- Preheat the oven to 180°C (160° fan) / 350 F / gas 4 and oil a 12-hole silicone muffin tin.
- Beat the egg in a jug with the oil and milk until well mixed.
- Mix the flour, baking powder, sugar and peaches in a bowl, then pour in the egg mixture and stir just enough to combine.
- Divide the mixture between the moulds, then bake in the oven for 20 – 25 minutes.
- Test with a wooden toothpick, if it comes out clean, the muffins are done.
- Transfer the muffins to a wire rack and leave to cool completely.

Apricot Muffins

583

This recipe works equally well with apricots - just substitute the peaches for 4 stoned, chopped apricots.

584

MAKES 12

Raisin and Oat Muffins

PREPARATION TIME: 25 MINUTES

COOKING TIME: 25 MINUTES

INGREDIENTS

1 large egg
120 ml / 4 fl. oz / ½ cup sunflower oil
120 ml / 4 fl. oz / ½ cup milk
375 g / 12 ½ oz / 2 ½ cups self-raising flour, sifted
1 tsp baking powder
200 g / 7 oz / ¾ cup caster (superfine) sugar
75 g / 2 ½ oz / ½ cup raisins
75 g / 2 ½ oz / ½ cup porridge oats

- Preheat the oven to 180°C (160° fan) / 350 F / gas 4 and oil a 12-hole silicone muffin tin.
- Beat the egg in a jug with the oil and milk until well mixed.
- Mix the flour, baking powder, sugar, raisins and oats in a bowl, then pour in the egg mixture and stir just enough to combine.
- Divide the mixture between the paper cases, then bake in the oven for 20 – 25 minutes.
- Test with a wooden toothpick, if it comes out clean, the muffins are done.
- Serve the muffins warm with butter.

Breakfast Muffins

585

Add 5 tbsp chopped dried apricots and 2 tbsp of pumpkin seeds to the muffin mixture for tasty breakfast muffins.

586

MAKES 12

Coconut and Almond Muffins

- Preheat the oven to 180°C (160° fan) / 350 F / gas 4 and line a 12-hole muffin tin with greaseproof paper.
- Beat the egg in a jug with the oil and milk until well mixed.
- Mix the flour, baking powder, sugar, coconut and almonds in a bowl, then pour in the egg mixture and stir just enough to combine.
- Divide the mixture between the paper cases, then bake in the oven for 20 – 25 minutes.
- Test with a wooden toothpick, if it comes out clean, the muffins are done.
- Transfer the muffins to a wire rack and leave to cool completely.

PREPARATION TIME: 15 MINUTES

COOKING TIME: 25 MINUTES

INGREDIENTS

1 large egg
120 ml / 4 fl. oz / ½ cup sunflower oil
120 ml / 4 fl. oz / ½ cup milk
375 g / 12 ½ oz / 2 ½ cups self-raising flour, sifted
1 tsp baking powder
200 g / 7 oz / ¾ cup caster (superfine) sugar
75 g / 2 ½ oz / ½ cup desiccated coconut
75 g / 2 ½ oz / ½ cup flaked (slivered) almonds

Coconut and Marzipan Muffins

587

Try adding 110g / 4oz / ½ cup marzipan cut into chunks to bring out the almond flavour.

588

MAKES 12

Raisin and White Chocolate Muffins

- Preheat the oven to 180°C (160° fan) / 350 F / gas 4 and oil a 12-hole silicone muffin tin.
- Beat the egg in a jug with the oil and milk until well mixed.
- Mix the flour, baking powder, sugar, raisins and chocolate in a bowl, then pour in the egg mixture and stir just enough to combine.
- Divide the mixture between the paper cases, then bake in the oven for 20 – 25 minutes.
- Test with a wooden toothpick, if it comes out clean, the muffins are done.
- Transfer the muffins to a wire rack and leave to cool completely.

PREPARATION TIME: 15 MINUTES

COOKING TIME: 25 MINUTES

INGREDIENTS

1 large egg
120 ml / 4 fl. oz / ½ cup sunflower oil
120 ml / 4 fl. oz / ½ cup milk
375 g / 12 ½ oz / 2 ½ cups self-raising flour, sifted
1 tsp baking powder
200 g / 7 oz / ¾ cup caster (superfine) sugar
75 g / 2 ½ oz / ½ cup raisins
75 g / 2 ½ oz / ½ cup white chocolate, chopped

Date, Walnut and White Chocolate Muffins

589

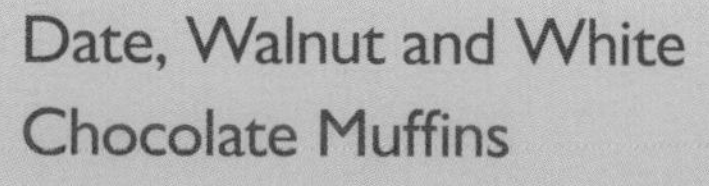

Replace the raisins with dates and add 85 g / 3 oz of chopped walnuts..

590

MAKES 12

Chocolate, Banana and Hazelnut Muffins

Chocolate Glazed Muffins

591

Mix 100g / 4oz / ½ cup icing sugar with 1 tbsp cocoa and enough boiling water to make a runny icing. Drizzle over the warm muffins.

Honey Glazed Muffins

592

Mix 100g / 4oz / ½ cup icing sugar with 1 tbsp honey and enough boiling water to make a runny icing. Drizzle over the warm muffins.

PREPARATION TIME: 10 MINUTES

COOKING TIME: 25 MINUTES

INGREDIENTS

1 large egg
120 ml / 4 fl. oz / ½ cup sunflower oil
120 ml / 4 fl. oz / ½ cup milk
375 g / 12 ½ oz / 2 ½ cups self-raising flour, sifted
55 g / 2 oz / ½ cup unsweetened cocoa powder, sifted
1 tsp baking powder
200 g / 7 oz / ¾ cup caster (superfine) sugar
110 g / 4 oz / ½ cup dark chocolate, minimum 60% cocoa solids, chopped
2 bananas, sliced
5 tbsp hazelnuts (cob nuts), chopped

- Preheat the oven to 180°C (160° fan) / 350 F / gas 4 and line a 12-hole muffin tin with paper cases.
- Beat the egg in a jug with the oil and milk until well mixed.
- Mix the flour, cocoa, baking powder, sugar, chocolate, banana and chopped hazelnuts in a bowl, then pour in the egg mixture and stir just enough to combine.
- Divide the mixture between the paper cases, then bake in the oven for 20 – 25 minutes.
- Test with a wooden toothpick, if it comes out clean, the muffins are done.
- Transfer the muffins to a wire rack and leave to cool completely.

593

MAKES 6

White Chocolate Muffins

- Oil 6 mini pudding basins and dust the insides with icing sugar.
- Melt the chocolate, butter and sugar together in a saucepan, stirring to dissolve the sugar.
- Leave to cool a little then beat in the eggs and egg yolks and fold in the flour.
- Divide the mixture between the pudding basins, then chill them for 30 minutes.
- Preheat the oven to 180°C (160° fan) / 350 F / gas 4 and put a baking tray in to heat.
- Transfer the fondants to the heated baking tray and bake in the oven for 8 minutes.
- Leave the fondants to cool for 2 minutes, then turn them out of their moulds and serve immediately.

PREPARATION TIME: 10 MINUTES

COOKING TIME: 10 MINUTES

INGREDIENTS

2 tbsp icing (confectioners') sugar
150 g / 6 oz / ⅔ cup white chocolate, chopped
150 g / 6 oz / ⅔ cup butter, chopped
85 g / 3 oz / ⅓ cup caster (superfine) sugar
3 large eggs
3 egg yolks
1 tbsp plain (all purpose) flour

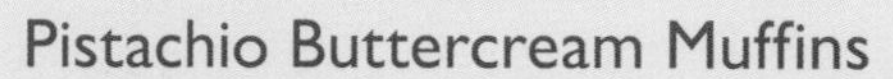

Pistachio Buttercream Muffins

594

Beat together 110g / 4 0z / ½ cup butter, 110g / 4 0z / ½ cup icing sugar, 2 tbsp ground pistachios and 2 tbsp milk until smooth. Pipe a rosette on top of each fondant.

595

MAKES 12

Chocolate and Vanilla Cream Muffins

- Preheat the oven to 180°C (160° fan) / 350 F / gas 4 and line a 12-hole muffin tin with paper cases.
- Beat the egg in a jug with the oil and milk until well mixed.
- Mix the flour, baking powder and sugar in a bowl, then pour in the egg mixture and chopped chocolate and stir just enough to combine.
- Divide the mixture between the paper cases, then bake in the oven for 20 – 25 minutes.
- Transfer the muffins to a wire rack and leave to cool completely. Whip the cream with the icing sugar and vanilla extract until thick.
- Spoon the vanilla cream into a piping bag fitted with a large star nozzle and pipe a big swirl on top of each cake.
- Melt the chocolate in a microwave or bain marie and leave to cool a little before spooning over the cakes.

PREPARATION TIME: 15 MINUTES

COOKING TIME: 25 MINUTES

INGREDIENTS

1 large egg
120 ml / 4 fl. oz / ½ cup sunflower oil
120 ml / 4 fl. oz / ½ cup milk
375 g / 12 ½ oz / 2 ½ cups self-raising flour, sifted
1 tsp baking powder
200 g / 7 oz / ¾ cup caster (superfine) sugar
110 g / 4 oz milk chocolate, chopped
To decorate
225 ml / 8 fl. oz / 1 cup double (heavy) cream
2 tbsp icing (confectioners') sugar
1 tsp vanilla extract
55 g / 2 oz / ¼ cup dark chocolate, minimum 60% cocoa solids

Chocolate and Mint Cream Muffins

596

Replace the vanilla extract with a few drops of peppermint essence. Top the muffins with a mint thin after drizzling with dark chocolate.

597

MAKES 12

Apricot and Sultana Muffins

PREPARATION TIME: 15 MINUTES

COOKING TIME: 25 MINUTES

INGREDIENTS

1 large egg
120 ml / 4 fl. oz / ½ cup sunflower oil
120 ml / 4 fl. oz / ½ cup milk
375 g / 12 ½ oz / 2 ½ cups self-raising flour, sifted
1 tsp baking powder
200 g / 7 oz / ¾ cup caster (superfine) sugar
75 g / 2 ½ oz / ½ cup dried apricots, chopped
75 g / 2 ½ oz / ½ cup sultanas

- Preheat the oven to 180°C (160° fan) / 350 F / gas 4 and oil a 12-hole silicone muffin tin.
- Beat the egg in a jug with the oil and milk until well mixed.
- Mix the flour, baking powder, sugar, apricots and sultanas in a bowl, then pour in the egg mixture and stir just enough to combine.
- Divide the mixture between the moulds, then bake in the oven for 20 – 25 minutes.
- Test with a wooden toothpick, if it comes out clean, the muffins are done.
- Transfer the muffins to a wire rack and leave to cool completely.

Apricot, Sultana and Oat Muffins

598

Add 2 tbsp rolled oats to the mixture to boost the fibre content.

599

MAKES 12

Bacon and Chive Muffins

PREPARATION TIME: 15 MINUTES

COOKING TIME: 25 MINUTES

INGREDIENTS

2 large eggs
120 ml / 4 fl. oz / ½ cup sunflower oil
180 ml / 6 fl. oz / ¾ cup Greek yogurt
110 g / 4 oz / 1 cup Parmesan, grated
75 g / 2 ½ oz / ½ cup streaky bacon, chopped
2 tbsp fresh chives, chopped
225 g / 8 oz / 1 ½ cups plain (all purpose) flour
2 tsp baking powder
½ tsp bicarbonate of (baking) soda
½ tsp salt

- Preheat the oven to 180°C (160° fan) / 350 F / gas 4 and line a 12-hole muffin tin with paper cases.
- Beat the egg in a jug with the oil, yoghurt and cheese until well mixed.
- Mix the bacon, chives, flour, raising agents and salt in a bowl, then pour in the egg mixture and stir just enough to combine.
- Divide the mixture between the paper cases, then bake in the oven for 20 – 25 minutes.
- Test with a wooden toothpick, if it comes out clean, the muffins are done.
- Transfer the muffins to a wire rack and leave to cool.

Bacon and Egg Muffins

600

For bacon and egg muffins, fold 2 chopped soft boiled eggs into the mixture before baking.

601

MAKES 12

Lemon Muffins with Cream Cheese Icing

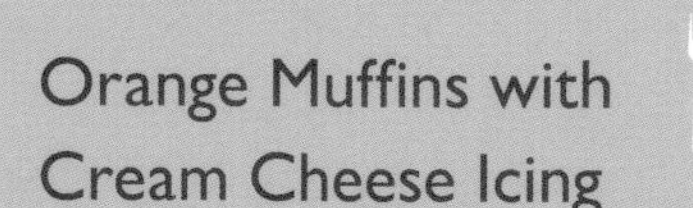

Orange Muffins with Cream Cheese Icing

602

Try this recipe with orange juice and zest in the mixture and orange marmalade in the cream cheese mixture.

Lime Muffins with Cream Cheese Icing

603

Try this recipe with lime juice and zest in the mixture and lime marmalade in the cream cheese mixture.

PREPARATION TIME: 15 MINUTES

COOKING TIME: 25 MINUTES

INGREDIENTS

1 large egg
120 ml / 4 fl. oz / ½ cup sunflower oil
120 ml / 4 fl. oz / ½ cup milk
1 lemon, juiced
375 g / 12 ½ oz / 2 ½ cups self-raising flour, sifted
1 tsp baking powder
200 g / 7 oz / ¾ cup caster (superfine) sugar
1 tbsp lemon zest, finely grated
To decorate
225 g / 8 oz / 1 cup cream cheese
110 g / 4 oz / ½ cup butter, softened
225 g / 8 oz / 2 cups icing (confectioners') sugar
2 tbsp lemon marmalade

- Preheat the oven to 180°C (160° fan) / 350 F / gas 4 and oil a 12-hole silicone muffin tin.
- Beat the egg in a jug with the oil, milk and lemon juice until well mixed.
- Mix the flour, baking powder, sugar and lemon zest in a bowl, then pour in the egg mixture and stir just enough to combine.
- Divide the mixture between the moulds, then bake in the oven for 20 – 25 minutes.
- Test with a wooden toothpick, if it comes out clean, the muffins are done.
- Transfer the muffins to a wire rack and leave to cool completely.
- To make the icing, beat the cream cheese and butter together with a wooden spoon until light and fluffy then beat in the icing sugar a quarter at a time.
- Add the lemon marmalade then use a whisk to whip the mixture for 2 minutes or until smooth and light.
- Spoon on top of the muffins.

604

MAKES 12

Mini Apple Muffins

PREPARATION TIME: 15 MINUTES

COOKING TIME: 20 MINUTES

INGREDIENTS

1 large egg
120 ml / 4 fl. oz / ½ cup sunflower oil
120 ml / 4 fl. oz / ½ cup milk
375 g / 12 ½ oz / 2 ½ cups self-raising flour, sifted
1 tsp baking powder
200 g / 7 oz / ¾ cup caster (superfine) sugar
150 g / 5 oz / 1 cup apple, grated

- Preheat the oven to 180°C (160° fan) / 350 F / gas 4 and line a 24-hole mini muffin tin with paper cases.
- Beat the egg in a jug with the oil and milk until well mixed.
- Mix the flour, baking powder, sugar and grated apple in a bowl, then pour in the egg mixture and stir just enough to combine.
- Divide the mixture between the paper cases, then bake in the oven for 15 – 20 minutes.
- Test with a wooden toothpick, if it comes out clean, the muffins are done.
- Transfer the muffins to a wire rack and leave to cool completely.

Mini Apple and Cinnamon Muffins

605

For apple and cinnamon mini muffins, add 1 tsp ground cinnamon.

606

MAKES 12

Apricot and Cardamom Muffins

PREPARATION TIME: 15 MINUTES

COOKING TIME: 25 MINUTES

INGREDIENTS

1 large egg
120 ml / 4 fl. oz / ½ cup sunflower oil
120 ml / 4 fl. oz / ½ cup milk
375 g / 12 ½ oz / 2 ½ cups self-raising flour, sifted
1 tsp baking powder
200 g / 7 oz / ¾ cup caster (superfine) sugar
75 g / 2 ½ oz / ½ cup dried apricots, chopped
½ tsp ground cardamom

- Preheat the oven to 180°C (160° fan) / 350 F / gas 4 and oil a 12-hole silicone muffin tin.
- Beat the egg in a jug with the oil and milk until well mixed.
- Mix the flour, baking powder, sugar, apricots and cardamom in a bowl, then pour in the egg mixture and stir just enough to combine.
- Divide the mixture between the paper cases, then bake in the oven for 20 – 25 minutes.
- Test with a wooden toothpick, if it comes out clean, the muffins are done.
- Transfer the muffins to a wire rack and leave to cool completely.

Apricot and Date Muffins

607

Try adding 5 tbsp of chopped dates to the muffin mixture along with the apricots.

608

MAKES 12

Summer Fruit Muffins

- Preheat the oven to 180°C (160° fan) / 350 F / gas 4 and line a 12-hole muffin tin with paper cases.
- Beat the egg in a jug with the oil and milk until well mixed.
- Mix the flour, baking powder, sugar and summer fruits in a bowl, then pour in the egg mixture and stir just enough to combine.
- Divide the mixture between the moulds, then bake in the oven for 20 – 25 minutes.
- Test with a wooden toothpick, if it comes out clean, the muffins are done.
- Transfer the muffins to a wire rack and leave to cool.

PREPARATION TIME: 15 MINUTES

COOKING TIME: 25 MINUTES

INGREDIENTS

1 large egg
120 ml / 4 fl. oz / ½ cup sunflower oil
120 ml / 4 fl. oz / ½ cup milk
375 g / 12 ½ oz / 2 ½ cups self-raising flour, sifted
1 tsp baking powder
200 g / 7 oz / ¾ cup caster (superfine) sugar
150 g / 5 oz / 1 cup mixed summer fruits

With Extra Fruity Flavour

609

Add the grated zest of 1 orange and 1 lemon for an extra citrusy tang.

610

MAKES 12

Sun-dried Tomato and Basil Muffins

- Preheat the oven to 180°C (160° fan) / 350 F / gas 4 and line a 12-hole muffin tin with paper cases.
- Beat the egg in a jug with the oil, yoghurt and cheese until well mixed.
- Mix the sundried tomatoes, basil, flour, raising agents and salt in a bowl, then pour in the egg mixture and stir just enough to combine.
- Divide the mixture between the paper cases, then bake in the oven for 20 – 25 minutes.
- Test with a wooden toothpick, if it comes out clean, the muffins are done.
- Transfer the muffins to a wire rack and leave to cool completely.

PREPARATION TIME: 15 MINUTES

COOKING TIME: 25 MINUTES

INGREDIENTS

2 large eggs
120 ml / 4 fl. oz / ½ cup sunflower oil
180 ml / 6 fl. oz / ¾ cup Greek yogurt
110 g / 4 oz / 1 cup Parmesan, grated
75 g / 2 ½ oz / ½ cup sundried tomatoes, chopped
2 tbsp basil leaves, shredded
225 g / 8 oz / 1 ½ cups plain (all purpose) flour
2 tsp baking powder
½ tsp bicarbonate of (baking) soda
½ tsp salt

Sun-dried Tomato and Feta Muffins

611

Try adding 100 g / 4 oz of feta cheese to the muffin mixture before cooking.

612

MAKES 36

Banana and Coffee Mini Muffins

Banana and Lime Muffins

613

Replace the coffee powder with the grated zest of 2 limes for banana and lime mini muffins.

Banana and Almond Muffins

614

Replace the coffee powder with 2 tbsp of almond extract in the muffin mixture.

PREPARATION TIME: 15 MINUTES

COOKING TIME: 20 MINUTES

INGREDIENTS

3 very ripe bananas
110 g / 4 oz / ⅔ cup soft light brown sugar
2 large eggs
120 ml / 4 fl. oz / ½ cup sunflower oil
225 g / 8 oz / 1 ½ cups plain (all purpose) flour
1 tsp bicarbonate of (baking) soda
1 tsp instant espresso powder
2 tbsp porridge oats

TO DECORATE
36 chocolate coated coffee beans

- Preheat the oven to 200°C (180° fan) / 400 F / gas 6 and line a 36-hole mini muffin tin with paper cases.
- Mash 3 of the bananas with a fork then whisk in the sugar, eggs and oil.
- Sieve the flour and bicarbonate of soda into the bowl and add the coffee powder and oats, then stir just enough to evenly mix all the ingredients together.
- Divide the mixture between the paper cases then transfer the tin to the oven and bake for 15 – 20 minutes.
- Test with a wooden toothpick, if it comes out clean, the muffins are done.
- Transfer the muffins to a wire rack and leave to cool completely then top with the chocolate coated coffee beans.

615

MAKES 12

Seaweed Muffins

- Preheat the oven to 180°C (160° fan) / 350 F / gas 4 and line a 12-hole muffin tin with paper cases.
- Soak the seaweed in water for 5 minutes, then drain and chop.
- Beat the egg in a jug with the oil, yoghurt, cheese and seaweed until well mixed.
- Mix the flour, raising agents and salt in a bowl, then pour in the egg mixture and stir just enough to combine.
- Divide the mixture between the paper cases, then bake in the oven for 20 – 25 minutes.
- Test with a wooden toothpick, if it comes out clean, the muffins are done.
- Serve warm.

PREPARATION TIME: 15 MINUTES

COOKING TIME: 25 MINUTES

INGREDIENTS

28 g / 1 oz dried sea vegetable salad mix
2 large eggs
120 ml / 4 fl. oz / ½ cup sunflower oil
180 ml / 6 fl. oz / ¾ cup Greek yogurt
110 g / 4 oz / 1 cup Parmesan, grated
225 g / 8 oz / 1 cup plain flour
2 tsp baking powder
½ tsp bicarbonate of (baking) soda
½ tsp salt

With Feta & Sour Cream

616

Try adding 75g / 3 oz / ⅓ cup of cubed feta to the wet ingredients before mixing. Alternatively, serve the muffins with a dollop of sour cream and more soaked, chopped seaweed on top.

617

MAKES 12

Orange and Hazelnut Muffins

- Preheat the oven to 180°C (160° fan) / 350 F / gas 4 and oil a 12-hole silicone muffin tin.
- Beat the egg in a jug with the oil and milk until well mixed.
- Mix the flour, baking powder, sugar, nuts and orange zest in a bowl, then pour in the egg mixture and stir just enough to combine.
- Divide the mixture between the paper cases, then bake in the oven for 20 minutes.
- Test with a wooden toothpick, if it comes out clean, the muffins are done.
- Transfer the muffins to a wire rack and leave to cool completely.
- Decorate the muffins with a few shreds of orange zest on the top.

PREPARATION TIME: 10 MINUTES

COOKING TIME: 20 MINUTES

INGREDIENTS

1 large egg
120 ml / 4 fl. oz / ½ cup sunflower oil
120 ml / 4 fl. oz / ½ cup milk
375 g / 12 ½ oz / 2 ½ cups self-raising flour, sifted
1 tsp baking powder
200 g / 7 oz / ¾ cup caster (superfine) sugar
75 g / 2 ½ oz / ½ cup hazelnuts (cob nuts), chopped
1 orange, zest finely grated

TO DECORATE
1 orange, zest finely pared

Lemon and Hazelnut Muffins

618

Replace the orange with lemon.

619

MAKES 12

Dried Mango and Coconut Muffins

PREPARATION TIME: 15 MINUTES

COOKING TIME: 25 MINUTES

INGREDIENTS

1 large egg
120 ml / 4 fl. oz / ½ cup sunflower oil
120 ml / 4 fl. oz / ½ cup milk
375 g / 12 ½ oz / 2 ½ cups self-raising flour, sifted
1 tsp baking powder
200 g / 7 oz / ¾ cup caster (superfine) sugar
28 g / 1 oz / ⅛ cup desiccated coconut
150 g / 5 oz / 1 cup dried mango, chopped

- Preheat the oven to 180°C (160° fan) / 350 F / gas 4 and oil a 12-hole silicone muffin tin.
- Beat the egg in a jug with the oil and milk until well mixed.
- Mix the flour, baking powder, sugar, coconut and mango in a bowl, then pour in the egg mixture and stir just enough to combine.
- Divide the mixture between the moulds, then bake in the oven for 20 – 25 minutes.
- Test with a wooden toothpick, if it comes out clean, the muffins are done.
- Transfer the muffins to a wire rack and leave to cool completely.

Fresh Mango and Lime Muffins

620

Try using fresh mango in this recipe and add the grated zest of a lime.

621

MAKES 12

Dark Chocolate and Star Anise Muffins

PREPARATION TIME: 15 MINUTES

COOKING TIME: 25 MINUTES

INGREDIENTS

1 large egg
120 ml / 4 fl. oz / ½ cup sunflower oil
120 ml / 4 fl. oz / ½ cup milk
375 g / 12 ½ oz / 2 ½ cups self-raising flour, sifted
55 g / 2 oz / ½ cup unsweetened cocoa powder, sifted
1 tsp baking powder
200 g / 7 oz / ¾ cup caster (superfine) sugar
110 g / 4 oz / ½ cup dark chocolate, minimum 60% cocoa solids, chopped
2 tsp ground star anise

- Preheat the oven to 180°C (160° fan) / 350 F / gas 4 and line a 12-hole muffin tin with paper cases.
- Beat the egg in a jug with the oil and milk until well mixed.
- Mix the flour, cocoa, baking powder, sugar, chocolate and star anise in a bowl, then pour in the egg mixture and stir just enough to combine.
- Divide the mixture between the paper cases, then bake in the oven for 20 – 25 minutes.
- Test with a wooden toothpick, if it comes out clean, the muffins are done.
- Transfer the muffins to a wire rack and leave to cool completely.

Liquorice Cream Muffins

Chop 55g / 2 oz of black liquorice and heat it in a small saucepan with 150ml / 6 oz double cream until it dissolves. Leave to cool then refrigerate for 1 hour before whipping to soft peaks. Spread onto the muffins.

623

MAKES 12

Redcurrant Muffins

Blackcurrant Muffins

Replace the redcurrants with blackcurrants.

625

Redcurrant and Almond Muffins

Add 85 g / 3 oz of flaked almonds to the mixture.

PREPARATION TIME: 25 MINUTES

COOKING TIME: 25 MINUTES

INGREDIENTS

large egg
120 ml / 4 fl. oz / ½ cup sunflower oil
120 ml / 4 fl. oz / ½ cup milk
375 g / 12 ½ oz / 2 ½ cups self-raising flour, sifted
1 tsp baking powder
200 g / 7 oz / ¾ cup caster sugar
150 g / 5 oz / 1 cup redcurrants

- Preheat the oven to 180°C (160° fan) / 350F / gas 4 and line a 12-hole muffin tin with paper cases.
- Beat the egg in a jug with the oil and milk until well mixed.
- Mix the flour, baking powder, sugar and redcurrants in a bowl, then pour in the egg mixture and stir just enough to combine.
- Divide the mixture between the moulds, then bake in the oven for 20 – 25 minutes.
- Test with a wooden toothpick, if it comes out clean, the cakes are done.
- Transfer the cakes to a wire rack and leave to cool completely.

626

MAKES 24

Almond and Cherry Jam Mini Muffins

- Preheat the oven to 180°C (160° fan) / 350 F / gas 4 and oil a 24 small dariole moulds.
- Beat the egg in a jug with the oil and milk until well mixed.
- Mix the flour, baking powder, sugar and ground almonds in a bowl, then pour in the egg mixture and stir just enough to combine.
- Divide half the mixture between the moulds, and top each one with a spoon of cherry jam.
- Top with the rest of the muffin mixture, then bake in the oven for 15 – 20 minutes.
- Test with a wooden toothpick, if it comes out clean, the muffins are done.
- Transfer the muffins to a wire rack and leave to cool.

PREPARATION TIME: 15 MINUTES

COOKING TIME: 20 MINUTES

INGREDIENTS

1 large egg
120 ml / 4 fl. oz / ½ cup sunflower oil
120 ml / 4 fl. oz / ½ cup milk
375 g / 12 ½ oz / 2 ½ cups self-raising flour, sifted
1 tsp baking powder
200 g / 7 oz / ¾ cup caster (superfine) sugar
55 g / 2 oz / ½ cup ground almonds
110 g / 4 oz / ½ cup cherry jam (jelly)
75 g / 2 ½ oz / ½ cup flaked (slivered) almonds

627

MAKES 12

Blackcurrant and Granola Muffins

PREPARATION TIME: 15MINUTES

COOKING TIME: 25 MINUTES

INGREDIENTS

1 large egg
120 ml / 4 fl. oz / ½ cup sunflower oil
120 ml / 4 fl. oz / ½ cup milk
375 g / 12 ½ oz / 2 ½ cups self-raising flour, sifted
1 tsp baking powder
200 g / 7 oz / ¾ cup caster (superfine) sugar
150 g / 5 oz / 1 cup blackcurrants
75 g / 2 ½ oz / ½ cup plain granolaced
basil, to garnish

- Preheat the oven to 180°C (160° fan) / 350 F / gas 4 and line a 12-hole muffin tin with paper cases.
- Beat the egg in a jug with the oil and milk until well mixed.
- Mix the flour, baking powder, sugar and blackcurrants in a bowl, then pour in the egg mixture and stir just enough to combine.
- Divide the mixture between the moulds and sprinkle with granola then bake in the oven for 20 – 25 minutes.
- Test with a wooden toothpick, if it comes out clean, the muffins are done.
- Transfer the muffins to a wire rack and leave to cool completely.

628

MAKES 12

Raspberry and Orange Muffins

PREPARATION TIME: 15 MINUTES

COOKING TIME: 25 MINUTES

INGREDIENTS

1 large egg
120 ml / 4 fl. oz / ½ cup sunflower oil
120 ml / 4 fl. oz / ½ cup milk
1 orange, zest finely grated
375 g / 12 ½ oz / 2 ½ cups self-raising flour, sifted
1 tsp baking powder
200 g / 7 oz / ¾ cup caster (superfine) sugar
150 g / 5 oz / 1 cup raspberries
75 g / 2 ½ oz / ½ cup candied orange peel, chopped

TO DECORATE
12 raspberries

- Preheat the oven to 180°C (160° fan) / 350 F / gas 4 and oil a 12-hole silicone muffin tin.
- Beat the egg in a jug with the oil, milk and orange zest until well mixed.
- Mix the flour, baking powder, sugar, raspberries and candied peel in a bowl, then pour in the egg mixture and stir just enough to combine.
- Divide the mixture between the moulds, then bake in the oven for 20 – 25 minutes.
- Test with a wooden toothpick, if it comes out clean, the muffins are done.
- Transfer the muffins to a wire rack and leave to cool completely.

629

MAKES 12

Chocolate and Coffee Syrup Muffins

- Preheat the oven to 190°C (170° fan) / 375 F / gas 5 and oil a 12-hole silicone cupcake mould.
- Combine the flour, sugar, butter and eggs in a bowl and whisk together for 2 minutes or until smooth.
- Fold in ¾ of the chocolate chips then divide the mixture between the moulds.
- Sprinkle the rest of the chocolate chips on top then bake for 15 – 20 minutes. Transfer the muffins to a wire rack and leave to cool completely.
- To make the syrup, mix the sugar and espresso powder together in a small saucepan with 55ml water. Stir over a medium heat to dissolve the sugar, then boil for 2 minutes or until syrupy.
- Leave to cool and thicken, then drizzle over the cupmuffins.

PREPARATION TIME: 15 MINUTES

COOKING TIME: 20 MINUTES

INGREDIENTS

110 g / 4 oz / ½ cup self-raising flour, sifted
110 g / 4 oz / ½ cup caster (superfine) sugar
110 g / 4 oz / ½ cup butter, softened
2 large eggs
1 tsp instant espresso powder
150 g / 5 oz / 1 cup chocolate chips

TO DECORATE

55 g / 2 oz / ¼ cup caster (superfine) sugar
¼ tsp instant espresso powder

Chocolate and Honey Syrup Muffins

630

Replace the coffee powder with 1 tbsp of honey.

631

MAKES 12

Sugar Nib Muffins

- Preheat the oven to 180°C (160° fan) / 350 F / gas 4 and line a 12-hole muffin tin with paper cases.
- Beat the egg in a jug with the oil and milk until well mixed.
- Mix the flour, baking powder and sugar in a bowl, then pour in the egg mixture and stir just enough to combine.
- Divide the mixture between the paper cases and sprinkle with sugar nibs, then bake in the oven for 20 – 25 minutes.
- Test with a wooden toothpick, if it comes out clean, the muffins are done.
- Transfer the muffins to a wire rack and leave to cool completely.

PREPARATION TIME: 15 MINUTES

COOKING TIME: 25 MINUTES

INGREDIENTS

1 large egg
120 ml / 4 fl. oz / ½ cup sunflower oil
120 ml / 4 fl. oz / ½ cup milk
375 g / 12 ½ oz / 2 ½ cups self-raising flour, sifted
1 tsp baking powder
200 g / 7 oz / ¾ cup caster (superfine) sugar
1 tsp vanilla extract
75 g / 2 ½ oz / ½ cup sugar nibs

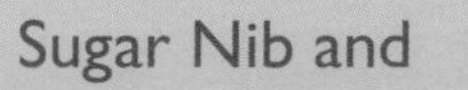

Sugar Nib and Summer Berry Muffins

632

Add 110g / 4 oz / ½ cup of summer berries to the mixture.

633

MAKES 12

Cranberry Muffins

PREPARATION TIME: 15 MINUTES

COOKING TIME: 25 MINUTES

INGREDIENTS

1 large egg
120 ml / 4 fl. oz / ½ cup sunflower oil
120 ml / 4 fl. oz / ½ cup milk
375 g / 12 ½ oz / 2 ½ cups self-raising flour, sifted
1 tsp baking powder
200 g / 7 oz / ¾ cup caster (superfine) sugar
75 g / 2 ½ oz / ½ cup dried cranberries

- Preheat the oven to 180°C (160° fan) / 350 F / gas 4 and oil a 12 metal muffin tins.
- Beat the egg in a jug with the oil and milk until well mixed.
- Mix the flour, baking powder, sugar and cranberries in a bowl, then pour in the egg mixture and stir just enough to combine.
- Divide the mixture between the tins, then bake in the oven for 20 – 25 minutes.
- Test with a wooden toothpick, if it comes out clean, the muffins are done.
- Transfer the muffins to a wire rack and leave to cool completely.

Cranberry and Orange Muffins

634

Add finely grated zest of 1 orange to the muffin mixture.

635

MAKES 12

Ginger and Marmalade Muffins

PREPARATION TIME: 15 MINUTES

COOKING TIME: 25 MINUTES

INGREDIENTS

1 large egg
120 ml / 4 fl. oz / ½ cup sunflower oil
120 ml / 4 fl. oz / ½ cup milk
2 tbsp marmalade
375 g / 12 ½ oz / 2 ½ cups self-raising flour, sifted
1 tsp baking powder
200 g / 7 oz / ¾ cup caster (superfine) sugar
75 g / 2 ½ oz / ½ cup stem ginger, chopped

TO DECORATE
2 tbsp orange marmalade

- Preheat the oven to 180°C (160° fan) / 350 F / gas 4 and oil a 12-hole silicone muffin tin.
- Beat the egg in a jug with the oil, milk and marmalade until well mixed.
- Mix the flour, baking powder, sugar and stem ginger in a bowl, then pour in the egg mixture and stir just enough to combine.
- Divide the mixture between the paper cases, then bake in the oven for 20 – 25 minutes.
- Test with a wooden toothpick, if it comes out clean, the muffins are done.
- As soon as the muffins come out of the oven, brush them with marmalade to glaze.
- Transfer the muffins to a wire rack and leave to cool completely.

Ginger and Lime Marmalade Muffins

636

Replace the orange marmalade with lime marmalade.

637

MAKES 24

Pecan Mini Muffins

- Preheat the oven to 180°C (160° fan) / 350 F / gas 4 and oil a 24-hole silicone mini muffin mould.
- Beat the egg in a jug with the oil and milk until well mixed.
- Mix the flour, baking powder, sugar and chopped pecans in a bowl, then pour in the egg mixture and stir just enough to combine.
- Press a pecan half into the top of each cake.
- Divide the mixture between the moulds, then bake in the oven for 15 – 20 minutes.
- Test with a wooden toothpick, if it comes out clean, the muffins are done.
- Transfer the muffins to a wire rack and leave to cool completely.

PREPARATION TIME: 10 MINUTES

COOKING TIME: 20 MINUTES

INGREDIENTS

1 large egg
120 ml / 4 fl. oz / ½ cup sunflower oil
120 ml / 4 fl. oz / ½ cup milk
375 g / 12 ½ oz / 2 ½ cups self-raising flour, sifted
1 tsp baking powder
200 g / 7 oz / ¾ cup caster (superfine) sugar
75 g / 2 ½ oz / ½ cup pecans, chopped
24 pecan halves

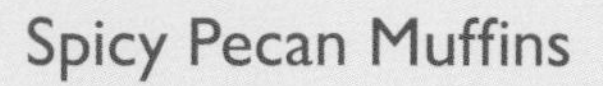

Spicy Pecan Muffins

638

Try adding ½ tsp freshly grated nutmeg to add some warming spice.

639

MAKES 12

Mixed Pepper Muffins

- Preheat the oven to 180°C (160° fan) / 350 F / gas 4 and line a 12-hole muffin tin with paper cases.
- Fry the peppers in the olive oil for 10 minutes or until soft.
- Beat the egg in a jug with the oil, yogurt and cheese until well mixed then stir in the peppers.
- Mix the flour, raising agents and salt in a bowl, then pour in the egg mixture and stir just enough to combine.
- Divide the mixture between the paper cases, then bake in the oven for 20 – 25 minutes.
- Test with a wooden toothpick, if it comes out clean, the muffins are done.
- Serve warm.

PREPARATION TIME: 15 MINUTES

COOKING TIME: 25 MINUTES

INGREDIENTS

1 red pepper, deseeded and sliced
1 orange pepper, deseeded and sliced
1 green pepper, deseeded and sliced
2 tbsp olive oil
2 large eggs
120 ml / 4 fl. oz / ½ cup sunflower oil
180 ml / 6 fl. oz / ¾ cup Greek yogurt
110 g / 4 oz / 1 cup Parmesan, grated
225 g / 8 oz / 1 ½ cups plain (all purpose) flour
2 tsp baking powder
½ tsp bicarbonate of (baking) soda
½ tsp salt

Mixed Pepper and Mozzarella Muffins

640

Try adding 2 tbsp of pesto to the mixture before baking. Alternatively, try adding 5 tbsp of cubed mozzarella.

641

MAKES 12

Strawberry and Pistachio Muffins

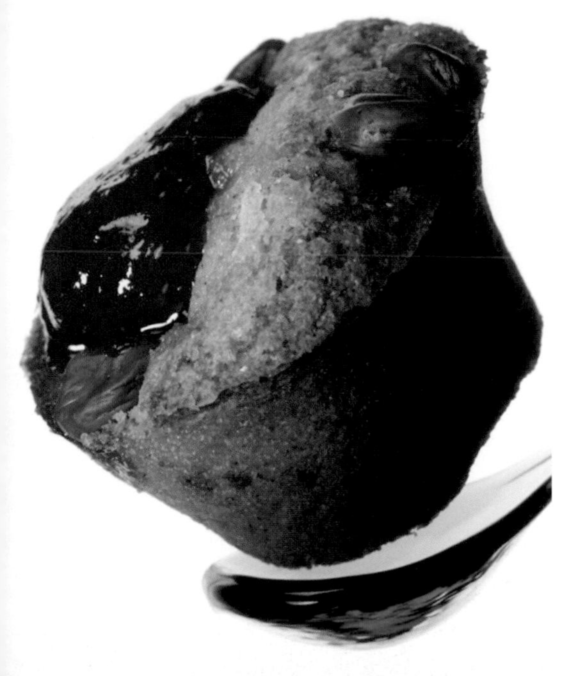

PREPARATION TIME: 15 MINUTES

COOKING TIME: 25 MINUTES

INGREDIENTS

1 large egg
120 ml / 4 fl. oz / ½ cup sunflower oil
120 ml / 4 fl. oz / ½ cup milk
225 g / 7 ½ oz / 1 ½ cups self-raising flour, sifted
1 tsp baking powder
150 g / 5 oz / 1 ¼ cups ground pistachios
200 g / 7 oz / ¾ cup caster (superfine) sugar
4 strawberries, chopped

TO DECORATE
6 strawberries, halved
2 tbsp honey
2 tbsp pistachios

- Preheat the oven to 180°C (160° fan) / 350 F / gas 4 and line a 12-hole muffin tin with paper cases.
- Beat the egg in a jug with the oil and milk until well mixed.
- Mix the flour, baking powder, ground pistachios, sugar and chopped strawberries in a bowl, then pour in the egg mixture and stir just enough to combine.
- Divide the mixture between the paper cases and bake in the oven for 20 – 25 minutes.
- Test with a wooden toothpick, if it comes out clean, the muffins are done.
- Transfer the muffins to a wire rack and leave to cool.
- Top each muffin with half a strawberry.
- Warm the honey in a microwave and brush it over the strawberries and finish with a few whole pistachios.

With Fresh Apricots

642

This recipe works really well if you replace the strawberries with chopped fresh apricots.

643

MAKES 12

Treacle Gingerbread Muffins

PREPARATION TIME: 15 MINUTES

COOKING TIME: 25 MINUTES

INGREDIENTS

250 g / 9 oz / 1 ¾ cups self-raising flour
1 tsp bicarbonate of (baking) soda
2 tsp ground ginger
200 g / 8 ½ oz / ½ cup treacle
125 g / 4 ½ oz / ½ cup butter
125 g / 4 ½ oz / ¾ cup dark brown sugar
2 large eggs, beaten
240 ml / 8 fl. oz / 1 cup milk
4 pieces stem ginger, chopped

- Preheat the oven to 190°C (170° fan) / 375 F / gas 5 and line a 12-hole cupcake tin with paper cases.
- Sieve the flour, bicarbonate of soda and ground ginger together into a bowl.
- Put the golden syrup, butter and brown sugar in a small saucepan and boil gently for 2 minutes, stirring to dissolve the sugar.
- Pour the butter and sugar mixture onto the flour with the eggs, milk and stem ginger and fold it all together until smooth.
- Divide the mixture between the paper cases, then transfer the tin to the oven and bake for 20 – 25 minutes.
- Test with a wooden toothpick, if it comes out clean, the muffins are done.
- Transfer the muffins to a wire rack and leave to cool completely.

Gingerbread and Syrup Muffins

644

For a lighter cake, use golden syrup instead of the treacle and light brown sugar instead of dark brown sugar.

645

MAKES 12

Wholemeal Blueberry Muffins

Blueberry and Oat Muffins

646

Add 2 tbsp of porridge oats and 2 tbsp of marmalade to the mixture before baking for healthy breakfast muffins.

Wholemeal Blackberry Muffins

647

Replace the blueberries with blackberries..

PREPARATION TIME: 15 MINUTES

COOKING TIME: 25 MINUTES

INGREDIENTS

1 large egg
120 ml / 4 fl. oz / ½ cup sunflower oil
120 ml / 4 fl. oz / ½ cup milk
375 g / 12 ½ oz / 2 ½ cups wholemeal flour
2 tsp baking powder
200 g / 7 oz / ¾ cup caster (superfine) sugar
150 g / 5 oz / 1 cup blueberries

- Preheat the oven to 180°C (160° fan) / 350 F / gas 4 and line a 12-hole muffin tin with paper cases.
- Beat the egg in a jug with the oil and milk until well mixed.
- Mix the flour, baking powder, sugar and blueberries in a bowl, then pour in the egg mixture and stir just enough to combine.
- Divide the mixture between the moulds, then bake in the oven for 20 – 25 minutes.
- Test with a wooden toothpick, if it comes out clean, the muffins are done.
- Transfer the muffins to a wire rack and leave to cool completely.

648

MAKES 12

Glace Cherry Muffins

Candied Fruit Muffins

649

Try adding 110g / 4oz / ½ cup chopped candied angelica and 110g / 4oz / ½ cup candied pineapple pieces for a jewelled effect.

650

Dried Fruit and Nut Muffins

Replace the cherries with sultanas and raisins and add 85 g / 3 oz of chopped mixed nuts.

Glace Cherry and Coconut Muffins

Add 2 tbsp of desiccated coconut to the muffin mixture before cooking.

PREPARATION TIME: 15 MINUTES

COOKING TIME: 25 MINUTES

INGREDIENTS

1 large egg
120 ml / 4 fl. oz / ½ cup sunflower oil
120 ml / 4 fl. oz / ½ cup milk
375 g / 12 ½ oz / 2 ½ cups self-raising flour, sifted
1 tsp baking powder
200 g / 7 oz / ¾ cup caster (superfine) sugar
150 g / 5 oz / 1 cup glace cherries, halved

- Preheat the oven to 180°C (160° fan) / 350 F / gas 4 and line a 12-hole muffin tin with paper cases.
- Beat the egg in a jug with the oil and milk until well mixed.
- Mix the flour, baking powder, sugar and cherries in a bowl, then pour in the egg mixture and stir just enough to combine.
- Divide the mixture between the moulds, then bake in the oven for 20 – 25 minutes.
- Test with a wooden toothpick, if it comes out clean, the muffins are done.
- Transfer the muffins to a wire rack and leave to cool completely.

652

MAKES 12

Chocolate Fudge Chunk Muffins

- Preheat the oven to 180°C (160° fan) / 350 F / gas 4 and line a 12-hole muffin tin with paper cases.
- Beat the egg in a jug with the oil and milk until well mixed.
- Mix the flour, cocoa, baking powder, sugar, chocolate and fudge in a bowl, then pour in the egg mixture and stir just enough to combine.
- Divide the mixture between the paper cases, then bake in the oven for 20 – 25 minutes.
- Test with a wooden toothpick, if it comes out clean, the muffins are done.
- Transfer the muffins to a wire rack and leave to cool completely.

PREPARATION TIME: 15 MINUTES

COOKING TIME: 25 MINUTES

INGREDIENTS

1 large egg
120 ml / 4 fl. oz / ½ cup sunflower oil
120 ml / 4 fl. oz / ½ cup milk
375 g / 12 ½ oz / 2 ½ cups self-raising flour, sifted
55 g / 2 oz / ½ cup unsweetened cocoa powder, sifted
1 tsp baking powder
200 g / 7 oz / ¾ cup caster (superfine) sugar
110 g / 4 oz / ½ cup dark chocolate, minimum 60% cocoa solids, chopped
110 g / 4 oz / ½ cup fudge, cubed

Vanilla Fudge Chunk Muffins

653

Leave out the cocoa powder and flavour the muffins with 1 tsp of vanilla extract instead.

654

MAKES 36

Banana and Chocolate Chip Muffins

- Preheat the oven to 200°C (180° fan) / 400 F / gas 6 and line a 36-hole mini muffin tin with paper cases.
- Mash 3 of the bananas with a fork then whisk in the sugar, eggs and oil.
- Sieve the flour and bicarbonate of soda into the bowl and add the chocolate chips, then stir just enough to evenly mix all the ingredients together.
- Divide the mixture between the paper cases.
- Slice the last 2 bananas and add a slice to the top of each cake.
- Transfer the tin to the oven and bake for 15 – 20 minutes.
- Test with a wooden toothpick, if it comes out clean, the muffins are done.
- Transfer the muffins to a wire rack and leave to cool completely.

PREPARATION TIME: 15 MINUTES

COOKING TIME: 20 MINUTES

INGREDIENTS

5 very ripe bananas
110g / 4 oz / 2/3 cup soft light brown sugar
2 large eggs
120ml / 4 fl oz / ½ cup sunflower oil
225g / 8 oz / 1 ½ cups plain (all purpose) flour
1 tsp bicarbonate of (baking) soda
75g / 2 ½ oz / ½ cup chocolate chips

Pear and Chocolate Chip Muffins

655

Replace the bananas with pears .

656

MAKES 12

Orange and Poppy Seed Muffins

PREPARATION TIME: 10 MINUTES

COOKING TIME: 25 MINUTES

INGREDIENTS

1 large egg
120 ml / 4 fl. oz / ½ cup sunflower oil
120 ml / 4 fl. oz / ½ cup milk
375 g / 12 ½ oz / 2 ½ cups self-raising flour, sifted
1 tsp baking powder
200 g / 7 oz / ¾ cup caster (superfine) sugar
1 orange, zest finely grated
1 tbsp poppy seeds
2 tbsp sugar nibs

- Preheat the oven to 180°C (160° fan) / 350 F / gas 4 and line a 12-hole muffin tin with paper cases.
- Beat the egg in a jug with the oil and milk until well mixed.
- Mix the flour, baking powder, sugar, orange zest and poppy seeds in a bowl, then pour in the egg mixture and stir just enough to combine.
- Divide the mixture between the cases and sprinkle with sugar nibs, then bake in the oven for 20 – 25 minutes.
- Test with a wooden toothpick, if it comes out clean, the muffins are done.
- Transfer the muffins to a wire rack and leave to cool completely.

Lemon and Lavender Muffins

657

Try this recipe with lemon zest instead of the orange and swap the poppy seeds for 1 tsp lavender flowers.

658

MAKES 12

Walnut and Coffee Muffins

PREPARATION TIME: 10 MINUTES

COOKING TIME: 20 MINUTES

INGREDIENTS

110 g / 4 oz / 1 cup self-raising flour, sifted
110 g / 4 oz / ½ cup caster (superfine) sugar
110 g / 4 oz / ½ cup butter, softened
2 large eggs
2 tsp instant espresso powder
75 g / 2 ½ oz / ½ cup walnuts, chopped
12 walnut halves

- Preheat the oven to 190°C (170° fan) / 375 F / gas 5 and line a 12-hole cupcake tin with paper cases.
- Combine the flour, sugar, butter, eggs, espresso powder and chopped walnuts in a bowl and whisk together for 2 minutes or until smooth.
- Divide the mixture between the paper cases, then transfer the tin to the oven and bake for 15 – 20 minutes.
- Test with a wooden toothpick, if it comes out clean, the muffins are done.
- Transfer the muffins to a wire rack and leave to cool completely.
- Top each cake with a walnut half to finish.

Coconut and Coffee Muffins

659

Replace the walnuts with 3 tbsp of desiccated coconut and add 1 tsp of coconut rum to the muffin mixture before cooking.

660

MAKES 24

Chocolate Mini Muffins

Chocolate and Coffee Mini Muffins

661

Add 1 tbsp instant espresso powder to the muffin mixture.

Chocolate Peppermint Mini Muffins

662

Add a few drops of peppermint essence to the muffin mixture.

Chocolate Cranberry Mini Muffins

663

Add 2 tbsp of cranberry juice and 60 g / 2 oz of cranberries to the muffin mixture before cooking.

PREPARATION TIME: 10 MINUTES

COOKING TIME: 15 – 20 MINUTES

INGREDIENTS

1 large egg
120 ml / 4 fl. oz / ½ cup sunflower oil
120 ml / 4 fl. oz / ½ cup milk
375 g / 12 ½ oz / 2 ½ cups self-raising flour, sifted
55 g / 2 oz / ½ cup unsweetened cocoa powder, sifted
1 tsp baking powder
200 g / 7 oz / ¾ cup caster (superfine) sugar
110 g / 4 oz dark chocolate, minimum 60% cocoa solids, choppedmozzarella
basil, to garnish

- Preheat the oven to 180°°C (160° fan) / 350 F / gas 4 and oil a 24-hole silicone mini muffin mould.
- Beat the egg in a jug with the oil and milk until well mixed.
- Mix the flour, cocoa, baking powder, sugar and chocolate in a bowl, then pour in the egg mixture and stir just enough to combine.
- Divide the mixture between the paper cases, then bake in the oven for 15 – 20 minutes.
- Test with a wooden toothpick, if it comes out clean, the muffins are done.
- Transfer the muffins to a wire rack and leave to cool.

664

MAKES 12

Butterscotch Cream Cupcakes

PREPARATION TIME: 10 MINUTES

COOKING TIME: 20 MINUTES

INGREDIENTS

CUPCAKES

110 g / 4 oz / 1 cup self-raising flour, sifted
110 g / 4 oz / ½ cup caster sugar
110 g / 4 oz / ½ cup butter, softened
2 large eggs
1 tsp vanilla extract

BUTTERSCOTCH SAUCE

85 g / 3 oz / ½ cup butter
85 ml / 3 fl. oz / ⅓ cup double (heavy) cream
85 g / 3 oz / ¼ cup golden syrup
85 g / 3 oz / ½ cup dark brown sugar

TO DECORATE

225 ml / 8 fl. oz / 1 cup double (heavy) cream
2 tbsp icing (confectioners') sugar
½ tsp vanilla extract

- Preheat the oven to 190°C (170° fan) / 375 F / gas 5 and line a 12-hole cupcake tin with paper cases.
- Combine the flour, sugar, butter, eggs and vanilla extract in a bowl and whisk together for 2 minutes.
- Divide the mixture between the paper cases, then bake for 15 – 20 minutes. Transfer the cakes to a wire rack and leave to cool completely.
- To make the butterscotch sauce, put the butter, cream, golden syrup and brown sugar in a small saucepan and boil for 2 minutes, stirring to dissolve the sugar.
- Leave to cool completely. Whisk the cream with the icing sugar and vanilla until thick.
- Remove the paper cases from the cup cakes and cut each one in half horizontally.
- Add a spoonful of cream to the bottom half of each cake, drizzle over the butterscotch sauce and sandwich the cakes back together.

Cream Cupcakes with Peanuts

665

Add 5 tbsp chopped peanuts and 5 tbsp chocolate chips to the cake mixture before baking.

666

MAKES 12

Honey and Spice Muffins

PREPARATION TIME: 10 MINUTES

COOKING TIME: 25 MINUTES

INGREDIENTS

1 large egg
120 ml / 4 fl. oz / ½ cup sunflower oil
120 ml / 4 fl. oz / ½ cup milk
110 g / 4 oz / ½ cup honey
375 g / 12 ½ oz / 2 ½ cups self-raising flour, sifted
1 tsp baking powder
200 g / 7 oz / ¾ cup caster (superfine) sugar
1 tsp ground cinnamon
1 tsp ground ginger
½ tsp ground cardamom
½ tsp freshly ground nutmeg

TO SERVE

110 g / 4 oz / ½ cup honey
2 tbsp pistachio nuts, chopped

- Preheat the oven to 180°C (160° fan) / 350 F / gas 4 and oil a 12-hole silicone muffin mould.
- Beat the egg in a jug with the oil, milk and honey until well mixed.
- Mix the flour, baking powder, sugar and spices in a bowl, then pour in the egg mixture and stir just enough to combine.
- Divide the mixture between the moulds and bake in the oven for 20 – 25 minutes.
- Test with a wooden toothpick, if it comes out clean, the muffins are done.
- Mix the honey with the chopped pistachios and drizzle over the muffins as soon as they come out of the oven.

With Pistachio and Orange

667

Try adding 5 tbsp of chopped pistachios to the muffin mixture with the finely grated zest of 1 orange.

668

MAKES 12

Pecan Muffins with Chocolate Icing

- Preheat the oven to 180°C (160° fan) / 350 F / gas 4 and oil a 12-hole silicone muffin tin.
- Beat the egg in a jug with the oil and milk until well mixed.
- Mix the flour, baking powder, sugar and nuts in a bowl, then pour in the egg mixture and stir just enough to combine.
- Divide the mixture between the paper cases, then bake in the oven for 20 – 25 minutes.
- Transfer the muffins to a wire rack and leave to cool completely.
- Chop the chocolate and transfer to a mixing bowl.
- Heat the cream until it starts to simmer, then pour over the chopped chocolate and stir until the mixture has cooled and thickened.
- Spread on top of the muffins with a palette knife and sprinkle with chopped pecans.

PREPARATION TIME: 10 MINUTES

COOKING TIME: 25 MINUTES

INGREDIENTS

1 large egg
120ml / 4 fl. oz / ½ cup sunflower oil
120ml / 4 fl. oz / ½ cup milk
375 g / 12 ½ oz / 2 ½ cups self-raising flour, sifted
1 tsp baking powder
200 g / 7 oz / ¾ cup caster (superfine) sugar
75 g / 2 ½ oz / ½ cup pecan nuts, chopped

TO DECORATE

225 g / 8 oz / 1 cup dark chocolate, minimum 60% cocoa solids
225ml / 8 fl. oz / 1 cup double (heavy) cream
2 tbsp pecan nuts, chopped

669

Pecan Muffins with Chocolate Icing

For extra indulgence, add 110g / 4oz / ½ cup of milk chocolate chunks to the muffin mixture.

670

MAKES 12

Blueberry and White Chocolate Muffins

- Preheat the oven to 180°C (160° fan) / 350 F / gas 4 and line a 12-hole muffin tin with paper cases.
- Beat the egg in a jug with the oil and milk until well mixed.
- Mix the flour, baking powder, sugar, chocolate buttons and blueberries in a bowl, then pour in the egg mixture and stir just enough to combine.
- Divide the mixture between the moulds, then bake in the oven for 20 – 25 minutes.
- Test with a wooden toothpick, if it comes out clean, the muffins are done.
- Transfer the muffins to a wire rack an d leave to cool completely.

PREPARATION TIME: 10 MINUTES

COOKING TIME: 25 MINUTES

INGREDIENTS

1 large egg
120 ml / 4 fl. oz / ½ cup sunflower oil
120 ml / 4 fl. oz / ½ cup milk
375 g / 12 ½ oz / 2 ½ cups self-raising flour, sifted
1 tsp baking powder
200 g / 7 oz / ¾ cup caster (superfine) sugar
110 g / 4 oz / ½ cup white chocolate buttons
150 g / 5 oz / 1 cup blueberries

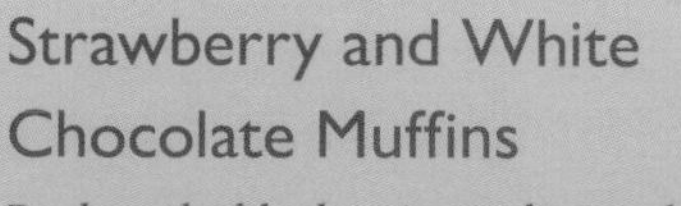

Strawberry and White Chocolate Muffins

671

Replace the blueberries with strawberries.

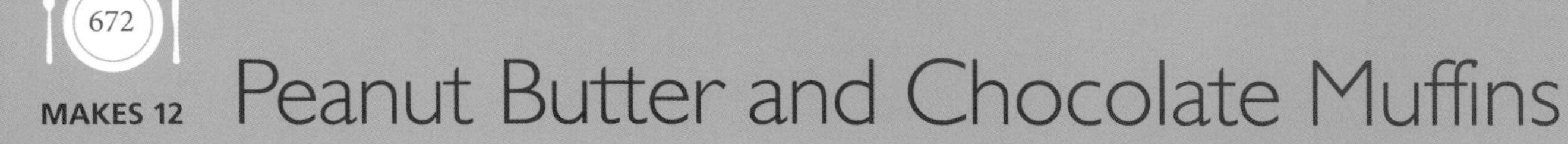

672

MAKES 12

Peanut Butter and Chocolate Muffins

Almond Butter and Chocolate Muffins

673

Replace the peanut butter with almond butter.

Peanut Butter and Hazelnut Muffins

674

Add 110 g / 4 oz of hazelnut chocolate spread.

Peanut Butter and Walnut Muffins

675

Add 85 g / 3 oz of chopped walnuts to the cupcake mixture.

PREPARATION TIME: 15 MINUTES

COOKING TIME: 25 MINUTES

INGREDIENTS

1 large egg
120 ml / 4 fl. oz / ½ cup sunflower oil
120 ml / 4 fl. oz / ½ cup milk
375 g / 12 ½ oz / 2 ½ cups self-raising flour, sifted
1 tsp baking powder
200 g / 7 oz / ¾ cup caster (superfine) sugar
110 g / 4 oz / ⅔ cup chocolate chips
110 g / 4 oz / ½ cup crunchy peanut butter

- Preheat the oven to 180°C (160° fan) / 350 F / gas 4 and oil a 12-hole silicone muffin tin.
- Beat the egg in a jug with the oil and milk until well mixed.
- Mix the flour, baking powder and sugar in a bowl, then pour in the egg mixture and stir just enough to combine.
- Divide the half the mixture between the paper cases.
- Mix the chocolate chips with the peanut butter and put a big spoonful into each muffin case.
- Top with the rest of the muffin mixture then bake in the oven for 20 – 25 minutes.
- Test with a wooden toothpick, if it comes out clean, the muffins are done.
- Transfer the muffins to a wire rack and leave to cool completely.

676

MAKES 12

Chocolate and Cream Muffins

- Preheat the oven to 180°C (160° fan) / 350 F / gas 4 and line a 12-hole muffin tin with paper cases.
- Beat the egg in a jug with the oil and milk until well mixed.
- Mix the flour, cocoa, baking powder, sugar and chocolate in a bowl, then pour in the egg mixture and stir just enough to combine.
- Divide the mixture between the paper cases, then bake in the oven for 20 – 25 minutes.
- Transfer the muffins to a wire rack and leave to cool completely.
- To make the filling, whisk the cream with the icing sugar and vanilla until thick, then fill a piping bag fitted with a large star nozzle.
- Cut each muffin in half horizontally, pipe a swirl of cream onto the bottom halves and sandwich back together again.

Chocolate and Jam Muffins

677

Add a tbsp of cherry jam on top of the cream before sandwiching back together to make a miniature black forest gateau.

PREPARATION TIME: 15 MINUTES

COOKING TIME: 25 MINUTES

INGREDIENTS

1 large egg
120 ml / 4 fl. oz / ½ cup sunflower oil
120 ml / 4 fl. oz / ½ cup milk
375 g / 12 ½ oz / 2 ½ cups self-raising flour, sifted
55 g / 2 oz / ½ cup unsweetened cocoa powder, sifted
1 tsp baking powder
200 g / 7 oz / ¾ cup caster (superfine) sugar
110 g / 4 oz / ⅔ cup dark chocolate, minimum 60% cocoa solids, chopped

TO DECORATE

225 ml / 8 fl. oz / 1 cup double (heavy) cream
2 tbsp icing (confectioners') sugar
½ tsp vanilla extract

678

MAKES 12

Dark Chocolate Muffins

- Preheat the oven to 180°C (160° fan) / 350 F / gas 4 and line a 12-hole muffin tin with paper cases.
- Beat the egg in a jug with the oil and milk until well mixed.
- Mix the flour, cocoa, baking powder, sugar and chocolate in a bowl, then pour in the egg mixture and stir just enough to combine.
- Divide the mixture between the paper cases, then bake in the oven for 20 – 25 minutes.
- Test with a wooden toothpick, if it comes out clean, the muffins are done.
- Transfer the muffins to a wire rack and leave to cool completely.

Dark Chocolate and Raisin Muffins

Add 85 g / 3 oz of raisins to the muffin mixture before cooking.

PREPARATION TIME: 10 MINUTES

COOKING TIME: 25 MINUTES

INGREDIENTS

1 egg
120 ml / 4 fl. oz / ½ cup sunflower oil
120 ml / 4 fl. oz / ½ cup milk
375 g / 12 ½ oz / 2 ½ cups self-raising flour, sifted
55 g / 2 oz / ½ cup unsweetened cocoa powder, sifted
1 tsp baking powder
200 g / 7 oz / ¾ cup caster (superfine) sugar
110 g / 4 oz dark chocolate, chopped

680

MAKES 12

Fresh Fig and Almond Muffin

PREPARATION TIME: 15 MINUTES

COOKING TIME: 20 MINUTES

INGREDIENTS

55 g / 2 oz / ½ cup self-raising flour, sifted
55 g / 2 oz / ½ cup ground almonds
110 g / 4 oz / ½ cup caster (superfine) sugar
110 g / 4 oz / ½ cup butter, softened
2 large eggs
1 tsp almond essence
2 fresh figs, thinly sliced
basil, to garnish

- Preheat the oven to 190°C (170° fan) / 375 F / gas 5 and line a 12-hole cupcake tin with greaseproof paper.
- Combine the flour, ground almonds, sugar, butter, eggs and almond essence in a bowl and whisk together for 2 minutes or until smooth.
- Fold in the fresh fig slices, then spoon into the prepared tin.
- Transfer the tin to the oven and bake for 15 – 20 minutes.
- Test with a wooden toothpick, if it comes out clean, the muffins are done.
- Transfer the muffins to a wire rack and leave to cool completely.

Fig, Orange and Ginger Muffins

681

A little grated orange zest goes very well with the figs or why not try adding 2 tbsp of chopped stem ginger for an extra kick.

682

MAKES 36

Mini Pumpkin and Nutmeg Muffins

PREPARATION TIME: 25 MINUTES

COOKING TIME: 45 MINUTES

INGREDIENTS

175 g / 6 oz / ½ cup soft brown sugar
2 large eggs
150 ml / 5 fl. oz / ¾ cup sunflower oil
175 g / 6 oz / 1 ¼ cups wholemeal flour
3 tsp baking powder
½ tsp freshly grated nutmeg
200 g / 7 oz pumpkin, coarsely grated

- Preheat the oven to 190°C (170° fan) / 375 F / gas 5 and line a 36-hole mini cupcake tin with paper cases.
- Whisk the sugar, eggs and oil together for 3 minutes until thick.
- Fold in the flour, baking powder and nutmeg, followed by the grated pumpkin.
- Divide the mixture between the paper cases, then bake in the oven for 20 - 25 minutes.
- Test with a wooden toothpick, if it comes out clean, the muffins are done.
- Transfer the muffins to a wire rack and leave to cool completely.

Pumpkin, Nutmeg and Orange Muffins

683

Add the finely grated zest of 1 orange to the mixture. Mix together 2 tbsp of orange juice with 2 tbsp of soft brown sugar and spoon over the muffins when they come out of the oven.

684

MAKES 24

Wholemeal Carob Mini Muffins

Carob and Cranberry Muffins

685

Add 85 g / 3 oz of cranberries to the mixture before cooking.

Carob and Raisin Muffins

686

Add 85 g / 3 oz of raisins to the mixture before cooking.

Carob and Coconut Muffins

687

Add 3 tbsp of desiccated coconut to the muffin mixture.

PREPARATION TIME: 15 MINUTES

COOKING TIME: 20 MINUTES

INGREDIENTS

1 large egg
120 ml / 4 fl. oz / ½ cup sunflower oil
120 ml / 4 fl. oz / ½ cup milk
375 g / 12 ½ oz / 2 ½ cups wholemeal flour
2 tsp baking powder
200 g / 7 oz / ¾ cup caster (superfine) sugar
75 g / 2 ½ oz / ½ cup carob drops

- Preheat the oven to 180°C (160° fan) / 350 F / gas 4 and line a 24-hole mini muffin tin with paper cases.
- Beat the egg in a jug with the oil and milk until well mixed.
- Mix the flour, baking powder, sugar and carob drops in a bowl, then pour in the egg mixture and stir just enough to combine.
- Divide the mixture between the moulds and bake in the oven for 15 – 20 minutes.
- Test with a wooden toothpick, if it comes out clean, the muffins are done.
- Transfer the muffins to a wire rack and leave to cool.

688

MAKES 12

Blueberry and Ginger Muffins

PREPARATION TIME: 10 MINUTES

COOKING TIME: 20 MINUTES

INGREDIENTS

250 g / 9 oz / 1 ¾ cups self-raising flour
1 tsp bicarbonate of (baking) soda
2 tsp ground ginger
200 g / 8 ½ oz / ½ cup golden syrup
125 g / 4 ½ oz / ½ cup butter
125 g / 4 ½ oz / ¾ cup light brown sugar
2 large eggs, beaten
240 ml / 8 fl. oz / 1 cup milk
150 g / 5 oz / 1 cup blueberries

- Preheat the oven to 190°C (170° fan) / 375 F / gas 5 and line a 12-hole muffin tin with paper cases.
- Sieve the flour, bicarbonate of soda and ground ginger together into a bowl.
- Put the golden syrup, butter and brown sugar in a small saucepan and boil gently for 2 minutes, stirring to dissolve the sugar.
- Pour the butter and sugar mixture onto the flour with the eggs and milk and fold it all together with the blueberries until smooth.
- Divide the mixture between the muffin cases and bake in the oven for 20 – 25 minutes.
- Test with a wooden toothpick, if it comes out clean, the muffins are done.
- Transfer the muffins to a wire rack and leave to cool.

Blueberry and Cinnamon Muffins

689

Replace the ginger with 2 tsp of cinnamon. Mix 1 tsp of ground cinnamon with 1 tbsp of caster sugar and sprinkle over the muffins.

690

MAKES 12

Cheese and Tomato Muffins

PREPARATION TIME: 10 MINUTES

COOKING TIME: 20-25 MINUTES

INGREDIENTS

2 large eggs
120 ml / 4 fl. oz / ½ cup sunflower oil
180 ml / 6 fl. oz / ¾ cup Greek yoghurt
110 g / 4 oz / 1 cup cheddar, grated
225 g / 8 oz / 1 ½ cups plain flour
2 tsp baking powder
½ tsp bicarbonate of (baking) soda
½ tsp salt
110 g / 4 oz / 1 cup tomato chutney

- Preheat the oven to 180°°C (160° fan) / 350 F / gas 4 and oil a 12-hole silicone muffin mould.
- Beat the egg in a jug with the oil, yoghurt and cheese until well mixed.
- Mix the flour, raising agents and salt in a bowl, then pour in the egg mixture and chutney and stir just enough to combine.
- Divide the mixture between the moulds, then bake in the oven for 20 – 25 minutes.
- Test with a wooden toothpick, if it comes out clean, the muffins are done.
- Transfer the muffins to a wire rack and leave to cool completely.

Stilton and Onion Muffins

691

Replace the cheddar with 110 g of crumbled Stilton and replace the tomato chutney with onion marmalade.

692

MAKES 12

Black Sesame Seed Muffin

- Preheat the oven to 180°C (160° fan) / 350 F / gas 4 and oil a 12-hole silicone muffin tin.
- Beat the egg in a jug with the oil, milk and sesame oil until well mixed.
- Mix the flour, baking powder, sugar and ¾ of the sesame seeds in a bowl, then pour in the egg mixture and stir just enough to combine.
- Divide the mixture between the moulds and sprinkle with the remaining sesame seeds, then bake in the oven for 20 – 25 minutes.
- Test with a wooden toothpick, if it comes out clean, the muffins are done.
- Transfer the muffins to a wire rack and leave to cool completely.

PREPARATION TIME: 10 MINUTES

COOKING TIME: 45 MINUTES

INGREDIENTS

1 large egg
120 ml / 4 fl. oz / ½ cup sunflower oil
120 ml / 4 fl. oz / ½ cup milk
2 tbsp toasted sesame oil
375 g / 12 ½ oz / 2 ½ cups self-raising flour, sifted
1 tsp baking powder
200 g / 7 oz / ¾ cup caster (superfine) sugar
75 g / 2 ½ oz / ¼ cup black sesame seeds

Black Sesame Seed and Candied Peel Muffins

693

Add 75g / 3 oz / ⅓ cup chopped mixed candied peel to the muffin mixture.

694

MAKES 12

Fig and Honey Muffins

- Preheat the oven to 180°C (160° fan) / 350 F / gas 4 and oil a 12 silicone muffin moulds.
- Beat the egg in a jug with the oil, milk and honey until well mixed.
- Mix the flour, baking powder, sugar and figs in a bowl, then pour in the egg mixture and stir just enough to combine.
- Divide the mixture between the moulds and bake in the oven for 20 – 25 minutes.
- Test with a wooden toothpick, if it comes out clean, the muffins are done.
- Transfer the muffins to a wire rack to cool.

PREPARATION TIME: 10 MINUTES

COOKING TIME: 25 MINUTES

INGREDIENTS

1 large egg
120 ml / 4 fl. oz / ½ cup sunflower oil
120 ml / 4 fl. oz / ½ cup milk
110 g / 4 oz / ½ cup honey
375 g / 12 ½ oz / 2 ½ cups self-raising flour, sifted
1 tsp baking powder
200 g / 7 oz / ¾ cup caster (superfine) sugar
150 g / 5 oz / 1 cup fresh figs, chopped
75 g / 2 ½ oz / ½ cup dried figs, chopped

Fig, Walnut and Honey Muffins

Add 75g / 3oz / ⅓ cup of chopped walnuts to the muffin mixture.

MAKES 12

Wholemeal Honey Mini Muffins

PREPARATION TIME: 10 MINUTES

COOKING TIME: 25 MINUTES

INGREDIENTS

1 large egg
120 ml / 4 fl. oz / ½ cup sunflower oil
120 ml / 4 fl. oz / ½ cup milk
110 g / 4 oz / ½ cup honey
375 g / 12 ½ oz / 2 ½ cups wholemeal flour
2 tsp baking powder
55 g / 2 oz / ½ cup ground almonds

FOR THE SOAKING SYRUP
1 lemon, juiced
110 g / 4 oz / ½ cup honey
1 tsp ground cinnamon

- Preheat the oven to 180°C (160° fan) / 350 F / gas 4 and oil a 24 small dariole moulds.
- Beat the egg in a jug with the oil, milk and honey until well mixed.
- Mix the flour, baking powder and ground almonds in a bowl, then pour in the egg mixture and stir just enough to combine.
- Divide the mixture between the moulds and bake in the oven for 15 – 20 minutes.
- Test with a wooden toothpick, if it comes out clean, the muffins are done.
- While the muffins are cooking, make the soaking syrup. Put the lemon juice, honey and cinnamon in a small saucepan and boil for 2 minutes.
- When the muffins are ready, spoon over the soaking syrup and leave them to cool in their moulds.

Honey and Oat Muffins

Add 100 g / 4 oz of oats to the muffin mixture before cooking. .

Honey and Candied Fruit Muffins

Add 85 g / 3 oz of candied fruit tot he mixture before cooking.

699

MAKES 12

Peanut Muffins

- Preheat the oven to 180°C (160° fan) / 350 F / gas 4 and line a 12-hole muffin tin with paper cases.
- Beat the egg in a jug with the oil and milk until well mixed.
- Mix the flour, baking powder, sugar and ¾ of the peanuts in a bowl, then pour in the egg mixture and stir just enough to combine.
- Divide the mixture between the paper cases and sprinkle with the rest of the nuts, then bake in the oven for 20 – 25 minutes.
- Test with a wooden toothpick, if it comes out clean, the muffins are done.
- Transfer the muffins to a wire rack and leave to cool.

PREPARATION TIME: 15 MINUTES

COOKING TIME: 25 MINUTES

INGREDIENTS

1 large egg
120 ml / 4 fl. oz / ½ cup sunflower oil
120 ml / 4 fl. oz / ½ cup milk
375 g / 12 ½ oz / 2 ½ cups self-raising flour, sifted
1 tsp baking powder
200 g / 7 oz / ¾ cup caster (superfine) sugar
75 g / 2 ½ oz / ½ cup peanuts

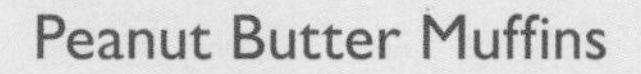

Peanut Butter Muffins

700

Divide half of the muffin mixture between the paper cases and top each one with 1 tbsp smooth peanut butter. Spoon the rest of the muffin mixture on top and bake as above.

701

MAKES 12

Chocolate and Pecan Muffins

- Preheat the oven to 180°C (160° fan) / 350 F / gas 4 and line 12 paper drinking cups with greaseproof paper.
- Beat the egg in a jug with the oil and milk until well mixed.
- Mix the flour, cocoa, baking powder, sugar, chocolate and ¾ of the pecans in a bowl, then pour in the egg mixture and stir just enough to combine.
- Divide the mixture between the paper cups and sprinkle with the remaining pecans, then bake in the oven for 20 – 25 minutes.
- Test with a wooden toothpick, if it comes out clean, the muffins are done.
- Transfer the muffins to a wire rack and leave to cool completely.

PREPARATION TIME: 15 MINUTES

COOKING TIME: 25 MINUTES

INGREDIENTS

1 large egg
120 ml / 4 fl. oz / ½ cup sunflower oil
120 ml / 4 fl. oz / ½ cup milk
375 g / 12 ½ oz / 2 ½ cups self-raising flour, sifted
55 g / 2 oz / ½ cup unsweetened cocoa powder, sifted
1 tsp baking powder
200 g / 7 oz / ¾ cup caster (superfine) sugar
110 g / 4 oz / ½ cup dark chocolate, minimum 60% cocoa solids, chopped
110 g / 4 oz pecan nuts, chopped

Chocolate, Pecan and Cherry Muffins

702

Add 75g / 3 oz / ⅓ cup of halved glace cherries to the dry ingredients before mixing together.

703

MAKES 12

Orange and Chocolate Chip Muffins

PREPARATION TIME: 20 MINUTES

COOKING TIME: 20 MINUTES

INGREDIENTS

110 g / 4 oz / 1 cup self-raising flour, sifted
110 g / 4 oz / ½ cup caster (superfine) sugar
110 g / 4 oz / ½ cup butter, softened
2 large eggs
1 orange, zest finely grated
2 tsp ground cinnamon
150 g / 5 oz / 1 cup chocolate chips

FOR THE GLAZE
½ orange, juiced
60 ml / 2 fl. oz / ¼ cup honey
1 cinnamon stick

- Preheat the oven to 190°C (170° fan) / 375 F / gas 5 and line a 12-hole cupcake tin with paper cases.
- Combine the flour, sugar, butter, eggs, orange zest and cinnamon in a bowl and whisk together for 2 minutes or until smooth, then fold in ¾ of the chocolate chips.
- Divide the mixture between the paper cases and sprinkle the rest of the chocolate chips on top, then transfer the tin to the oven and bake for 15 – 20 minutes.
- Test with a wooden toothpick, if it comes out clean, the muffins are done.
- Transfer the muffins to a wire rack and leave to cool completely.
- To make the glaze, combine the ingredients in a small saucepan and boil for 2 minutes or until syrupy.
- Remove the cinnamon stick and leave to cool then spoon on top of the muffins.

Orange, Cinnamon and Raisin Muffins

704

Replace the chocolate chips with 110g / 4 oz / ½ cup raisins that have been soaked in the juice of 1 orange for an hour.

705

MAKES 12

Almond and Raspberry Cream Muffins

PREPARATION TIME: 40 MINUTES

COOKING TIME: 25 MINUTES

INGREDIENTS

1 large egg
120 ml / 4 fl. oz / ½ cup sunflower oil
120 ml / 4 fl. oz / ½ cup milk
375 g / 12 ½ oz / 2 ½ cups self-raising flour, sifted
1 tsp baking powder
200 g / 7 oz / ¾ cup caster (superfine) sugar
75 g / 2 ½ oz / ½ cup ground almonds

TO DECORATE
225 ml / 8 fl. oz / 1 cup double (heavy) cream
2 tbsp icing (confectioners') sugar
2 tbsp raspberry syrup
150 g / 5 oz / 1 cup raspberries
75 g / 2 ½ oz / ½ cup toasted, flaked (slivered) almonds

- Preheat the oven to 180°C (160° fan) / 350 F / gas 4 and line a 12-hole muffin tin with paper cases.
- Beat the egg in a jug with the oil and milk until well mixed.
- Mix the flour, baking powder, sugar and ground almonds in a bowl, then pour in the egg mixture and stir just enough to combine.
- Divide the mixture between the paper cases and bake for 20 – 25 minutes. Transfer the muffins to a wire rack and leave to cool completely.
- Whip the cream with the icing sugar and raspberry syrup until thick.
- Spoon the raspberry cream into a piping bag fitted with a large plain nozzle and pipe a big swirl on top of each cake.
- Top with fresh raspberries and flaked almonds.

Almond and Strawberry Cream Muffins

706

Replace the raspberry syrup in the cream with strawberry syrup and top the muffins with fresh strawberries and flaked almond.

707

MAKES 12

Blackberry Crumble Muffins

PREPARATION TIME: 45 MINUTES

COOKING TIME: 25 MINUTES

INGREDIENTS

1 large egg
120 ml / 4 fl. oz / ½ cup sunflower oil
120 ml / 4 fl. oz / ½ cup milk
375 g / 12 ½ oz / 2 ½ cups self-raising flour, sifted
1 tsp baking powder
200 g / 7 oz / ¾ cup caster (superfine) sugar
150 g / 5 oz / 1 cup blackberries
2 tsp ground cinnamon

FOR THE CRUMBLE TOPPING
55 g / 2 oz / ¼ cup butter, cubed and chilled
110 g / 4 oz / ¾ cup plain (all purpose) flour
2 tbsp caster (superfine) sugar

- Preheat the oven to 180°C (160° fan) / 350 F / gas 4 and line a 12-hole muffin tin with paper cases.
- Beat the egg in a jug with the oil and milk until well mixed.
- Mix the flour, baking powder, sugar and blackberries in a bowl, then pour in the egg mixture and stir just enough to combine.
- Divide the mixture between the paper cases.
- To make the crumble topping, rub the butter into the flour until the mixture resembles fine breadcrumbs. Stir in the sugar, then clump the mixture together in your hands and crumble it over the top of the muffins.
- Transfer the tin to the oven and bake for 20 - 25 minutes.
- Test with a wooden toothpick, if it comes out clean, the muffins are done.
- Transfer the muffins to a wire rack and leave to cool completely.

708

Spiced Plum Crumble Muffins

Replace the blackberries with 3 stoned, chopped plums and add 1 tsp mixed spice and ½ tsp ground cloves.

709

Cranberry Crumble Muffins

Replace the blackberries with cranberries and the cinnamon with vanilla extract.

710

Bun and Raisin Crumble Muffins

Replace the blackberries with raisins and add 85 g / 4 oz of chopped mixed nuts.

711

MAKES 12

Peanut Macaroons

- Oil and line a large baking tray with baking parchment. Grind the ground almonds, hazelnuts and icing sugar together in a food processor to a very fine powder.
- Whisk the egg whites to stiff peaks then carefully fold in the nut and sugar mixture. Spoon the mixture into a piping bag fitted with a large plain nozzle and pipe 2 ½cm / 1" rounds onto the baking tray.
- Sprinkle with chopped hazelnuts then leave the to stand for 30 minutes to form a skin.
- Preheat the oven to 170°C (150° fan) / 325 F / gas 3. Bake for 10 – 15 minutes. Slide the paper onto a cold work surface and leave the macaroons to cool completely.
- Beat the butter until light and fluffy then beat in the icing sugar. Add the milk, then whisk for 2 minutes.
- Spoon the buttercream into a piping bag fitted with a plain nozzle and pipe an even round onto half of the macaroons. Sandwich together with the other half.

PREPARATION TIME: 1 HOUR 15 MINUTES

COOKING TIME: 15 MINUTES

INGREDIENTS

110 g / 4 oz / 1 cup ground almonds
55 g / 2 oz / ½ cup ground hazelnuts
175 g / 6 oz / 1 ½ cups icing sugar
2 large egg whites
2 tbsp hazelnuts, finely chopped

TO DECORATE

110 g / 4 oz / ½ cup butter, softened
225 g / 8 oz / 2 cups icing sugar

712

Plain Almond Macaroons

MAKES 18

PREPARATION TIME: 1 HOUR 15 MINUTES

COOKING TIME: 15 MINUTES

INGREDIENTS

175 g / 6 oz / 1 ½ cups ground almonds
175 g / 6 oz / 1 ½ cups icing sugar
2 large egg whites

- Oil and line a large baking sheet with baking parchment.
- Grind the ground almonds and icing sugar together in a food processor to a very fine powder.
- Whisk the egg whites to stiff peaks in a very clean bowl then carefully fold in the almond and sugar mixture.
- Spoon the mixture into a piping bag fitted with a large plain nozzle and pipe 2 ½ cm / 1" rounds onto the baking tray.
- Leave the uncooked macaroons to stand for 30 minutes to form a skin.
- Preheat the oven to 170°C (150° fan) / 325 F / gas 3.
- Bake for 10 – 15 minutes or until crisp on the outside and still a bit chewy in the middle.
- Slide the greaseproof paper onto a cold work surface and leave the macaroons to cool completely.

713

Strawberry Macaroons

MAKES 18

PREPARATION TIME: 1 HOUR 15 MINUTES

COOKING TIME: 15 MINUTES

INGREDIENTS

175 g / 6 oz / 1 ½ cups ground almonds
175 g / 6 oz / 1 ½ cups icing sugar
2 large egg whites
1 tbsp strawberry syrup
10 drops pink food colouring

TO DECORATE

110 g / 4 oz / ½ cup butter, softened
225 g / 8 oz / 2 cups icing sugar
1 tbsp strawberry syrup

- Oil and line a large baking sheet with baking parchment. Grind the almonds and icing sugar together to a very fine powder.
- Whisk the egg whites to stiff peaks then carefully fold in the almond and sugar mixture with the strawberry syrup and food colouring.
- Spoon the mixture into a piping bag fitted with a large plain nozzle and pipe 2 ½cm / 1" rounds onto the baking tray.
- Leave them to stand for 30 minutes to form a skin. Preheat the oven to 170°C (150° fan) / 325 F / gas 3. Bake for 10 – 15 minutes.
- Slide the paper onto a cold work surface and leave to cool.
- Beat the butter until light and fluffy then beat in the icing sugar. Add the strawberry syrup, then whisk for 2 minutes.
- Spoon the buttercream into a piping bag fitted with a plain nozzle and pipe an even round onto half of the macaroons.
- Sandwich together with the other half.

714

MAKES 18

Golden Chocolate Macaroons

- Oil and line a large baking tray with baking parchment.
- Grind the almonds, icing sugar and cocoa powder together to a very fine powder. Whisk the egg whites to stiff peaks then fold in the almond and sugar mixture.
- Spoon the mixture into a piping bag fitted with a plain nozzle and pipe 2 ½ cm / 1" rounds onto the tray.
- Leave them to stand for 30 minutes to form a skin.
- Preheat the oven to 170°C (150° fan) / 325 F / gas 3.
- Bake for 10 – 15 minutes. Slide the paper onto a cold work surface and leave them to cool completely.
- Beat the butter until light and fluffy then beat in the icing sugar. Mix the milk and cocoa together then add to the buttercream and whisk for 2 minutes.
- Spoon the buttercream into a piping bag fitted with a plain nozzle and pipe an even round onto half of the macaroons. Sandwich together with the other half.
- Carefully apply the gold leaf with a dry brush.

PREPARATION TIME:1 HOUR 15 MINUTES

COOKING TIME: 15 MINUTES

INGREDIENTS

175 g / 6 oz / 1 ½ cups ground almonds
175 g / 6 oz / 1 ½ cups icing (confectioners') sugar
2 tbsp unsweetened cocoa powder
2 large egg whites

TO DECORATE

110 g / 4 oz / ½ cup butter, softened
225 g / 8 oz / 2 cups icing (confectioners') sugar
1 tbsp milk
1 tbsp unsweetened cocoa powder
3 sheets of gold leaf

Golden Almond Macaroons

715

Add 2 tsp of almond extract for an intense almond flavour.

716

SERVES 6

Cocoa Meringues with White Chocolate Cream

- Preheat the oven to 140°C (120° fan) / 275 F / gas 1 and oil and line a large baking tray with greaseproof paper.
- Whisk the egg whites until stiff, then gradually whisk in half the sugar until the mixture is very shiny.
- Fold in the remaining sugar with the cocoa then spoon the mixture into a piping bag fitted with a large plain nozzle.
- Pipe 24 rounds onto the baking tray, then bake in the oven for 35 minutes or until the meringues are crisp.
- Leave to cool completely.
- To make the white chocolate cream, melt the white chocolate in a microwave or bain marie and leave to cool a little.
- Whisk the cream until it forms soft peaks, then fold in the chocolate and spoon into glasses.
- Serve with the cocoa meringues.

PREPARATION TIME: 1 HOUR 15 MINUTES

COOKING TIME: 15 MINUTES

INGREDIENTS

4 large egg whites
110 g / 4 oz / 1 cup caster (superfine) sugar
1 tbsp cocoa powder

TO DECORATE

110 g / 4 oz / ½ cup white chocolate, chopped
225 ml / 8 fl. oz / 1 cup double cream

Cocoa Meringues with Milk Chocolate Cream

717

You can make a milk chocolate cream by replacing the white chocolate with milk chocolate and marbling it through the whipped cream.

718

MAKES 18

Hazelnut Chocolate Macaroons

Peanut Butter and Almond Macaroons

719

Replace the hazelnut chocolate spread with peanut butter.

Almond Butter Macaroons

720

Replace the hazelnut chocolate spread with almond butter.

Hazelnut Chocolate and Orange Macaroons

721

Add a few drops of orange essence to the mixture.

PREPARATION TIME:
1 HOUR 15 MINUTES

COOKING TIME: 15 MINUTES

INGREDIENTS

110 g / 4 oz / 1 cup ground almonds
55 g / 2 oz / ½ cup ground hazelnuts (cob nuts)
175 g / 6 oz / 1 ½ cups icing (confectioners') sugar
2 large egg whites

TO DECORATE
110 g / 4 oz / ½ cup hazelnut chocolate spread

- Oil and line a large baking sheet with baking parchment.
- Grind the ground almonds, hazelnuts and icing sugar together in a food processor to a very fine powder.
- Whisk the egg whites to stiff peaks in a very clean bowl then carefully fold in the nut and sugar mixture.
- Spoon the mixture into a piping bag fitted with a large plain nozzle and pipe 2 ½ cm / 1" rounds onto the baking tray.
- Leave the uncooked macaroons to stand for 30 minutes to form a skin.
- Preheat the oven to 170°C (150° fan) / 325 F / gas 3.
- Bake for 10 – 15 minutes or until crisp on the outside and still a bit chewy in the middle.
- Slide the greaseproof paper onto a cold work surface and leave the macaroons to cool completely.
- Spoon the hazelnut chocolate spread into a piping bag fitted with a medium plain nozzle and pipe an even round onto half of the macaroons.
- Sandwich together with the other half.

722

MAKES 18

Peanut Butter Macaroons

- Oil and line a large baking tray with baking parchment.
- Grind the almonds, peanuts and icing sugar together to a very fine powder. Whisk the egg whites to stiff peaks then carefully fold in the nut and sugar mixture.
- Spoon the mixture into a piping bag fitted with a large plain nozzle and pipe 2 ½cm / 1" rounds onto the baking tray.
- Leave the uncooked macaroons to stand for 30 minutes to form a skin.
- Preheat the oven to 170°C (150° fan) / 325 F / gas 3.
- Bake for 10 – 15 minutes or until crisp on the outside and still a bit chewy in the middle.
- Slide the greaseproof paper onto a cold work surface and leave the macaroons to cool completely.
- Sandwich the macaroons together with peanut butter.

PREPARATION TIME: 1 HOUR 15 MINUTES

COOKING TIME: 15 MINUTES

INGREDIENTS

110 g / 4 oz / 1 cup ground almonds
55 g / 2 oz / ½ cup ground peanuts
175 g / 6 oz / 1 ½ cups icing (confectioners') sugar
2 large egg whites

TO DECORATE

110 g / 4 oz / ½ cup smooth peanut butter

Chocolate Peanut Butter Macaroons

723

For chocolate peanut butter macaroons, grind 1 tbsp cocoa powder with the almonds, peanuts and icing sugar and proceed as above.

724

MAKES 36

Amaretti Biscuits

- Preheat the oven to 170°°C (150° fan) / 325 F / gas 3 and oil a large baking tray.
- Whisk the egg whites to stiff peaks in a very clean bowl then carefully fold in the almonds, sugar and amaretto.
- Spoon the mixture into a piping bag fitted with a large plain nozzle and pipe 2 ½ cm / 1" rounds onto the baking tray.
- Bake for 15 – 20 minutes or until golden brown and crisp.
- Transfer to a wire rack to cool.

PREPARATION TIME: 15 MINUTES

COOKING TIME: 15-20 MINUTES

INGREDIENTS

2 large egg whites
175 g / 6 oz / 1 ½ cups ground almonds
175 g / 6 oz / 1 ½ cups icing (confectioners') sugar
1 tbsp amaretto liqueur

Coffee Amaretti Biscuits

Replace the amaretto liqueur with coffee liqueur and add ½ tsp of instant espresso powder.

726

MAKES 18

Lemon Macaroons

PREPARATION TIME:
1 HOUR 15 MINUTES

COOKING TIME: 15 MINUTES

INGREDIENTS

175 g / 6 oz / 1 ½ cups ground almonds
175 g / 6 oz / 1 ½ cups icing (confectioners') sugar
2 tsp lemon zest, finely grated
2 large egg whites
10 drops yellow food colouring

TO DECORATE
110 g / 4 oz / ½ cup lemon curd
basil, to garnish

- Oil and line a large baking tray with baking parchment.
- Grind the ground almonds, icing sugar and lemon zest together in a food processor to a very fine powder.
- Whisk the egg whites to stiff peaks in a very clean bowl then carefully fold in the almond and sugar mixture with the food colouring.
- Spoon the mixture into a piping bag fitted with a large plain nozzle and pipe 2 ½cm / 1" rounds onto the baking tray.
- Leave them to stand for 30 minutes to form a skin.
- Preheat the oven to 170°C (150° fan) / 325 F / gas 3.
- Bake for 10 – 15 minutes or until crisp on the outside and still a bit chewy in the middle.
- Slide the greaseproof paper onto a cold work surface and leave the macaroons to cool completely.
- Sandwich together with the lemon curd.

Lime Macaroons

727

For lime macaroons, replace the lemon zest with lime zest and colour the macaroons green. Sandwich together with lime curd.

728

MAKES 24

Pistachio Macaroons

PREPARATION TIME: 1 HOUR

COOKING TIME: 35 MINUTES

INGREDIENTS

4 large egg whites
110 g / 4 oz / 1 cup caster (superfine) sugar
55 g / 2 oz / ½ cup ground pistachios

TO DECORATE
225 g / 8 oz / 1 cup dark chocolate, minimum 60% cocoa solids
225 ml / 8 fl. oz / 1 cup double (heavy) cream
2 tbsp pistachio nuts, chopped

- Preheat the oven to 140°C (120° fan) / 275 F / gas 1 and oil and line a large baking tray with greaseproof paper.
- Whisk the egg whites until stiff, then gradually whisk in half the sugar until the mixture is very shiny.
- Fold in the remaining sugar with the ground pistachios then spoon the mixture into a piping bag fitted with a large plain nozzle.
- Pipe 24 rounds onto the baking tray, then bake in the oven for 35 minutes or until the meringues are crisp.
- Leave to cool completely.
- Chop the chocolate and transfer to a mixing bowl.
- Heat the cream until it starts to simmer, then pour over the chopped chocolate and stir until the mixture has cooled and thickened.
- Sandwich the meringues together with the ganache and sprinkle with chopped pistachios.

Pistachio and Lemon Macaroons

729

Add 2 tbsp of lemon juice to the mixture before cooking.

730

MAKES 18

Raspberry Macaroons

Raspberry and Orange Macaroons

731

Add 2 tsp of finely grated orange zest to the macaroon mixture.

Peppermint and Lemon Macaroons

732

Replace the raspberry jam with lemon curd and the raspberry syrup with peppermint syrup.

Strawberry Macaroons

733

Replace the raspberry jam with strawberry jam and the raspberry syrup with strawberry syrup.

PREPARATION TIME: 1 HOUR 15 MINUTES

COOKING TIME: 15 MINUTES

INGREDIENTS

175 g / 6 oz / 1 ½ cups ground almonds
175 g / 6 oz / 1 ½ cups icing (confectioners') sugar
2 large egg whites
1 tbsp raspberry syrup
10 drops pink food colouring

TO DECORATE

110 g / 4 oz / ½ cup raspberry jam (jelly)

- Oil and line a large baking sheet with baking parchment.
- Grind the ground almonds and icing sugar together in a food processor to a very fine powder.
- Whisk the egg whites to stiff peaks in a very clean bowl then carefully fold in the almond and sugar mixture with the raspberry syrup and food colouring.
- Spoon the mixture into a piping bag fitted with a large plain nozzle and pipe 2 ½cm / 1" rounds onto the baking tray.
- Leave the uncooked macaroons to stand for 30 minutes to form a skin.
- Preheat the oven to 170°C (150° fan) / 325 F / gas 3.
- Bake for 10 – 15 minutes or until crisp on the outside and still a bit chewy in the middle.
- Slide the greaseproof paper onto a cold work surface and leave the macaroons to cool completely.
- Sandwich the macaroons together with jam.

734

MAKES 12

Mint Chocolate Macaroons

With Coloured Buttercream

735

Use a few drops of green or blue food colouring in the buttercream to depict the mint flavour.

736

Fresh Mint Macaroons

Replace the peppermint essence with 1 tbsp finely chopped fresh mint leaves.

PREPARATION TIME: 1 HOUR 15 MINUTES

COOKING TIME: 15 MINUTES

INGREDIENTS

175 g / 6 oz / 1 ½ cups ground almonds
175 g / 6 oz / 1 ½ cups icing (confectioners') sugar
28 g / 1 oz / ¼ cup unsweetened cocoa powder
2 large egg whites

TO DECORATE
110 g / 4 oz / ½ cup butter, softened
225 g / 8 oz / 2 cups icing (confectioners') sugar
2 tbsp milk
5 drops peppermint essence

- Oil and line a large baking tray with baking parchment.
- Grind the ground almonds, icing sugar and cocoa together in a food processor to a very fine powder.
- Whisk the egg whites to stiff peaks then carefully fold in the almond mixture. Spoon the mixture into a piping bag fitted with a large plain nozzle and pipe 2 ½cm / 1" rounds onto the baking tray.
- Leave them to stand for 30 minutes to form a skin.
- Preheat the oven to 170°C (150° fan) / 325 F / gas 3.
- Bake for 10 – 15 minutes or until crisp on the outside and still a bit chewy in the middle.
- Slide the greaseproof paper onto a cold work surface and leave the macaroons to cool completely.
- Beat the butter with a wooden spoon until light and fluffy then beat in the icing sugar a quarter at a time.
- Use a whisk to incorporate the milk and peppermint essence, then whisk for 2 minutes or until smooth and well whipped.
- Spoon the buttercream into a piping bag fitted with a medium plain nozzle and pipe an even round onto half of the macaroons.
- Sandwich together with the other half.

737

MAKES 18

Apricot Macaroons

Cranberry Macaroons

738

Replace the cocoa powder with 1 tbsp of cranberry juice and add a few drops of red food colouring.

Lemon Macaroons

739

Replace the cocoa powder and apricot syrup with 3 tbsp of lemon juice and add a few drops of yellow food colouring.

PREPARATION TIME:
1 HOUR 15 MINUTES

COOKING TIME: 15 MINUTES

INGREDIENTS

175 g / 6 oz / 1 ½ cups ground almonds
175 g / 6 oz / 1 ½ cups icing (confectioners') sugar
2 large egg whites
1 tbsp apricot syrup
1 drop of orange food colouring

TO DECORATE

110 g / 4 oz / ½ cup butter, softened
225 g / 8 oz / 2 cups icing (confectioners') sugar
2 tbsp apricot syrup
1 drop orange food colouring

- Oil and line a large baking sheet with baking parchment.
- Grind the ground almonds and icing sugar together in a food processor to a very fine powder.
- Whisk the egg whites to stiff peaks in a very clean bowl then carefully fold in the almond and sugar mixture with the apricot syrup and food colouring.
- Spoon the mixture into a piping bag fitted with a large plain nozzle and pipe 2 ½cm / 1" rounds onto the baking tray.
- Leave the uncooked macaroons to stand for 30 minutes to form a skin.
- Preheat the oven to 170°C (150° fan) / 325 F / gas 3.
- Bake for 10 – 15 minutes or until crisp on the outside and still a bit chewy in the middle.
- Slide the greaseproof paper onto a cold work surface and leave the macaroons to cool completely.
- Beat the butter with a wooden spoon until light and fluffy then beat in the icing sugar a quarter at a time.
- Whisk in the syrup and food colouring then continue to whisk for 2 minutes or until smooth and well whipped.
- Spoon the buttercream into a piping bag fitted with a medium plain nozzle and pipe an even round onto half of the macaroons.
- Sandwich together with the other half.

740

MAKES 18

Orange Crunch Macaroons

PREPARATION TIME:
I HOUR 15 MINUTES

COOKING TIME: 15 MINUTES

INGREDIENTS

175 g / 6 oz / 1 ½ cups ground almonds
175 g / 6 oz / 1 ½ cups icing (confectioners') sugar
2 large egg whites
2 tsp orange zest, finely grated
8 drops orange food colouring

TO DECORATE
110 g / 4 oz / ½ cup butter, softened
225 g / 8 oz / 2 cups icing (confectioners') sugar
1 tbsp orange juice
2 tbsp cornflakes, crushed
55 g / 2 oz dark chocolate
1 tsp ground pistachios
basil, to garnish

- Oil and line a large baking tray with baking parchment.
- Grind the almonds and icing sugar together to a very fine powder. Whisk the egg whites to stiff peaks then fold in the almond and sugar mixture with the orange zest and food colouring.
- Spoon the mixture into a piping bag fitted with a plain nozzle and pipe 2 ½cm / 1" rounds onto the baking tray.
- Leave the m to stand for 30 minutes to form a skin.
- Preheat the oven to 170°C (150° fan) / 325 F / gas 3.
- Bake for 10 – 15 minutes or until crisp on the outside and still a bit chewy in the middle.
- Slide the greaseproof paper onto a cold work surface and leave the macaroons to cool completely.
- Beat the butter until light and fluffy then beat in the icing sugar. Add the orange juice, then whisk for 2 minutes. Spoon the buttercream into a piping bag fitted with a plain nozzle and pipe an even round onto half of the macaroons.
- Sandwich together with the other half then dip the edges in the crushed cornflakes.
- Melt the chocolate in a microwave or bain marie and fill a small piping bag.
- Decorate the macaroons with the chocolate and finish with a sprinkling of ground pistachios.

741

MAKES 6

Giant Lemon and Raspberry Macaroons

PREPARATION TIME: I HOUR 15 MINUTES

COOKING TIME: 15 MINUTES

INGREDIENTS

175 g / 6 oz / 1 ½ cups ground almonds
175 g / 6 oz / 1 ½ cups icing (confectioners') sugar
2 large egg whites
1 tbsp raspberry syrup

TO DECORATE
110 g / 4 oz / ½ cup lemon curd
150 g / 5 oz / 1 cup raspberries
chocolate sprinkles

- Oil and line a large baking tray with baking parchment.
- Grind the almonds and icing sugar to a fine powder. Whisk the egg whites to stiff peaks in a then fold in the almond and sugar mixture with the raspberry syrup.
- Spoon the mixture into a piping bag fitted with a large plain nozzle and pipe 12 circles of 8m / 3" onto the baking tray.
- Leave them to stand for 30 minutes to form a skin.
- Preheat the oven to 170°C (150° fan) / 325 F / gas 3.
- Bake for 15 - 20 minutes or until crisp on the outside and still a bit chewy in the middle.
- Slide the greaseproof paper onto a cold work surface and leave the macaroons to cool completely.
- Divide the lemon curd between 6 of the macaroons and dot round the edge with raspberries.
- Top with the final 6 macaroons.

Giant Lime and Raspberry Macaroons

742

Replace the lemon curd with lime marmalade.

743

MAKES 18

Chocolate and Raspberry Macaroons

744

Chocolate and Strawberry Macaroons

Replace the raspberry jam with strawberry jam.

745

Chocolate and Plum Macaroons

Replace the raspberry jam with plum jam.

746

Chocolate and Fig Macaroons

Replace the raspberry jam with fig jam.

PREPARATION TIME: 1 HOUR 15 MINUTES

COOKING TIME: 15 MINUTES

INGREDIENTS

175 g / 6 oz / 1 ½ cups ground almonds
175 g / 6 oz / 1 ½ cups icing (confectioners') sugar
2 tbsp unsweetened cocoa powder
2 large egg whites

TO DECORATE

55 g / 2 oz / ¼ cup butter, softened
110 g / 4 oz / 1 cup icing (confectioners') sugar
2 tsp milk
2 tbsp raspberry jam (jelly)

- Oil and line a large baking sheet with baking parchment.
- Grind the ground almonds, icing sugar and cocoa powder together in a food processor to a very fine powder.
- Whisk the egg whites to stiff peaks in a very clean bowl then carefully fold in the almond and sugar mixture.
- Spoon the mixture into a piping bag fitted with a small plain nozzle and pipe 36 heart shapes onto the tray.
- Leave the uncooked macaroons to stand for 30 minutes to form a skin.
- Preheat the oven to 170°C (150° fan) / 325 F / gas 3.
- Bake for 10 – 15 minutes or until crisp on the outside and still a bit chewy in the middle.
- Slide the greaseproof paper onto a cold work surface and leave the macaroons to cool completely.
- Beat the butter with a wooden spoon until light and fluffy then beat in the icing sugar a quarter at a time.
- Use a whisk to incorporate the milk into the buttercream then whisk for 2 minutes or until smooth and well whipped.
- Fold the jam into the buttercream until it looks marbled and use it to sandwich the macaroons together in pairs.

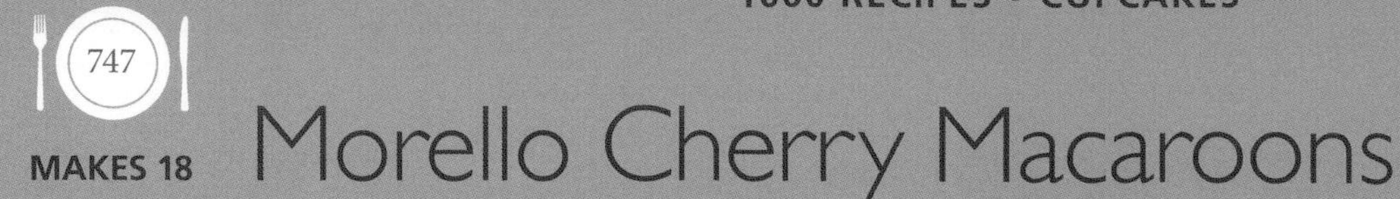

747

MAKES 18

Morello Cherry Macaroons

Cherry and Chocolate Hazelnut Macaroons

748

Add a layer of chocolate hazelnut spread between the macaroons.

PREPARATION TIME:
1 HOUR 15 MINUTES

COOKING TIME: 10 - 15 MINUTES

INGREDIENTS

175 g / 6 oz / 1 ½ cups ground almonds
175 g / 6 oz / 1 ½ cups icing (confectioners') sugar
2 large egg whites
1 tbsp cherry syrup
a few drops of pink food colouring

TO DECORATE
110 g / 4 oz / ½ cup butter, softened
225 g / 8 oz / 2 cups icing (confectioners') sugar
1 tbsp cherry syrup
a few drops of pink food colouring
9 fresh morello cherries with stalks

- Oil and line a large baking sheet with baking parchment.
- Grind the almonds and icing sugar together in a food processor to a fine powder.
- Whisk the egg whites in a bowl, then fold in the almond and sugar mixture with the cherry syrup and food colouring.
- Spoon the mixture into a piping bag and pipe 2 ½ cm / 1" rounds onto the baking tray.
- Leave the uncooked macaroons to stand for 30 minutes.
- Preheat the oven to 170°°C (150° fan) / 325 F / gas 3.
- Bake for 10 – 15 minutes.
- Place the greaseproof paper onto a work surface and leave the macaroons to cool.
- Beat the butter until fluffy then beat in the icing sugar a quarter at a time.
- Mix the cherry syrup and food colouring, then whisk for 2 minutes.
- Spoon the buttercream into a piping bag and pipe an even round onto the back of the macaroons, then halve and stone the cherries.
- Top half of the macaroons with half a cherry and sandwich together with the other half of the macaroons.

749

MAKES 18

Matcha Green Tea Macaroons

- Oil and line a large baking tray with baking parchment.
- Grind the almonds, icing sugar and half the matcha powder together to a very fine powder.
- Whisk the egg whites to stiff peaks then fold in the almond and sugar mixture.
- Spoon the mixture into a piping bag fitted with a plain nozzle and pipe 2 ½cm / 1" rounds onto the baking tray.
- Sprinkle with matcha powder then leave them to stand for 30 minutes to form a skin.
- Preheat the oven to 170°C (150° fan) / 325F / gas 3.
- Bake for 10 – 15 minutes or until crisp on the outside and still a bit chewy in the middle.
- Slide the greaseproof paper onto a cold work surface and leave the macaroons to cool completely.
- Beat the butter until light and fluffy then beat in the icing sugar.
- Use a whisk to incorporate the milk and matcha powder, then whisk for 2 minutes or until smooth and well whipped.
- Spoon the buttercream into a piping bag fitted with a medium plain nozzle and pipe an even round onto half of the macaroons.
- Sandwich together with the other half.

PREPARATION TIME:
1 HOUR 15 MINUTES

COOKING TIME: 15 MINUTES

INGREDIENTS

175 g / 6 oz / 1 ½ cups ground almonds
175 g / 6 oz / 1 ½ cups icing (confectioners') sugar
2 tsp matcha green tea powder
2 large egg whites

TO DECORATE

110 g / 4 oz / ½ cup butter, softened
225 g / 8 oz / 2 cups icing (confectioners') sugar
1 tbsp milk
1 tsp matcha green tea powder

750

MAKES 18

Coffee and Walnut Macaroons

- Oil and line a large baking tray with baking parchment.
- Grind the almonds, walnuts and icing sugar together to a very fine powder. Whisk the egg whites to stiff peaks then carefully fold in the nut and sugar mixture.
- Spoon the mixture into a piping bag fitted with a plain nozzle and pipe 2 ½ cm / 1" rounds onto the baking tray. Leave them to stand for 30 minutes to form a skin.
- Preheat the oven to 170°C (150° fan) / 325 F / gas 3.
- Bake for 10 – 15 minutes. Slide the greaseproof paper onto a cold work surface and leave to cool completely.
- Beat the butter until light and fluffy then beat in the icing sugar. Add the milk and espresso powder, then whisk for 2 minutes or until smooth and well whipped.
- Spoon the buttercream into a piping bag fitted with a medium plain nozzle and pipe an even round onto half of the macaroons.
- Sandwich together with the other hal

PREPARATION TIME:
1 HOUR 15 MINUTES

COOKING TIME: 15 MINUTES

INGREDIENTS

110 g / 4 oz / ½ cup ground almonds
55 g / 2 oz / ½ cup ground walnuts
175 g / 6 oz / 1 ½ cups icing (confectioners') sugar
2 large egg whites

TO DECORATE

110 g / 4 oz / ½ cup butter, softened
225 g / 8 oz / 2 cups icing (confectioners') sugar
1 tbsp milk
1 tbsp instant espresso powder

Maple Syrup Macaroons

751

Try filling the macaroons with maple buttercream – just replace the milk and espresso powder with 2 tbsp of maple syrup.

752

MAKES 18

Chocolate and Pistachio Macaroons

PREPARATION TIME: 1 HOUR MINUTES

COOKING TIME: 10 – 15 MINUTES

INGREDIENTS

175 g / 6 oz / 1 ½ cups ground almonds
175 g / 6 oz / 1 ½ cups icing (confectioners') sugar
28g / 1 oz / ¼ cup unsweetened cocoa powder
2 large egg whites

TO DECORATE
110 g / 4 oz dark chocolate, minimum 60% cocoa solids
110 ml / 4 fl. oz / 1 cup double (heavy) cream
2 tbsp pistachio nuts, chopped

- Oil and line a large baking tray with baking parchment.
- Grind the almonds, icing sugar and cocoa together to a very fine powder. Whisk the egg whites to stiff peaks then carefully fold in the almond mixture.
- Spoon the mixture into a piping bag fitted with a large plain nozzle and pipe 2 ½ cm / 1" rounds onto the baking tray.
- Leave them to stand for 30 minutes to form a skin. Preheat the oven to 170°C (150° fan) / 325F / gas 3. Bake for 10 – 15 minutes.
- Slide the paper onto a cold work surface and leave them to cool. Chop the chocolate and place in a bowl.
- Heat the cream until it starts to simmer, then pour over the chopped chocolate and stir until the mixture has cooled and thickened. Chill until thick enough to pipe.
- Spoon the ganache into a piping bag fitted with a medium plain nozzle and pipe an even round onto half of the macaroons.
- Sandwich together with the other half, then dip the edges in chopped pistachios.

753

MAKES 18

White Chocolate Cream Macaroons

PREPARATION TIME: 1 HOUR 15 MINUTES

COOKING TIME: 15 MINUTES

INGREDIENTS

175 g / 6 oz / 1 ½ cups ground almonds
175 g / 6 oz / 1 ½ cups icing (confectioners') sugar
2 large egg whites

TO DECORATE
110 g / 4 oz / ½ cup white chocolate
110 ml / 4 fl. oz / ½ cup double (heavy) cream

- Oil and line a large baking tray with baking parchment.
- Grind the ground almonds and icing sugar together in a food processor to a very fine powder.
- Whisk the egg whites to stiff peaks in a very clean bowl then carefully fold in the almond and sugar mixture.
- Spoon the mixture into a piping bag fitted with a large plain nozzle and pipe 2 ½cm / 1" rounds onto the baking tray.
- Leave them to stand for 30 minutes to form a skin.
- Preheat the oven to 170°C (150° fan) / 325 F / gas 3.
- Bake for 10 – 15 minutes. Slide the paper onto a cold work surface and leave them to cool completely.
- Chop the chocolate and transfer to a bowl. Heat the cream until it starts to simmer, then pour over the chopped chocolate and stir until the mixture has cooled and thickened.
- Chill until thick enough to pipe.
- Spoon the ganache into a piping bag fitted with a medium plain nozzle and pipe an even round onto half of the macaroons.
- Sandwich together with the other half.

MAKES 18

Lemon and Passion Fruit Macaroons

Lemon and Lime

755

For lemon and lime macaroons, substitute the lemon zest for lime zest and sandwich together with lemon curd.

Blackcurrant and Lemon Macaroons

756

Replace the passion fruit curd with blackcurrant jam.

Lemon and Orange Macaroons

757

For lemon and orange macaroons, substitute the lemon zest for orange zest and sandwich together with lemon curd.

PREPARATION TIME:
1 HOUR 15 MINUTES

COOKING TIME: 15 MINUTES

INGREDIENTS

175 g / 6 oz / 1 ½ cups ground almonds
175 g / 6 oz / 1 ½ cups icing (confectioners') sugar
2 tsp lemon, zest finely grated
2 large egg whites

TO DECORATE
110 g / 4 oz / ½ cup passion fruit curd

- Oil and line a large baking sheet with baking parchment.
- Grind the ground almonds, icing sugar and lemon zest together in a food processor to a very fine powder.
- Whisk the egg whites to stiff peaks in a very clean bowl then carefully fold in the almond and sugar mixture.
- Spoon the mixture into a piping bag fitted with a large plain nozzle and pipe 2 ½ cm / 1" rounds onto the baking tray.
- Leave the uncooked macaroons to stand for 30 minutes to form a skin.
- Preheat the oven to 170°C (150° fan) / 325 F / gas 3.
- Bake for 10 – 15 minutes or until crisp on the outside and still a bit chewy in the middle.
- Slide the greaseproof paper onto a cold work surface and leave the macaroons to cool completely.
- Sandwich together with the passion fruit curd.

BROWNIES AND MINI CAKES

762

MAKES 12

Nutty Chocolate Brownies

PREPARATION TIME: 25 MINUTES

COOKING TIME: 20 MINUTES

INGREDIENTS

110 g / 4 oz / ½ cup milk chocolate, chopped
85 g / 3 oz / ¾ cup unsweetened cocoa powder, sifted
225 g / 8 oz / 1 cup butter
450 g / 15 oz / 2 ½ cups light brown sugar
4 large eggs
110 g / 4 oz / 1 cup self-raising flour
75 g / 2 ½ oz / ½ cup almonds, chopped
75 g / 2 ½ oz / ½ cup walnuts, chopped
75 g / 2 ½ oz / ½ cup cashews, chopped

- Preheat the oven to 170°C (150° fan) / 325 F / gas 3 and oil and line a 20cm x 20cm / 8" x 8" square cake tin.
- Melt the chocolate, cocoa and butter together in a saucepan, then leave to cool a little.
- Whisk the sugar and eggs together with an electric whisk for 3 minutes or until very light and creamy.
- Pour in the chocolate mixture and sieve over the flour, then fold everything together until evenly mixed.
- Scrape into the tin and sprinkle over the nuts.
- Bake for 35 – 40 minutes or until the outside is set, but the centre is still quite soft, as it will continue to cook as it cools.
- Leave the brownie to cool completely before cutting into 12 rectangles.

Cherry Chocolate Brownies

763

Try adding 75g / 3 oz / ⅓ cup of halved glacé cherries to the mixed nut topping.

764

MAKES 12

Hazelnut Brownies

PREPARATION TIME: 25 MINUTES

COOKING TIME: 20 MINUTES

INGREDIENTS

110 g / 4 oz / ½ cup dark chocolate, chopped
85 g / 3 oz / ¾ cup unsweetened cocoa powder, sifted
225 g / 8 oz / 1 cup butter
110 g / 4 oz / ½ cup chocolate hazelnut spread
450 g / 15 oz / 2 ½ cups light brown sugar
4 large eggs
110 g / 4 oz / 1 cup self-raising flour
75 g / 2 ½ oz / ½ cup hazelnuts

- Preheat the oven to 170°C (150° fan) / 325 F / gas 3 and oil and line a 20cm x 20cm / 8" x 8" square cake tin.
- Melt the chocolate, cocoa and butter together in a saucepan, then leave to cool a little before stirring in the chocolate hazelnut spread.
- Whisk the sugar and eggs together with an electric whisk for 3 minutes or until very light and creamy.
- Pour in the chocolate mixture and sieve over the flour, then fold everything together with the hazelnuts until evenly mixed.
- Scrape into the tin and bake for 35 – 40 minutes or until the outside is set, but the centre is still quite soft, as it will continue to cook as it cools.
- Leave the brownie to cool completely before cutting into 12 rectangles.

Hazelnut and Raisin Brownies

Add 85 g / 3 oz of raisins to the mixture for a fruity twist.

766

MAKES 9

Marbled Brownies

- Preheat the oven to 170°C (150 fan) / 325 F / gas 3 and oil and line a 20cm x 20cm / 8" x 8" square cake tin.
- Melt the dark chocolate, cocoa and butter together in a saucepan, then leave to cool a little.
- Whisk the sugar and eggs together with an electric whisk for 3 minutes or until very light and creamy.
- Pour in the chocolate mixture and sieve over the flour, then fold everything together until evenly mixed.
- Make the white chocolate mixture in the same way, folding in the ground almonds with the flour at the end.
- Put alternate spoonfuls of each mixture into the prepared tin, then marble together by drawing a toothpick through the mixture.
- Bake for 35 – 40 minutes until the outside is set.
- Leave the brownie to cool completely before cutting into squares.

PREPARATION TIME: 25 MINUTES

COOKING TIME: 20 MINUTES

INGREDIENTS

55 g / 2 oz / ¼ cup dark chocolate, minimum 60% cocoa solids, chopped
40 g / 1 ½ oz / ⅓ cup unsweetened cocoa powder, sifted
110 g / 4 oz / ½ cup butter
225 g / 7 ½ oz / 1 ¼ cups light brown sugar
2 large eggs
55 g / 2 oz / ½ cup self-raising flour

FOR THE WHITE CHOCOLATE MIXTURE

55 g / 2 oz / ¼ cup white chocolate, chopped
110 g / 4 oz / ½ cup butter
225 g / 7 ½ oz / 1 ¼ cups light brown sugar
2 large eggs
55 g / 2 oz / ½ cup self-raising flour
2 tbsp ground almonds

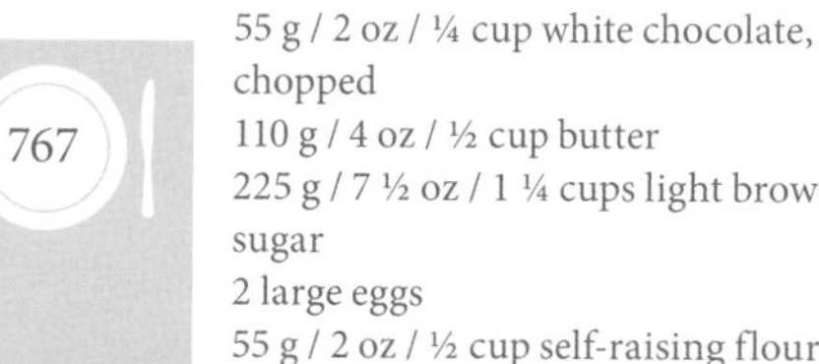

Nutty Marbled Brownies

767

Add 75g / 3 oz / ⅓ cup of chopped mixed nuts to the dark chocolate brownie mixture.

768

MAKES 9

Chocolate and Ginger Brownies

- Preheat the oven to 170°C (150° fan) / 325 F / gas 3 and oil and line a 20cm x 20cm / 8" x 8" square cake tin.
- Melt the chocolate, cocoa and butter together in a saucepan, then leave to cool a little.
- Whisk the sugar and eggs together with an electric whisk for 3 minutes or until very light and creamy.
- Pour in the chocolate mixture and sieve over the flour and ground ginger, then fold everything together with the stem ginger until evenly mixed.
- Scrape into the tin and bake for 35 – 40 minutes or until the outside is set, but the centre is still quite soft, as it will continue to cook as it cools.
- Leave the brownie to cool completely before cutting into 9 squares and topping with the cake sprinkles.

PREPARATION TIME: 25 MINUTES

COOKING TIME: 20 MINUTES

INGREDIENTS

110 g / 4 oz / ½ cup milk chocolate, chopped
85 g / 3 oz / ¾ cup unsweetened cocoa powder, sifted
225 g / 8 oz / 1 cup butter
450 g / 15 oz / 2 ½ cups light brown sugar
4 large eggs
110 g / 4 oz / 1 cup self-raising flour
2 tsp ground ginger
75 g / 2 ½ oz / ½ cup stem ginger, finely chopped

TO DECORATE

Hundreds and thousands

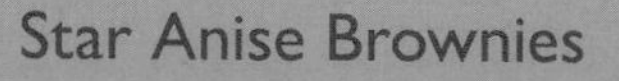

Star Anise Brownies

769

Try replacing the milk chocolate with dark chocolate and use 1 tsp of ground star anise instead of the ground ginger.

MAKES 9

Chocolate and Blueberry Brownies

White Chocolate and Cherry Brownies

Try replacing the blueberries with stoned fresh cherries.

Milk Chocolate and Cherry Brownies

772

Try replacing the white chocolate with dark chocolate.

White Chocolate and Raisin Brownies

773

Replace the blueberries with 150 g / 5 oz / 1 cup of raisins.

PREPARATION TIME: 25 MINUTES

COOKING TIME: 20 MINUTES

INGREDIENTS

110 g / 4 oz / ½ cup white chocolate, chopped
225 g / 8 oz / 1 cup butter
450 g / 15 oz / 2 ½ cups light brown sugar
4 large eggs
110 g / 4 oz / ½ cup self-raising flour
55 g / 2 oz / ½ cup ground almonds
150 g / 5 oz / 1 cup blueberries

- Preheat the oven to 170°C (150° fan) / 325 F / gas 3 and oil and line a 20cm x 20cm / 8" x 8" square cake tin.
- Melt the chocolate and butter together in a saucepan, then leave to cool a little.
- Whisk the sugar and eggs together with an electric whisk for 3 minutes or until very light and creamy.
- Pour in the chocolate mixture and sieve over the flour, then fold everything together with the ground almonds and blueberries until evenly mixed.
- Scrape into the tin and bake for 35 – 40 minutes or until the outside is set, but the centre is still quite soft, as it will continue to cook as it cools.
- Leave the brownie to cool completely before cutting into 9 squares.

774

MAKES 12

Chocolate and Salted Peanut Brownies

- Preheat the oven to 170°C (150° fan) / 325 F / gas 3 and oil and line a 20cm x 20cm / 8" x 8" square cake tin.
- Melt the chocolate, cocoa and butter together in a saucepan, then leave to cool a little.
- Whisk the sugar and eggs together with an electric whisk for 3 minutes or until very light and creamy.
- Pour in the chocolate mixture and sieve over the flour, then fold everything together with the peanuts until evenly mixed.
- Scrape into the tin and bake for 35 – 40 minutes or until the outside is set, but the centre is still quite soft, as it will continue to cook as it cools.
- Leave the brownie to cool completely before cutting into 12 rectangles and scattering over some more peanuts.

PREPARATION TIME: 25 MINUTES

COOKING TIME: 20 MINUTES

INGREDIENTS

110g / 4 oz dark chocolate, minimum 60% cocoa solids
85g / 3 oz / ¾ cup unsweetened cocoa powder, sifted
225g / 8 oz / 1 cup butter
450g /15 oz / 2 ½ cups light brown sugar
4 large eggs
110g / 4 oz / 1 cup self-raising flour
75g / 2 ½ oz / ½ cup salted peanuts

TO DECORATE
75g / 2 ½ oz / ½ cup salted peanuts

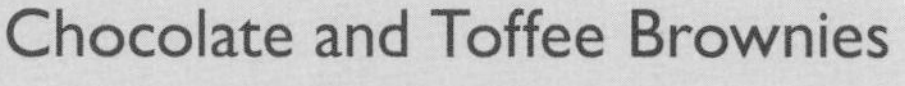

Chocolate and Toffee Brownies

775

Add 75g / 3oz chopped chewy toffee pieces to the brownie mixture.

776

MAKES 9

Gluten-free Chocolate and Pistachio Brownies

- Preheat the oven to 170°C (150° fan) / 325°F / gas 3 and oil and line a 20cm x 20cm / 8" x 8" square cake tin.
- Melt the chocolate, cocoa and butter together in a saucepan, then leave to cool a little.
- Whisk the sugar and eggs together with an electric whisk for 3 minutes or until very light and creamy.
- Pour in the chocolate mixture and sieve over the flour, then fold everything together with the peanuts until evenly mixed.
- Scrape into the tin and bake for 35 – 40 minutes or until the outside is set, but the centre is still quite soft, as it will continue to cook as it cools.
- Leave the brownie to cool completely before cutting into 12 rectangles and scattering over some more peanuts.

PREPARATION TIME: 25 MINUTES

COOKING TIME: 40 MINUTES

INGREDIENTS

110g / 4 oz / ½ cup dark chocolate, minimum 60% cocoa solids, chopped
85g / 3 oz / ¾ cup unsweetened cocoa powder, sifted
225g / 8 oz / 1 cup butter
450g /15 oz / 2 ½ cups light brown sugar
4 large eggs
110g / 4 oz / 1 cup ground pistachios

TO DECORATE
75g / 2 ½ oz / ½ cup pistachio nuts, chopped

Gluten-free Chocolate and Almond Brownies

777

Replace the ground pistachio nuts with ground almonds and sprinkle the brownies with 75g / 3 oz / ⅓ cup flaked (slivered) almonds after baking.

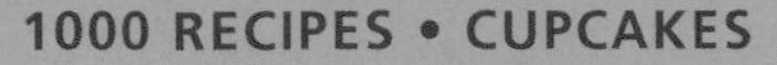

778

MAKES 9

Almond and Chocolate Brownies

PREPARATION TIME: 25 MINUTES

COOKING TIME: 20 MINUTES

INGREDIENTS

110 g / 4 oz / ½ cup dark chocolate, minimum 60% cocoa solids, chopped
85 g / 3 oz / ¾ cup unsweetened cocoa powder, sifted
225 g / 8 oz / 1 cup butter
450 g / 15 oz / 2 ½ cups light brown sugar
4 large eggs
110 g / 4 oz / 1 cup self-raising flour
75 g / 2 ½ oz / ½ cup flaked (slivered) almonds

TO DECORATE

75 g / 2 ½ oz / ½ cup flaked (slivered) almonds
Icing (confectioners') sugar to dust

- Preheat the oven to 170°C (150° fan) / 325 F / gas 3 and oil and line a 20cm x 20cm / 8" x 8" square cake tin.
- Melt the chocolate, cocoa and butter together in a saucepan, then leave to cool a little.
- Whisk the sugar and eggs together with an electric whisk for 3 minutes or until very light and creamy.
- Pour in the chocolate mixture and sieve over the flour, then fold everything together with the flaked almonds until evenly mixed.
- Scrape into the tin and bake for 35 – 40 minutes or until the outside is set, but the centre is still a quite soft, as it will continue to cook as it cools.
- Leave the brownie to cool completely before cutting into 9 squares and topping with more flaked almonds and a dusting of icing sugar.

Marzipan Brownies

779

For extra almond flavour, add 110g / 4oz / ½ cup of marzipan in cubes to the brownie mixture.

780

MAKES 24

Mini Chocolate Brownies

PREPARATION TIME: 25 MINUTES

COOKING TIME: 20 MINUTES

INGREDIENTS

110 g / 4 oz / ⅔ cup dark chocolate, minimum 60% cocoa solids, chopped
85 g / 3 oz / ¾ cup unsweetened cocoa powder, sifted
225 g / 8 oz / 1 cup butter
450 g / 15 oz / 2 ½ cups light brown sugar
4 large eggs
110 g / 4 oz / 1 cup self-raising flour

- Preheat the oven to 170°C (150° fan) / 325 F / gas 3 and line a 24-hole muffin tin with paper cases.
- Melt the chocolate, cocoa and butter together in a saucepan, then leave to cool a little.
- Whisk the sugar and eggs together with an electric whisk for 3 minutes or until very light and creamy.
- Pour in the chocolate mixture and sieve over the flour, then fold everything together until evenly mixed.
- Spoon into the muffin cases and bake for 15 – 20 minutes or until the outside is set, but the centre is still a quite soft, as they will continue to cook as they cool.

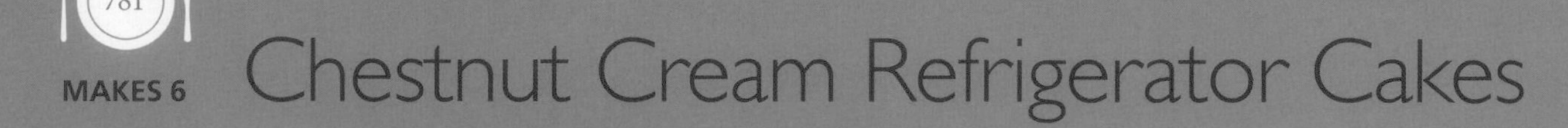

781

MAKES 6

Chestnut Cream Refrigerator Cakes

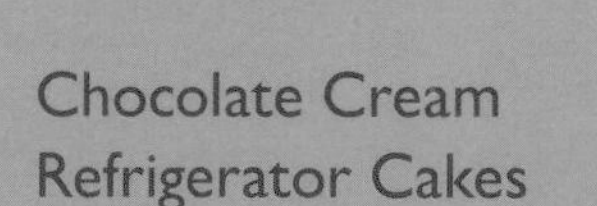

Chocolate Cream Refrigerator Cakes

782

Replace the chestnut puree with melted milk chocolate. Decorate with milk chocolate curls.

Orange Cream Refrigerator Cakes

783

Replace the chestnut puree in the chestnut cream with 1 tbsp grated orange zest. Decorate with candied peel.

PREPARATION TIME: 25 MINUTES
COOKING TIME : 15 MINUTES

INGREDIENTS

2 plain cakes
55 g / 2 oz / ¼ cup chestnut puree

FOR THE CHOCOLATE GANACHE
110 g / 4 oz / ½ cup dark chocolate, minimum 60% cocoa solids
110 ml / 4 fl. oz / ½ cup double (heavy) cream

FOR THE CHESTNUT CREAM
225 ml / 8 fl. oz / 1 cup double (heavy) cream
2 tbsp icing (confectioners') sugar
½ tsp vanilla extract
110 g / 4 oz / ½ cup chestnut puree
2 tbsp mixed nuts, finely chopped
Gold leaf

- Put the cakes in a food processor and process to fine crumbs.
- Stir in the chestnut puree and press the mixture into the bottom of 6 sundae glasses.
- Chop the chocolate and transfer to a mixing bowl.
- Heat the cream until it starts to simmer, then pour over the chopped chocolate and stir until the mixture has cooled and thickened.
- Spoon on top of the cake mixture and chill until firm.
- Whip the cream with the icing sugar and vanilla extract, then whisk in the chestnut puree.
- Spoon the chestnut cream on top of the chocolate ganache and top with chopped nuts and gold leaf.

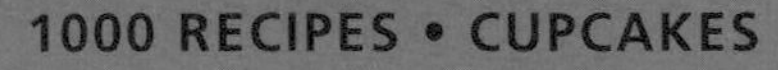

784

MAKES 9

Chocolate and Pecan Brownies

PREPARATION TIME: 25 MINUTES

COOKING TIME: 40 MINUTES

INGREDIENTS

110 g / 4 oz / ½ cup dark chocolate, minimum 60% cocoa solids, chopped
85 g / 3 oz / ¾ cup unsweetened cocoa powder, sifted
225 g / 8 oz / 1 cup butter
450 g / 15 oz / 2 ½ cups light brown sugar
4 large eggs
110 g / 4 oz / 1 cup self-raising flour
75 g / 2 ½ oz / ½ cup pecan nuts, chopped

TO DECORATE
18 pecan halves

- Preheat the oven to 170°C (150° fan) / 325 F / gas 3 and oil and line a 20cm x 20cm / 8" x 8" square cake tin.
- Melt the chocolate, cocoa and butter together in a saucepan, then leave to cool a little.
- Whisk the sugar and eggs together with an electric whisk for 3 minutes or until very light and creamy.
- Pour in the chocolate mixture and sieve over the flour, then fold everything together with the chopped pecans until evenly mixed.
- Scrape into the tin and bake for 35 – 40 minutes or until the outside is set, but the centre is still quite soft, as it will continue to cook as it cools.
- Leave the brownie to cool completely before cutting into 9 squares.
- Top each square with 2 pecan nuts.

Chocolate And Pistachio Brownies

785

Replace the pecan nuts with 75g / 3 oz / ⅓ cup of whole pistachio nuts and dust with unsweetened cocoa powder before serving.

786

MAKES 12

Peanut and Caramel Brownie Slices

PREPARATION TIME: 25 MINUTES

COOKING TIME: 40 MINUTES

INGREDIENTS

110 g / 4 oz milk chocolate
85 g / 3 oz / ¾ cup unsweetened cocoa powder, sifted
225 g / 8 oz / 1 cup butter
450 g / 15 oz / 2 ½ cups light brown sugar
4 large eggs
110 g / 4 oz / ½ cup self-raising flour
150 g / 5 oz / ⅔ cup peanuts, chopped

TO DECORATE
85 g / 3 oz / ½ cup butter
85 ml / 3 fl. oz / ⅓ cup double (heavy) cream
85 g / 3 oz / ¼ cup golden syrup
85 g / 3 oz / ½ cup dark brown sugar
110 g / 4 oz dark chocolate, minimum 60% cocoa solids
75 g / 2 ½ oz / ½ cup peanuts, roughly chopped

- Preheat the oven to 170°C (150° fan) / 325 F / gas 3 and oil and line a 20cm x 20cm / 8" x 8" square cake tin.
- Melt the chocolate, cocoa and butter together in a saucepan, then leave to cool a little.
- Whisk the sugar and eggs together for 3 minutes.
- Pour in the chocolate mixture and sieve over the flour, then fold everything together with the chopped peanuts until evenly mixed.
- Scrape into the tin and bake for 35 – 40 minutes or until the outside is set, but the centre is still quite soft, as it will continue to cook as it cools.
- Leave the brownie to cool completely in the tin.
- Put the butter, cream, golden syrup and brown sugar in a small saucepan and boil for 2 minutes, stirring to dissolve the sugar.
- Pour the caramel over the brownie and leave to set in the fridge until firm.
- Melt the chocolate in a microwave or bain marie and pour over the caramel layer.
- Scatter over the peanuts and cut into 12 slices.

787

MAKES 24

Almond and Orange Mini Cakes

Almond and Lemon Cakes

788

Replace the orange juice with lemon juice and the orange zest with lemon zest.

Iced Almond and Orange Mini Cakes

789

Decorate these little cakes with a drizzle of plain white icing: mix 200 g of icing sugar with just enough boiling water to make a thin icing.

PREPARATION TIME: 25 MINUTES

COOKING TIME: 20 MINUTES

INGREDIENTS

1 large egg
120 ml / 4 fl. oz / ½ cup sunflower oil
120 ml / 4 fl. oz / ½ cup milk
2 tbsp orange juice
375 g / 12 ½ oz / 2 ½ cups self-raising flour, sifted
1 tsp baking powder
200 g / 7 oz / ¾ cup caster (superfine) sugar
55 g / 2 oz / ½ cup ground almonds
1 tbsp orange zest, finely grated
75 g / 2 ½ oz / ½ cup flaked (slivered) almonds
icing sugar to dust

- Preheat the oven to 180°C (160° fan) / 350F / gas 4 and oil a 24-hole silicone mini muffin mould.
- Beat the egg in a jug with the oil, milk and orange juice until well mixed.
- Mix the flour, baking powder, sugar, ground almonds and orange zest in a bowl, then pour in the egg mixture and stir just enough to combine.
- Divide the mixture between the moulds and sprinkle with flaked almonds, then bake in the oven for 15 – 20 minutes.
- Test with a wooden toothpick, if it comes out clean, the cakes are done.
- Transfer the cakes to a wire rack and dust with icing sugar.

MAKES 12

Basil and Mozzarella Mini Loaf Cakes

Mozzarella and Tomato Loaf Cakes

791

Try marbling the muffin mixture with 2 tbsp of sun-dried tomato paste.

Mozzarella and Oregano Loaf Cakes

792

Replace the basil with fresh oregano.

PREPARATION TIME: 25 MINUTES

COOKING TIME: 20 MINUTES

INGREDIENTS

2 large eggs
120 ml / 4 fl. oz / ½ cup sunflower oil
180 ml / 6 fl. oz / ¾ cup Greek yogurt
110 g / 4 oz / 1 cup mozzarella, cubed
28 g / 1 oz / 1 cup basil leaves, shredded
225 g / 8 oz / 1 ½ cups plain (all purpose) flour
2 tsp baking powder
½ tsp bicarbonate of (baking) soda
½ tsp salt

- Preheat the oven to 180°C (160° fan) / 350 F / gas 4 and oil 12 mini loaf tins.
- Beat the egg in a jug with the oil, yogurt, cheese and basil until well mixed.
- Mix the flour, raising agents and salt in a bowl, then pour in the egg mixture and stir just enough to combine.
- Divide the mixture between the tins, then bake in the oven for 20 – 25 minutes.
- Test with a wooden toothpick, if it comes out clean, the cakes are done.
- Serve warm.

793

MAKES 12

Apricot, Date and Hazelnut Cakes

- Preheat the oven to 180°C (160° fan) / 350 F / gas 4 and oil a 12-hole silicone muffin tin.
- Beat the egg in a jug with the oil and milk until well mixed.
- Mix the flour, baking powder, sugar, apricots, dates and hazelnuts in a bowl, then pour in the egg mixture and stir just enough to combine.
- Divide the mixture between the moulds, then bake in the oven for 20 – 25 minutes.
- Test with a wooden toothpick, if it comes out clean, the cakes are done.
- Transfer the cakes to a wire rack and leave to cool completely.

PREPARATION TIME: 25 MINUTES

COOKING TIME: 25 MINUTES

INGREDIENTS

1 large egg
120 ml / 4 fl. oz / ½ cup sunflower oil
120 ml / 4 fl. oz / ½ cup milk
375 g / 12 ½ oz / 2 ½ cups self-raising flour, sifted
1 tsp baking powder
200 g / 7 oz / ¾ cup caster (superfine) sugar
75 g / 2 ½ oz / ½ cup dried apricots, chopped
75 g / 2 ½ oz / ½ cup dates, stoned and chopped
75 g / 2 ½ oz / ½ cup hazelnuts (cob nuts), chopped

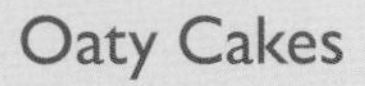

Oaty Cakes

794

Try adding 2 tbsp rolled oats to the mixture to boost the fibre content.

795

MAKES 12

Almond and Raspberry Jam Mini Cakes

- Preheat the oven to 190°C (170° fan) / 375 F / gas 5 and oil a 36-hole silicone mini cupcake mould.
- Combine the flour, baking powder, ground almonds, sugar, butter, eggs and almond essence in a bowl and whisk together for 2 minutes or until smooth.
- Divide half of the mixture between the moulds, then add a small spoonful of raspberry jam in the centre of each one.
- Top with the rest of the cake mixture then transfer the tin to the oven and bake for 10 – 15 minutes.
- Test with a wooden toothpick, if it comes out clean, the cakes are done.
- Transfer the cakes to a wire rack and leave to cool.

PREPARATION TIME: 20 MINUTES

COOKING TIME: 15 MINUTES

INGREDIENTS

55 g / 2 oz / ½ cup self-raising flour, sifted
2 tsp baking powder
55 g / 2 oz / ½ cup ground almonds
110 g / 4 oz / ½ cup caster (superfine) sugar
110 g / 4 oz / ½ cup butter, softened
2 large eggs
1 tsp almond essence
110 g / 4 oz / ½ cup raspberry jam (jelly)

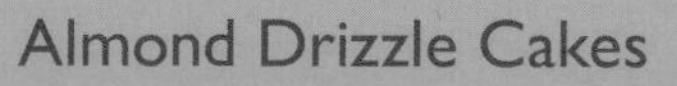

Almond Drizzle Cakes

796

Try making an almond drizzle to ice the cakes: mix 225g / 8 oz / 1 cup icing sugar with ½ tsp almond essence and just enough boiling water to make a runny glaze.

797

MAKES 12

Mango, Coconut and Lime Cakes

PREPARATION TIME: 35 MINUTES

COOKING TIME: 20 MINUTES

INGREDIENTS

110 g / 4 oz / ½ cup self-raising flour, sifted
110 g / 4 oz / ½ cup caster (superfine) sugar
110 g / 4 oz / ½ cup butter, softened
2 large eggs
2 tbsp mango puree
28 g / 1 oz / ⅛ cup desiccated coconut
1 lime, zest finely grated
150 g / 5 oz / 1 cup very ripe mango, finely chopped

TO DECORATE
2 tbsp desiccated coconut

- Preheat the oven to 190°C (170° fan) / 375 F / gas 5 and oil a 12-hole silicone cupcake mould.
- Combine the flour, sugar, butter, eggs, mango puree, coconut and lime zest in a bowl and whisk together for 2 minutes or until smooth.
- Fold in the chopped mango then divide the mixture between the moulds.
- Bake in the oven for 15 – 20 minutes.
- Test with a wooden toothpick, if it comes out clean, the cakes are done.
- Transfer the cakes to a wire rack and leave to cool then sprinkle with coconut.

Lime Drizzle Cakes

798

Try making a simple lime drizzle icing for the top of the cakes: sift 110g / 4oz / ½ cup icing (confectioners') sugar into a bowl and stir in just enough lime juice to make a runny icing.

799

MAKES 12

Pine Nut Cakes

PREPARATION TIME: 20 MINUTES

COOKING TIME: 20 MINUTES

INGREDIENTS

110 g / 4 oz / ½ cup self-raising flour, sifted
110 g / 4 oz / ½ cup caster (superfine) sugar
110 g / 4 oz / ½ cup butter, softened
2 large eggs
2 tbsp pine nuts
Icing (confectioners') sugar to dust

- Preheat the oven to 190°C (170° fan) / 375 F / gas 5 and oil 12 dariole moulds.
- Combine the flour, sugar, butter, eggs and pine nuts in a bowl and whisk together for 2 minutes or until smooth.
- Divide the mixture between the moulds and bake in the oven for 15 – 20 minutes.
- Test with a wooden toothpick, if it comes out clean, the cakes are done.
- Transfer the cakes to a wire rack and leave to cool before dusting with icing sugar.

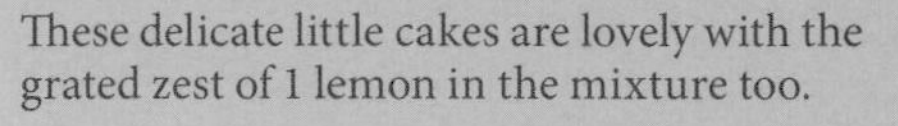

Pine Nut and Lemon Cakes

800

These delicate little cakes are lovely with the grated zest of 1 lemon in the mixture too.

801

MAKES 12

Almond and Chocolate Chip Loaf Cakes

PREPARATION TIME: 25 MINUTES

COOKING TIME: 25 MINUTES

INGREDIENTS

250 g / 9 oz / 1 ¾ cups self-raising flour
1 tsp bicarbonate of (baking) soda
200 g / 8 ½ oz / ½ cup golden syrup
125 g / 4 ½ oz / ½ cup butter
125 g / 4 ½ oz / ¾ cup light brown sugar
2 large eggs, beaten
240 ml / 8 fl. oz / 1 cup milk
1 tsp almond essence
75 g / 2 ½ oz / ½ cup dark chocolate chips
75 g / 2 ½ oz / ½ cup flaked (slivered) almonds

- Preheat the oven to 190°C (170° fan) / 375 F / gas 5 and line a 12-hole mini loaf cake tin with paper cases.
- Sieve the flour and bicarbonate of soda together into a bowl.
- Put the golden syrup, butter and brown sugar in a small saucepan and boil gently for 2 minutes, stirring to dissolve the sugar.
- Pour the butter and sugar mixture onto the flour with the eggs, milk and almond essence and fold it all together with the chocolate chips until smooth.
- Divide the mixture between the paper cases and sprinkle with the flaked almonds.
- Transfer the tin to the oven and bake for 20 – 25 minutes.
- Test with a wooden toothpick, if it comes out clean, the cakes are done.
- Transfer the cakes to a wire rack and leave to cool completely.

802

Spiced Almond Mini Loaf Cakes

Replace the chocolate chips with 1 tsp mixed spice, 1 tsp ground ginger and 1 tsp ground cinnamon.

803

Ginger and Chocolate Chip Mini Loaf Cakes

Replace the almond essence with 2 tsp ground ginger and replace the flaked almonds on the top of the cakes with 75g / 3oz / ⅓ cup chopped crystallised ginger.

818

MAKES 12

Ratatouille Cakes

PREPARATION TIME: 25 MINUTES

COOKING TIME: 20-25 MINUTES

INGREDIENTS

1 shallot, chopped
1 medium courgettes (zucchini), sliced
½ aubergine, chopped
1 yellow pepper, chopped
4 tbsp olive oil
1 clove of garlic, chopped
2 large eggs
120 ml / 4 fl. oz / ½ cup sunflower oil
180 ml / 6 fl. oz / ¾ cup Greek yoghurt
225 g / 8 oz / 1 ½ cups plain flour
2 tsp baking powder
½ tsp bicarbonate of (baking) soda
½ tsp salt

- Fry the shallot, courgette, aubergine and pepper in the olive oil for 10 minutes until softened.
- Add the garli°C and continue to cook, stirring occasionally for 2 minutes, then leave to cool.
- Preheat the oven to 180°°C (160° fan) / 350 F / gas 4 and oil a 12-hole silicone muffin tin.
- Beat the egg in a jug with the oil, yoghurt and fried vegetables until well mixed.
- Mix the flour, raising agents and salt in a bowl, then pour in the egg mixture and stir just enough to combine.
- Divide the mixture between the moulds, then bake in the oven for 20 – 25 minutes.
- Test with a wooden toothpick, if it comes out clean, the cakes are done.
- Serve warm.

Ratatouille and Goats Cheese Cakes

819

Add 100 g of cubed goats cheese and 2 tbsp fresh oregano leaves to the muffin mixture.

820

MAKES 12

Coconut and Chocolate Mini Loaf Cakes

PREPARATION TIME: 20 MINUTES

COOKING TIME: 20 MINUTES

INGREDIENTS

110 g / 4 oz / ½ cup self-raising flour, sifted
110 g / 4 oz / ½ cup caster (superfine) sugar
110 g / 4 oz / ½ cup butter, softened
2 large eggs
1 tsp vanilla extract
28 g / 1 oz / ⅛ cup desiccated coconut
150 g / 5 oz / 1 cup chocolate chips

- Preheat the oven to 190°C (170° fan) / 375 F / gas 5 and oil a 12-hole silicone mini loaf cake mould.
- Combine the flour, sugar, butter and eggs in a bowl and whisk together for 2 minutes or until smooth.
- Fold in the coconut and chocolate chips then divide the mixture between the moulds.
- Transfer the mould to the oven and bake for 15 – 20 minutes.
- Test with a wooden toothpick, if it comes out clean, the cakes are done.
- Transfer the cakes to a wire rack and leave to cool completely.

White Chocolate and Coconut Mini Loaf Cakes

821

Try covering the cakes in melted white chocolate and rolling them in desiccated coconut before leaving to set on a wire rack.

822

MAKES 12

Orange Mini Loaf Cakes

Marmalade-glazed Mini Loaf Cakes

823

For a simple but effective glaze, heat 4 tbsp marmalade in a small saucepan and spoon over the cakes when they come out of the oven.

PREPARATION TIME: 20 MINUTES

COOKING TIME: 20 MINUTES

INGREDIENTS

110 g / 4 oz / ½ cup self-raising flour, sifted
110 g / 4 oz / ½ cup caster (superfine) sugar
110 g / 4 oz / ½ cup butter, softened
2 large eggs
1 orange, zest finely grated

- Preheat the oven to 190°C (170° fan) / 375 F / gas 5 and oil a 12-hole silicone mini loaf cake mould.
- Combine the flour, sugar, butter, eggs and orange zest in a bowl and whisk together for 2 minutes or until smooth.
- Divide the mixture between the moulds then transfer the mould to the oven and bake for 15 – 20 minutes.
- Test with a wooden toothpick, if it comes out clean, the cakes are done.
- Transfer the cakes to a wire rack and leave to cool completely.

824

MAKES 12

Artichoke Heart Cakes

PREPARATION TIME: 25 MINUTES

COOKING TIME: 25 MINUTES

INGREDIENTS

2 large eggs
120 ml / 4 fl. oz / ½ cup sunflower oil
180 ml / 6 fl. oz / ¾ cup Greek yogurt
110 g / 4 oz / 1 cup Parmesan, grated
225 g / 8 oz / 1 ½ cups plain (all purpose) flour
2 tsp baking powder
½ tsp bicarbonate of (baking) soda
½ tsp salt
12 artichoke hearts in oil, drained

- Preheat the oven to 180°C (160° fan) / 350 F / gas 4 and oil a 12-hole silicone muffin tin.
- Beat the egg in a jug with the oil, yogurt and cheese until well mixed.
- Mix the flour, raising agents and salt in a bowl, then pour in the egg mixture and stir just enough to combine.
- Divide the mixture between the moulds and press an artichoke heart into the top of each, then bake in the oven for 20 – 25 minutes.
- Test with a wooden toothpick, if it comes out clean, the cakes are done.
- Serve warm.

Melted Brie Cakes

825

Try stirring 110g / 4 oz / ½ cupf sliced Brie into the muffin mixture for a melting centre.

826

MAKES 36

Clementine Mini Cakes

PREPARATION TIME: 25 MINUTES

COOKING TIME: 15 MINUTES

INGREDIENTS

110 g / 4 oz / 1 cup self-raising flour, sifted
110 g / 4 oz / ½ cup caster (superfine) sugar
110 g / 4 oz / ½ cup butter, softened
2 large eggs
36 clementine segments
110 g / 4 oz / ½ cup honey

- Preheat the oven to 190°C (170° fan) / 375 F / gas 5 and oil a 36-hole mini silicone cupcake mould.
- Combine the flour, sugar, butter and eggs in a bowl and whisk together for 2 minutes or until smooth.
- Divide half the mixture between the moulds and top with a clementine segment.
- Top with the rest of the cake mixture and bake for 10 – 15 minutes.
- Test with a wooden toothpick, if it comes out clean, the cakes are done.
- Drizzle with honey then transfer the cakes to a wire rack and leave to cool completely.

827

MAKES 12

Chocolate and Strawberry Jam Cakes

- Preheat the oven to 190°C (170° fan) / 375 F / gas 5 and oil a 12-hole heart-shaped silicone cupcake mould.
- Combine the flour, cocoa, sugar, butter and eggs in a bowl and whisk together for 2 minutes or until smooth.
- Divide half of the mixture between the moulds, then add 1 tsp of strawberry jam in the centre of each one.
- Top with the rest of the cake mixture then transfer the tin to the oven and bake for 15 – 20 minutes.
- Test with a wooden toothpick, if it comes out clean, the cakes are done.
- Transfer the cakes to a wire rack and leave to cool.

PREPARATION TIME: 25 MINUTES

COOKING TIME: 20 MINUTES

INGREDIENTS

110 g / 4 oz / ½ cup self-raising flour, sifted
28 g / 1 oz / ¼ cup unsweetened cocoa powder, sifted
110 g / 4 oz / ½ cup caster (superfine) sugar
110 g / 4 oz / ½ cup butter, softened
2 large eggs
110 g / 4 oz / ½ cup strawberry jam (jelly)

828

White Chocolate and Strawberry Jam Cakes

Try adding 75g / 3oz / ⅓ cup white chocolate chips to the cake mixture.

829

MAKES 6

Chocolate and Fennel Fondants

- Oil 6 mini pudding basins and dust the insides with cocoa.
- Melt the chocolate, butter and sugar together in a saucepan, stirring to dissolve the sugar.
- Leave to cool a little then beat in the eggs and egg yolks and fold in the flour and fennel.
- Divide the mixture between the pudding basins, then chill them for 30 minutes.
- Preheat the oven to 180°C (160° fan) / 350 F / gas 4 and put a baking tray in to heat.
- Transfer the fondants to the heated baking tray and bake in the oven for 8 minutes.
- Leave the fondants to cool for 2 minutes, then turn them out of their moulds and serve immediately.

PREPARATION TIME 50 MINUTES

COOKING TIME 8 MINUTES

INGREDIENTS

2 tbsp unsweetened cocoa powder
150 g / 6 oz / ⅔ cup dark chocolate, minimum 60% cocoa solids, chopped
150 g / 6 oz / ⅔ cup butter, chopped
85 g / 3 oz / ⅓ cup caster (superfine) sugar
3 large eggs
3 egg yolks
1 tbsp plain (all purpose) flour
2 tsp ground fennel seeds

830

Chocolate and Star Anise Fondants

For a stronger aniseed flavour, use 2 tsp of ground star anise instead of the fennel.

831

MAKES 36

Mini Clementine Babas

Mini Lime Babas

832

Replace the clementine zest in the baba dough with lime zest and replace the clementine juice in the soaking syrup with lime juice.

PREPARATION TIME:
1 HOUR 35 MINUTES

COOKING TIME: 5 MINUTES

INGREDIENTS

150 g / 5 oz / ⅔ cup plain (all purpose) flour
2 tsp dried easy-blend yeast
1 tbsp caster (superfine) sugar
½ tsp salt
2 clementines, zest finely grated
3 large eggs, lightly beaten
75 g / 2 ½ oz / ⅓ cup butter, softened

FOR THE SOAKING SYRUP
450 g / 1 lb / 2 cups caster (superfine) sugar
4 clementines, juiced
240 ml / 8 fl. oz / 1 cup rum

- Oil a 36-hole silicone mini cupcake mould.
- Combine the flour, yeast, sugar, salt and clementine zest in a bowl and gradually whisk in half of the beaten egg with an electric whisk.
- Continuing to whisk, incorporate half of the butter, followed by the rest of the egg.
- Beat the remaining butter in with a wooden spoon, then divide the mixture between the moulds.
- Leave the babas to prove in a warm, draught-free place for 1 hour or until they have doubled in size.
- Preheat the oven to 200°C (180° fan) / 400 F / gas 6.
- Bake the babas for 5 minutes or until golden brown and cooked through, then turn them out onto a wire rack.
- Put the sugar in a saucepan with the clementine juice and 675ml / 1 ¼ pints water and stir over a medium heat to dissolve the sugar.
- Boil the sugar water for 5 minutes or until it starts to turn syrupy, then stir in the rum.
- Transfer the babas to a mixing bowl, pour over the syrup and leave to soak until cold, turning occasionally.

833

MAKES 12

Carambar Mini Loaf Cakes

Caramel Cakes

834

Try chopping 75g / 3oz of Carambars and adding them to the cake mixture before baking.

PREPARATION TIME: 20 MINUTES

COOKING TIME: 20 MINUTES

INGREDIENTS

110 g / 4 oz / ½ cup self-raising flour, sifted
110 g / 4 oz / ½ cup caster (superfine) sugar
1 tbsp cocoa powder
110 g / 4 oz / ½ cup butter, softened
2 large eggs

TO DECORATE

55 g / 2 oz milk chocolate, chopped
12 Carambars
Hundreds and thousands

- Preheat the oven to 190°C (170° fan) / 375 F / gas 5 and oil a 12-hole silicone mini loaf cake mould.
- Combine the flour, sugar, cocoa, butter and eggs in a bowl and whisk together for 2 minutes or until smooth.
- Divide the mixture between the moulds, then transfer the mould to the oven and bake for 15 – 20 minutes.
- Test with a wooden toothpick, if it comes out clean, the cakes are done.
- Transfer the cakes to a wire rack and leave to cool completely.
- Melt the chocolate in a microwave or bain marie.
- Dip one side of the Carambars in the chocolate then dip in the hundreds and thousands and stick to the top of each cake with a little more melted chocolate.

835

MAKES 12

Spiced Raisin Cakes

PREPARATION TIME: 25 MINUTES

COOKING TIME: 25 MINUTES

INGREDIENTS

1 large egg
120 ml / 4 fl. oz / ½ cup sunflower oil
120 ml / 4 fl. oz / ½ cup milk
375 g / 12 ½ oz / 2 ½ cups self-raising flour, sifted
1 tsp baking powder
200 g / 7 oz / ¾ cup caster (superfine) sugar
75 g / 2 ½ oz / ½ cup raisins
1 tsp ground cinnamon
1 tsp ground ginger
½ tsp ground cloves
½ tsp freshly grated nutmeg
Icing (confectioners') sugar to dust

- Preheat the oven to 180°C (160° fan) / 350 F / gas 4 and oil a 12 disposable pudding moulds.
- Beat the egg in a jug with the oil and milk until well mixed.
- Mix the flour, baking powder, sugar, raisins and spices in a bowl, then pour in the egg mixture and stir just enough to combine.
- Divide the mixture between the paper cases, then bake in the oven for 20 – 25 minutes.
- Test with a wooden toothpick, if it comes out clean, the cakes are done.
- Transfer to a wire rack to cool before dusting with icing sugar.

Spiced Raisin and Apple Cakes

836

Try adding 5 tbsp of grated apple to the wet ingredients for extra moist cakes.

837

MAKES 24

Mini Chocolate Tarts

PREPARATION TIME: 45 MINUTES

COOKING TIME: 15 MINUTES

INGREDIENTS

225 g / 8 oz / 1 ½ cups plain (all purpose) flour
110 g / 4 oz / ½ cup butter, cubed and chilled

TO DECORATE
225 g / 8 oz / 1 cup dark chocolate, minimum 60% cocoa solids
225 ml / 8 fl. oz / 1 cup double (heavy) cream
Edible gold leaf

- Preheat the oven to 200°C (180° fan) / 400 F / gas 6.
- Sieve the flour into a mixing bowl then rub in the butter until the mixture resembles fine breadcrumbs.
- Stir in just enough cold water to bring the pastry together into a pliable dough.
- Roll out the pastry on a floured surface and cut out 24 circles then use them to line a 24 mini tartlet tins.
- Line the tins with film, then fill with baking beans and bake for 10 minutes. Remove the film and beans and return the cases to the oven for 2 minutes or until cooked through. Leave to cool.
- Chop the chocolate and transfer to a mixing bowl.
- Heat the cream until it starts to simmer, then pour over the chopped chocolate and stir until smooth.
- Spoon into the pastry cases and leave to cool and set.
- Use a dry paint brush to carefully apply the gold leaf.

White Chocolate Tarts

Replace the dark chocolate with white chocolate and finish with white chocolate curls and a sprinkling of desiccated coconut.

839

MAKES 12

Lemon Marmalade Cakes

Marmalade Cakes

840

Try this recipe with orange or lime marmalade, but remember to buy thick cut.

PREPARATION TIME: 15 MINUTES

COOKING TIME: 20 MINUTES

INGREDIENTS

110 g / 4 oz / 1 cup self-raising flour, sifted
110 g / 4 oz / ½ cup caster (superfine) sugar
110 g / 4 oz / ½ cup butter, softened
2 large eggs
1 lemon, zest finely grated

TO DECORATE
110 g / 4 oz / ½ cup thick cut lemon marmalade

- Preheat the oven to 190°C (170° fan) / 375 F / gas 5 and line a 12-hole cupcake tin with paper cases.
- Combine the flour, sugar, butter, eggs and lemon zest in a bowl and whisk together for 2 minutes or until smooth.
- Divide the mixture between the paper cases, then transfer the tin to the oven and bake for 15 – 20 minutes.
- Test with a wooden toothpick, if it comes out clean, the cakes are done.
- Top each cake with a spoonful of lemon marmalade and return to the oven for 2 minutes. The heat of the oven will melt the jam into a glaze and leave the lemon zest as a garnish.
- Transfer the cakes to a wire rack and leave to cool completely.

841

MAKES 12

Crab and Coriander Mini Loaf Cakes

PREPARATION TIME: 25 MINUTES

COOKING TIME: 20 MINUTES

INGREDIENTS

2 large eggs
120 ml / 4 fl. oz / ½ cup sunflower oil
180 ml / 6 fl. oz / ¾ cup Greek yogurt
110 g / 4 oz / 1 cup fresh crab meat
1 shallot, finely chopped
1 green chilli, finely chopped
2 tbsp fresh coriander (cilantro), chopped
225 g / 8 oz / 1 ½ cups plain (all purpose) flour
2 tsp baking powder
½ tsp bicarbonate of (baking) soda
½ tsp salt

- Preheat the oven to 180°C (160° fan) / 350 F / gas 4 and line 12 mini loaf tins with paper cases.
- Beat the egg in a jug with the oil, yogurt, cheese, crab, shallots, chilli and coriander until well mixed.
- Mix the flour, raising agents and salt in a bowl, then pour in the egg mixture and stir just enough to combine.
- Divide the mixture between the tins, then bake in the oven for 20 – 25 minutes.
- Test with a wooden toothpick, if it comes out clean, the cakes are done.
- Serve warm.

Crab and Coriander Mini Loaf Cakes with Guacamole

842

Try splitting open the warm loaf cakes and filling with a dollop of guacamole.

843

MAKES 24

Carrot, Saffron and Sultana Mini Cakes

PREPARATION TIME: 25 MINUTES

COOKING TIME: 20 MINUTES

INGREDIENTS

120 ml / 4 fl. oz / ½ cup milk
1 pinch of saffron
1 large egg
120 ml / 4 fl. oz / ½ cup sunflower oil
375 g / 12 ½ oz / 2 ½ cups self-raising flour, sifted
1 tsp baking powder
200 g / 7 oz / ¾ cup caster (superfine) sugar
150 g / 5 oz / 1 cup carrot, coarsely grated
75 g / 2 ½ oz / ½ cup sultanas

- Preheat the oven to 180°C (160° fan) / 350 F / gas 4 and oil a 24-hole silicone mini muffin mould.
- Heat the milk until it starts to simmer, then take off the heat, add the saffron and leave to infuse for 20 minutes.
- Beat the egg in a jug with the oil and saffron milk until well mixed.
- Mix the flour, baking powder, sugar, carrot and sultanas in a bowl, then pour in the egg mixture and stir just enough to combine.
- Divide the mixture between the moulds, then bake in the oven for 15 – 20 minutes.
- Test with a wooden toothpick, if it comes out clean, the cakes are done.
- Transfer the cakes to a wire rack and leave to cool completely.

Spiced Mini Cakes

844

Try adding ½ tsp freshly grated nutmeg to add some warming spice.

845

MAKES 12

Cherry Brandy Cakes

- Preheat the oven to 190°°C (170° fan) / 375 F / gas 5 and oil 12 mini pudding basins.
- Combine the flour, ground almonds, sugar, butter, eggs and almond essence in a bowl and whisk together for 2 minutes or until smooth.
- Divide the mixture between the basins and top with the cherries.
- Sit the pudding basins on a baking tray and bake in the oven for 15 – 20 minutes.
- Test with a wooden toothpick, if it comes out clean, the cakes are done.
- Spoon over the cherry brandy and leave to cool.

PREPARATION TIME: 20 MINUTES

COOKING TIME: 15-20 MINUTES

INGREDIENTS

55 g / 2 oz / ½ cup self-raising flour, sifted
55 g / 2 oz / ½ cup ground almonds
110 g / 4 oz / ½ cup caster (superfine) sugar
110 g / 4 oz / ½ cup butter, softened
2 large eggs
1 tsp almond essence
150 g / 5 oz / 1 cup cherries in brandy, drained
60 ml / 2 fl. oz / ¼ cup cherry brandy

Apricot Brandy Cakes

846

Replace the cherries with fresh apricot halves and spoon over apricot brandy when the cakes come out of the oven.

847

MAKES 12

Mini Fruit Cakes

- Oil 6 ramekin dishes and dust the insides with icing sugar.
- Melt the chocolate, butter and sugar together in a saucepan, stirring to dissolve the sugar.
- Leave to cool a little then beat in the eggs and egg yolks and fold in the flour and prunes.
- Divide the mixture between the pudding basins, then chill them for 30 minutes.
- Preheat the oven to 180°C (160° fan) / 350 F / gas 4 and put a baking tray in to heat.
- Transfer the fondants to the heated baking tray and bake in the oven for 8 minutes.
- Serve the fondants immediately.

PREPARATION TIME: 30 MINUTES

COOKING TIME: 8 MINUTES

INGREDIENTS

2 tbsp icing (confectioners') sugar
150g / 6 oz white chocolate, chopped
150g / 6 oz / 2/3 cup butter, chopped
85g / 3 oz / 1/3 cup caster (superfine) sugar
3 large eggs
3 egg yolks
1 tbsp plain (all purpose) flour
75g / 2 ½ oz / ½ cup prunes, stoned and chopped

848

MAKES 6

Milk Chocolate Fondants

White Chocolate and Malt Fondants

849

Replace the milk chocolate with white chocolate and the cocoa powder for powdered malt.

PREPARATION TIME: 50 MINUTES

COOKING TIME: 8 MINUTES

INGREDIENTS

2 tbsp unsweetened cocoa powder
150 g / 6 oz milk chocolate, chopped
150 g / 6 oz / ⅔ cup butter, chopped
85 g / 3 oz / ⅓ cup caster (superfine) sugar
3 large eggs
3 egg yolks
1 tbsp plain (all purpose) flour

- Oil 6 mini pudding basins and dust the insides with cocoa.
- Melt the chocolate, butter and sugar together in a saucepan, stirring to dissolve the sugar.
- Leave to cool a little then beat in the eggs and egg yolks and fold in the flour.
- Divide the mixture between the pudding basins, then chill them for 30 minutes.
- Preheat the oven to 180°C (160° fan) / 350 F / gas 4 and put a baking tray in to heat.
- Transfer the fondants to the heated baking tray and bake in the oven for 8 minutes.
- Leave the fondants to cool for 2 minutes, then turn them out of their moulds and serve immediately.

850

MAKES 6

Tuile Cups with Bananas

Tuile Cups with Fruits

851

Replace the bananas with mixed summer berries and top with plain whipped cream.

Tuile Cups with Raisins

852

Replace the bananas with raisins and top with plain whipped cream.

PREPARATION TIME:
1 HOUR 15 MINUTES

COOKING TIME: 8 – 10 MINUTES

INGREDIENTS

55 g / 2 oz / ½ cup plain (all-purpose) flour
55 g / 2 oz / ¼ cup caster (superfine) sugar
2 large egg whites
55 g / 2 oz / ¼ cup butter, melted

TO DECORATE
225 ml / 8 fl. oz / 1 cup double (heavy) cream
6 bananas, chopped
2 tbsp hazelnuts, chopped

- Beat together the flour, sugar and egg whites until smooth, then beat in the melted butter.
- Refrigerate for 30 minutes.
- Preheat the oven to 180°°C (160° fan) / 350 F / gas 4 and oil a large baking tray.
- Spoon teaspoonfuls of the mixture onto the baking tray and spread out with the back of the spoon to make 15 cm / 6" circles.
- Bake for 8 – 10 minutes.
- As soon as the biscuits come out of the oven, lift them off the baking tray with a palette knife and mould them around a jam jar.
- When the biscuits are cool and crisp, remove from the jar.
- Whip the cream until thick and spoon into a piping bag fitted with a large star nozzle.
- Fill the tuile cups with chopped banana, then pipe a big swirl of cream on top and sprinkle with nuts.

853

MAKES 12

Caramel Cream Brownies

PREPARATION TIME: 25 MINUTES

COOKING TIME: 40 MINUTES

INGREDIENTS

110 g / 4 oz / ½ milk chocolate, chopped
85 g / 3 oz / ¾ cup unsweetened cocoa powder, sifted
225 g / 8 oz / 1 cup butter
450 g / 15 oz / 2 ½ cups light brown sugar
4 large eggs
110 g / 4 oz / 1 cup self-raising flour

TO DECORATE
85 g / 3 oz / ½ cup butter
85 g / 3 oz / ¼ cup golden syrup
85 g / 3 oz / ½ cup dark brown sugar
225 ml / 8 fl. oz / 1 cup double (heavy) cream

- Preheat the oven to 170°C (150° fan) / 325 F / gas 3 and oil a 12-hole silicone cupcake mould.
- Melt the chocolate, cocoa and butter together in a saucepan, then leave to cool a little.
- Whisk the sugar and eggs together with an electric whisk for 3 minutes or until very light and creamy.
- Pour in the chocolate mixture and sieve over the flour, then fold everything together until evenly mixed.
- Divide the mixture between the moulds and bake for 35 – 40 minutes or until the outside is set, but the centres are still quite soft, as they will continue to cook as they cool.
- Put the butter, golden syrup and brown sugar in a small saucepan and boil for 2 minutes, stirring to dissolve the sugar.
- Leave to cool completely.
- Whip the cream until thick, then fold in the cooled caramel mixture.
- Spoon into a piping bag fitted with a large star nozzle and pipe a generous swirl on top of each brownie.

854

MAKES 12

Rosemary and Sultana Cakes

PREPARATION TIME: 25 MINUTES

COOKING TIME: 25 MINUTES

INGREDIENTS

1 large egg
120ml / 4 fl oz / ½ cup sunflower oil
120ml / 4 fl oz / ½ cup milk
375g / 12 ½ oz / 2 ½ cups self-raising flour, sifted
1 tsp baking powder
200g / 7 oz / ¾ cup caster (superfine) sugar
2 tsp fresh rosemary, chopped
75g / 2 ½ oz / ½ cup sultanas

TO DECORATE
12 golden sultanas
12 rosemary leaves

- Preheat the oven to 180C (160C fan) / 350F / gas 4 and oil a 12-hole silicone muffin tin.
- Beat the egg in a jug with the oil and milk until well mixed.
- Mix the flour, baking powder, sugar, rosemary and sultanas in a bowl, then pour in the egg mixture and stir just enough to combine.
- Divide the mixture between the moulds, then bake in the oven for 20 – 25 minutes.
- Test with a wooden toothpick, if it comes out clean, the cakes are done.
- Transfer the cakes to a wire rack and leave to cool completely.
- Top each cake with a sultana and a rosemary leaf.

Apricot and Lemon Thyme Cakes

Replace the sultanas with chopped dried apricots and replace the chopped rosemary with fresh lemon thyme leaves.

MAKES 24

Wholemeal Nutmeg and Orange Mini Cakes

PREPARATION TIME: 25 MINUTES

COOKING TIME: 15-20 MINUTES

INGREDIENTS

1 large egg
120 ml / 4 fl. oz / ½ cup sunflower oil
120 ml / 4 fl. oz / ½ cup milk
375 g / 12 ½ oz / 2 ½ cups wholemeal flour
2 tsp baking powder
200 g / 7 oz / ¾ cup caster (superfine) sugar
1 tbsp orange zest, finely grated
1 tsp freshly grated nutmeg

- Preheat the oven to 180°°C (160° fan) / 350 F / gas 4 and oil a 24-hole silicone mini muffin mould.
- Beat the egg in a jug with the oil and milk until well mixed.
- Mix the flour, baking powder, sugar, orange zest and nutmeg in a bowl, then pour in the egg mixture and stir just enough to combine.
- Divide the mixture between the moulds then bake in the oven for 15 – 20 minutes.
- Test with a wooden toothpick, if it comes out clean, the cakes are done.
- Transfer the cakes to a wire rack and leave to cool.

857

MAKES 24

Candied Peel Mini Cakes

- Preheat the oven to 180°C (160° fan) / 350 F / gas 4 and oil a 24 mini brioche moulds.
- Beat the egg in a jug with the oil and milk until well mixed.
- Mix the flour, baking powder, sugar, ground almonds and candied peel in a bowl, then pour in the egg mixture and stir just enough to combine.
- Divide the mixture between the moulds and bake in the oven for 15 – 20 minutes.
- Test with a wooden toothpick, if it comes out clean, the cakes are done.
- Transfer the cakes to a wire rack to cool.

PREPARATION TIME: 25 MINUTES

COOKING TIME: 20 MINUTES

INGREDIENTS

1 large egg
120 ml / 4 fl. oz / ½ cup sunflower oil
120 ml / 4 fl. oz / ½ cup milk
375 g / 12 ½ oz / 2 ½ cups self-raising flour, sifted
1 tsp baking powder
200 g / 7 oz / ¾ cup caster (superfine) sugar
55 g / 2 oz / ½ cup ground almonds
75 g / 2 ½ oz / ½ cup mixed candied peel, chopped

858

MAKES 12

Chocolate and Walnut Cakes

- Preheat the oven to 180°C (160° fan) / 350 F / gas 4 and oil a 12-hole silicone muffin mould.
- Beat the egg in a jug with the oil and milk until well mixed.
- Mix the flour, baking powder, cocoa and sugar in a bowl, then pour in the egg mixture, chopped chocolate and walnuts and stir just enough to combine.
- Divide the mixture between the paper cases, then bake in the oven for 20 – 25 minutes.
- Test with a wooden toothpick, if it comes out clean, the cakes are done.
- Transfer the cakes to a wire rack and leave to cool.

PREPARATION TIME: 25 MINUTES

COOKING TIME: 25 MINUTES

INGREDIENTS

1 large egg
120 ml / 4 fl. oz / ½ cup sunflower oil
120 ml / 4 fl. oz / ½ cup milk
375 g / 12 ½ oz / 2 ½ cups self-raising flour, sifted
1 tsp baking powder
55 g / 2 oz / ½ cup unsweetened cocoa powder, sifted
200 g / 7 oz / ¾ cup caster (superfine) sugar
110 g / 4 oz / ½ cup dark chocolate, minimum 60% cocoa solids, chopped
75 g / 2 ½ oz / ½ cup walnut halves

859

MAKES 24

Mini Milk Chocolate Fondants

- Oil a 24-hole silicone mini muffin mould and dust the insides with cocoa. Melt the chocolate, butter and sugar together in a saucepan, stirring to dissolve the sugar.
- Leave to cool a little then beat in the eggs and egg yolks and fold in the flour.
- Divide the mixture between the moulds, then chill for 30 minutes.
- Preheat the oven to 180°C (160° fan) / 350 F / gas 4 and put a baking tray in to heat.
- Transfer the fondants to the heated baking tray and bake in the oven for 4 minutes.
- Leave the fondants to cool for 30 seconds, then turn them out of their moulds and serve immediately., if it comes out clean, the cakes are done.
- Transfer the cakes to a wire rack and leave to cool.

PREPARATION TIME: 50 MINUTES

COOKING TIME: 4 MINUTES

INGREDIENTS

2 tbsp unsweetened cocoa powder
150 g / 6 oz milk chocolate, chopped
150 g / 6 oz / ⅔ cup butter, chopped
85 g / 3 oz / ⅓ cup caster (superfine) sugar
3 large eggs
3 egg yolks
1 tbsp plain (all purpose) flour

860

MAKES 12

Mini Banana Frangipane Tarts

- Sieve the flour into a mixing bowl then rub in the butter until the mixture resembles fine breadcrumbs.
- Stir in just enough cold water to bring the pastry together into a pliable dough.
- Roll out the pastry on a floured surface and cut out 24 circles then use them to line a 24 mini tartlet tins and crimp around the edges.
- Leave the pastry to chill the fridge for 30 minutes.
- Preheat the oven to 200°°C (180° fan) / 400 F / gas 6.
- To make the frangipane, combine the ground almonds, sugar, butter, egg and almond essence in a bowl and whisk together for 2 minutes or until smooth.
- Fill the pastry cases with the frangipane mixture and top each one with a slice of banana.
- Bake for 15 – 20 minutes then transfer to a wire rack and leave to cool.

PREPARATION TIME: 2 HOURS

COOKING TIME:
12 – 15 MINUTES

INGREDIENTS

225 g / 8 oz / 1 ½ cups plain (all-purpose) flour
110 g / 4 oz / ½ cup butter, cubed and chilled

FOR THE FRANGIPANE
55 g / 2 oz / ½ cup ground almonds
55 g / 2 oz / ¼ cup caster (superfine) sugar
55 g / 2 oz / ¼ cup butter, softened
1 large egg
1 tsp almond essence
2 bananas, sliced

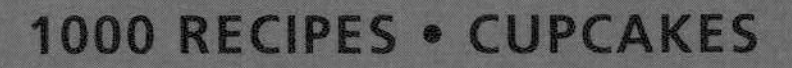

861

MAKES 12

Lemon and Almond Cakes

PREPARATION TIME: 20 MINUTES

COOKING TIME: 20 MINUTES

INGREDIENTS

55 g / 2 oz / ½ cup self-raising flour, sifted
2 tsp baking powder
55 g / 2 oz / ½ cup ground almonds
110 g / 4 oz / ½ cup caster (superfine) sugar
110 g / 4 oz / ½ cup butter, softened
2 large eggs
1 lemon, finely grated zest

TO DECORATE
12 pieces of candied lemon peel

- Preheat the oven to 190°C (170° fan) / 375 F / gas 5 and oil a 12-hole silicone cupcake mould.
- Combine the flour, baking powder, ground almonds, sugar, butter, eggs and lemon zest in a bowl and whisk together for 2 minutes or until smooth.
- Divide the mixture between the moulds and bake for 15 – 20 minutes.
- Test with a wooden toothpick, if it comes out clean, the cakes are done.
- Turn out the cakes onto a wire rack and leave to cool then decorate with a strip of candied lemon peel.

Grapefruit Cakes

862

These cakes work really well with grapefruit zest in the cake mixture and a strip of candied grapefruit peel.

863

MAKES 12

Pistachio Mini Cakes

PREPARATION TIME: 25 MINUTES

COOKING TIME: 15 MINUTES

INGREDIENTS

55 g / 2 oz / ¼ cup self-raising flour, sifted
2 tsp baking powder
55 g / 2 oz / ¼ cup ground pistachios
110 g / 4 oz / ½ cup caster (superfine) sugar
110 g / 4 oz / ½ cup butter, softened
2 large eggs
1 tsp almond essence

- Preheat the oven to 190°C (170° fan) / 375 F / gas 5 and oil a 36-hole silicone mini cupcake mould.
- Combine the flour, baking powder, ground pistachios, sugar, butter, eggs and almond essence in a bowl and whisk together for 2 minutes or until smooth.
- Divide the mixture between the moulds, then bake in the oven for 10 – 15 minutes.
- Test with a wooden toothpick, if it comes out clean, the cakes are done.
- Transfer the cakes to a wire rack and leave to cool.

Pistachio Mini Sandwiches

864

Try splitting these cakes in half horizontally before sandwiching together with cherry jam (jelly) and whipped cream.

MAKES 9

Chocolate and Marshmallow Brownies

Marshmallow Brownies

866

Try folding 110g / 4oz / ½ cup of untoasted mini marshmallows into the brownie mixture as well for extra marshmallow flavour.

PREPARATION TIME: 25 MINUTES

COOKING TIME: 40 MINUTES

INGREDIENTS

110 g / 4 oz / ½ cup marshmallows
110 g / 4 oz / ½ cup dark chocolate, minimum 60% cocoa solids, chopped
85 g / 3 oz / ¾ cup unsweetened cocoa powder, sifted
225 g / 8 oz / 1 cup butter
450 g / 15 oz / 2 ½ cups light brown sugar
4 large eggs
110 g / 4 oz / 1 cup self-raising flour

TO DECORATE
110 g / 4 oz / ½ cup marshmallows

- Preheat the oven to 170°C (150° fan) / 325 F / gas 3 and oil and line a 20cm x 20cm / 8" x 8" square cake tin.
- Spread the marshmallows out on a baking tray and bake in the oven for 4 – 5 minutes or until gooey and golden brown.
- Melt the chocolate, cocoa and butter together in a saucepan, then stir in the melted marshmallows and leave to cool a little.
- Whisk the sugar and eggs together with an electric whisk for 3 minutes or until very light and creamy.
- Pour in the chocolate mixture and sieve over the flour, then fold everything together until evenly mixed.
- Scrape into the tin and bake for 35 – 40 minutes or until the outside is set, but the centre is still quite soft, as it will continue to cook as it cools.
- Leave the brownie to cool completely before cutting into 9 squares.
- To decorate, divide the remaining marshmallows between the brownies and toast the tops briefly under a hot grill or with a cooks' blow torch.

867

MAKES 24

Apple and Date Mini Cakes

PREPARATION TIME: 25 MINUTES

COOKING TIME: 15 MINUTES

INGREDIENTS

1 large egg
120 ml / 4 fl. oz / ½ cup sunflower oil
120 ml / 4 fl. oz / ½ cup milk
375 g / 12 ½ oz / 2 ½ cups self-raising flour, sifted
1 tsp baking powder
200 g / 7 oz / ¾ cup caster (superfine) sugar
150 g / 5 oz / 1 cup apple, cored, quartered and sliced
75 g / 2 ½ oz / ½ cup dates, stoned and chopped

- Preheat the oven to 180°C (160° fan) / 350F / gas 4 and oil a 24-hole silicone mini muffin mould.
- Beat the egg in a jug with the oil and milk until well mixed.
- Mix the flour, baking powder, sugar, apple and dates in a bowl, then pour in the egg mixture and stir just enough to combine.
- Divide the mixture between the paper cases, then bake in the oven for 15 – 20 minutes.
- Test with a wooden toothpick, if it comes out clean, the cakes are done.
- Transfer the cakes to a wire rack and leave to cool completely.

868

MAKES 36

Spiced Carrot Mini Cakes

PREPARATION TIME: 35 MINUTES

COOKING TIME: 20 MINUTES

INGREDIENTS

175 g / 6 oz / 1 cup soft brown sugar
2 large eggs
150 ml / 5 fl. oz / ¾ cup sunflower oil
175 g / 6 oz / 1 ¼ cups wholemeal flour
3 tsp baking powder
1 tsp ground cinnamon
1 tsp mixed spice
½ tsp freshly grated nutmeg
200 g / 7 oz carrots, washed and coarsely grated

- Preheat the oven to 190°C (170° fan) / 375 F / gas 5 and oil a 36-hole silicone mini cupcake mould.
- Whisk the sugar, eggs and oil together for 3 minutes until thick.
- Fold in the flour, baking powder and spices, followed by the carrots.
- Divide the mixture between the moulds, then bake in the oven for 20 - 25 minutes.
- Test with a wooden toothpick, if it comes out clean, the cakes are done.
- Transfer the cakes to a wire rack and leave to cool completely.

Citrus Carrot Mini Cakes

869

To add a touch of citrus, include the finely grated zest of 1 orange and 1 lemon when you add the carrots.

MAKES 12

Courgette, Feta and Herb Mini Loaf Cakes

PREPARATION TIME: 25 MINUTES

COOKING TIME: 20 MINUTES

INGREDIENTS

2 large eggs
120 ml / 4 fl. oz / ½ cup sunflower oil
180 ml / 6 fl. oz / ¾ cup Greek yogurt
110 g / 4 oz / 1 cup feta cheese, cubed
2 medium courgettes (zucchini), coarsely grated
2 tbsp fresh mixed herbs, chopped
225 g / 8 oz / 1 cup plain (all purpose) flour
2 tsp baking powder
½ tsp bicarbonate of (baking) soda
½ tsp salt

- Preheat the oven to 180°C (160° fan) / 350 F / gas 4 and oil 12 mini loaf tins.
- Beat the egg in a jug with the oil, yoghurt, cheese, courgette and herbs until well mixed.
- Mix the flour, raising agents and salt in a bowl, then pour in the egg mixture and stir just enough to combine.
- Divide the mixture between the tins, then bake in the oven for 20 – 25 minutes.
- Test with a wooden toothpick, if it comes out clean, the cakes are done.
- Transfer the cakes to a wire rack and leave to cool.

871 Mini Loaf Cakes with Dill

These loaf cakes are particularly good with chopped fresh dill, but any herbs will do. Alternatively,

872 Mini Loaf Cakes with Capers

Add 1 tbsp capers to the mixture before baking.

873

MAKES 12

Lemon Curd Cakes

PREPARATION TIME: 15 MINUTES

COOKING TIME: 20 MINUTES

INGREDIENTS

110 g / 4 oz / ½ cup self-raising flour, sifted
110 g / 4 oz / ½ cup caster (superfine) sugar
110 g / 4 oz / ½ cup butter, softened
2 large eggs
1 lemon, zest finely grated
110 g / 4 oz / ½ cup lemon curd

TO DECORATE
225 g / 8 oz / 2 cups icing (confectioners') sugar
4 tsp lemon juice

- Preheat the oven to 190°C (170° fan) / 375 F / gas 5 and grease 12 dariole moulds.
- Combine the flour, sugar, butter, eggs and lemon zest in a bowl and whisk together for 2 minutes or until smooth.
- Divide half the mixture between the moulds, and top with a spoonful of lemon curd.
- Divide the rest of the cake mixture between the moulds then bake in the oven for 15 – 20 minutes.
- Transfer the cakes to a wire rack and leave to cool completely.
- Sieve the icing sugar into a bowl, then slowly stir in the lemon juice a few drops at a time until you have a thick icing.
- Pop the cakes out of their moulds and spoon over the icing.

Passion Fruit Cakes

874

Try this recipe with passion fruit curd in the centre and spoon some passion fruit seeds on top of the icing at the end.

875

MAKES 12

Strawberry Madeleines

PREPARATION TIME: 15 MINUTES

COOKING TIME: 15 MINUTES

INGREDIENTS

110 g / 4 oz / ½ cup butter
55 g / 2 oz / ⅓ cup plain (all purpose) flour
55 g / 2 oz / ½ cup ground almonds
110 g / 4 oz / 1 cup icing (confectioners') sugar
3 large egg whites
3 strawberries, quartered

- Heat the butter until it foams and starts to smell nutty, then leave to cool.
- Combine the flour, ground almonds and icing sugar in a bowl and whisk in the eggs whites.
- Pour the cooled butter through a sieve into the bowl and whisk into the mixture until evenly mixed.
- Leave the cake mixture to rest in the fridge for an hour.
- Preheat the oven to 170°C (150° fan) / 325 F / gas 3 and oil and flour a 12-hole Madeleine mould.
- Spoon the mixture into the moulds and press a strawberry quarter into the top of each one, then transfer the tin to the oven and bake for 10 – 15 minutes.
- Transfer the cakes to a wire rack to cool for 5 minutes. before serving in paper cupcake cases.

Raspberry Madeleines

876

Try this recipe with a fresh raspberries instead of the strawberries.

877

MAKES 12

Mirabelle Cakes

- Preheat the oven to 180°C (160° fan) / 350 F / gas 4 and oil a 12-hole silicone muffin tin.
- Beat the egg in a jug with the oil and milk until well mixed.
- Mix the flour, baking powder, sugar and Mirabelles in a bowl, then pour in the egg mixture and stir just enough to combine.
- Divide the mixture between the moulds, then bake in the oven for 20 – 25 minutes.
- Test with a wooden toothpick, if it comes out clean, the cakes are done.
- Transfer the cakes to a wire rack and leave to cool completely.

PREPARATION TIME: 25 MINUTES

COOKING TIME: 25 MINUTES

INGREDIENTS

1 large egg
120 ml / 4 fl. oz / ½ cup sunflower oil
120 ml / 4 fl. oz / ½ cup milk
375 g / 12 ½ oz / 2 ½ cups self-raising flour, sifted
1 tsp baking powder
200 g / 7 oz / ¾ cup caster (superfine) sugar
150 g / 5 oz / 1 cup Mirabelle plums, stoned and quartered

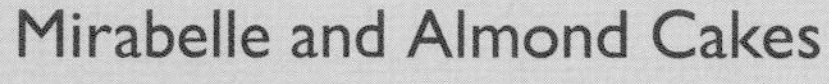

Mirabelle and Almond Cakes

878

Add 2 tbsp ground almonds to the mixture for extra moist cakes.

879

MAKES 12

Almond and Apricot Mini Cakes

- Preheat the oven to 180°C (160° fan) / 350 F / gas 4 and oil a 24-hole mini muffin tin.
- Beat the egg in a jug with the oil and milk until well mixed.
- Mix the flour, baking powder, sugar, ground almonds and apricots in a bowl, then pour in the egg mixture and stir just enough to combine.
- Divide the mixture between the moulds and scatter with flaked almonds, then bake in the oven for 15 – 20 minutes.
- Test with a wooden toothpick, if it comes out clean, the cakes are done.
- Transfer the cakes to a wire rack and leave to cool.

PREPARATION TIME: 25 MINUTES

COOKING TIME: 20 MINUTES

INGREDIENTS

1 large egg
120 ml / 4 fl. oz / ½ cup sunflower oil
120 ml / 4 fl. oz / ½ cup milk
375 g / 12 ½ oz / 2 ½ cups self-raising flour, sifted
1 tsp baking powder
200 g / 7 oz / ¾ cup caster (superfine) sugar
55 g / 2 oz / ½ cup ground almonds
75 g / 2 ½ oz / ½ cup dried apricots, chopped
2 tbsp flaked (slivered) almonds

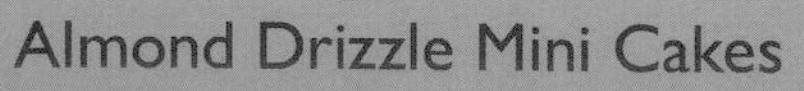

Almond Drizzle Mini Cakes

880

Try making an almond drizzle icing by mixing 225g / 8 oz / 1 cup icing sugar with ½ tsp almond essence and just enough boiling water to make a runny glaze.

881

MAKES 24

Vanilla Cranberry Cakes

PREPARATION TIME: 25 MINUTES

COOKING TIME: 25 MINUTES

INGREDIENTS

175 g/ 6 oz/ ¾ cup unsalted butter, softened
175 g/ 6oz/ 1 1/8 th cups self-raising flour
1 tsp baking powder
3 medium eggs lightly beaten
175g/6 oz/ ¾ cup golden caster sugar
75g/ 2 ½ oz/ ½ cup dried cranberries, chopped
1 tsp vanilla extract
24 paper cases

TO DECORATE
400g/ 7oz/ 1 cup unsalted butter
800g/ 14oz/ 3 cups icing sugar, sifted
a little pink food colouring
75g/ 2 ½ oz/ ½ cup dried cranberries, chopped

- Preheat oven to 180°C (160° fan) 375F, gas 5.
- Line cupcake tin with paper cases.
- Cream together in a food processor the sugar and butter until pale and fluffy.
- Add the eggs a little at a time if the mixture starts to curdle add a little of the measured flour.
- Add the vanilla extract to the mixture together with the dried cranberries.
- Spoon the mixture into the cases and bake for 18-20 minutes until risen and golden.
- Leave to cool on a wire rack.
- To decorate, beat the butter until soft. Add the icing sugar and beat again.
- Add a little pink food colouring and spoon onto the cooled cakes.
- Decorate with the chopped, dried cranberries

882

MAKES 24

Marmalade And Chocolate Mini Cakes

- Preheat the oven to 180°C (160° fan) / 350 F / gas 4 and oil a 24-hole silicone mini muffin mould.
- Beat the egg in a jug with the oil, milk and marmalade until well mixed.
- Mix the flour, baking powder, sugar and chocolate chunks in a bowl, then pour in the egg mixture and stir just enough to combine.
- Divide the mixture between the moulds, then bake in the oven for 15 – 20 minutes.
- Test with a wooden toothpick, if it comes out clean, the cakes are done.
- Transfer the cakes to a wire rack and leave to cool.

PREPARATION TIME: 25 MINUTES

COOKING TIME: 20 MINUTES

INGREDIENTS

1 large egg
120 ml / 4 fl. oz / ½ cup sunflower oil
120 ml / 4 fl. oz / ½ cup milk
110 g / 4 oz / ½ cup thick cut marmalade
375 g / 12 ½ oz / 2 ½ cups self-raising flour, sifted
1 tsp baking powder
200 g / 7 oz / ¾ cup caster (superfine) sugar
150 g / 5 oz / ⅔ cup dark chocolate, minimum 60% cocoa solids, chopped

Marmalade and Orange Chocolate Chunk Mini Cakes

883

Try using orange flavoured chocolate for the chunks for an even zestier taste.

884

MAKES 24

Almond Mini Cakes

- Preheat the oven to 180°C (160° fan) / 350 F / gas 4 and oil a 24-hole silicone mini muffin mould.
- Beat the egg in a jug with the oil, milk and honey until well mixed.
- Mix the flour, baking powder, sugar and ground almonds in a bowl, then pour in the egg mixture and stir just enough to combine.
- Divide the mixture between the moulds, then bake in the oven for 15 – 20 minutes.
- Test with a wooden toothpick, if it comes out clean, the cakes are done.
- Transfer the cakes to a wire rack and leave to cool.

PREPARATION TIME: 25 MINUTES

COOKING TIME: 20 MINUTES

INGREDIENTS

1 large egg
120 ml / 4 fl. oz / ½ cup sunflower oil
120 ml / 4 fl. oz / ½ cup milk
2 tbsp honey
375 g / 12 ½ oz / 2 ½ cups self-raising flour, sifted
1 tsp baking powder
200 g / 7 oz / ¾ cup caster (superfine) sugar
55 g / 2 oz / ½ cup ground almonds

Decorated Almond Mini Cakes

885

Try decorating these little cakes with a drizzle of plain white icing and a whole blanched almond on each one.

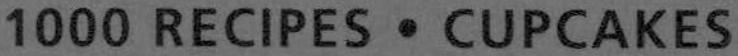

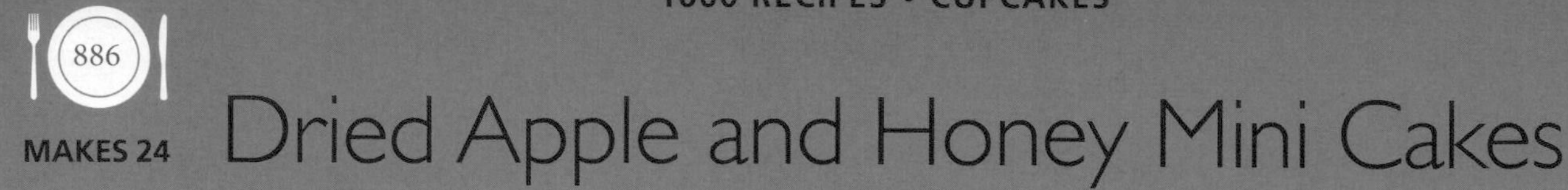

886

MAKES 24

Dried Apple and Honey Mini Cakes

PREPARATION TIME: 25 MINUTES

COOKING TIME: 20 MINUTES

INGREDIENTS

1 large egg
120 ml / 4 fl. oz / ½ cup sunflower oil
120 ml / 4 fl. oz / ½ cup milk
2 tbsp honey
375 g / 12 ½ oz / 2 ½ cups self-raising flour, sifted
1 tsp baking powder
200 g / 7 oz / ¾ cup caster (superfine) sugar
150 g / 5 oz / 1 cup dried apple slices, chopped
To decorate
24 dried apple slices

- Preheat the oven to 180°C (160° fan) / 350 F / gas 4 and oil a 24-hole silicone mini muffin mould.
- Beat the egg in a jug with the oil, milk and honey until well mixed.
- Mix the flour, baking powder, sugar and dried apple in a bowl, then pour in the egg mixture and stir just enough to combine.
- Divide the mixture between the moulds, then bake in the oven for 15 – 20 minutes.
- Test with a wooden toothpick, if it comes out clean, the cakes are done.
- Transfer the cakes to a wire rack and leave to cool, then top each one with a slice of dried apple.

Apple and Brandy Mini Cakes

887

Soak the dried apple in 3 tbsp of brandy for 1 hour before cooking for an extra touch of luxury.

888

MAKES 12

Apple Babas

Spiced Apple Babas

889

Add 1 tsp each of ground cinnamon, ground ginger and mixed spice to the baba dough.

Pear Babas

890

Replace the chopped apple with chopped pear.

PREPARATION TIME: 1 HOUR 15 MINUTES

COOKING TIME: 15 MINUTES

INGREDIENTS

150 g / 5 oz / ⅔ cup plain (all-purpose) flour
2 tsp dried easy-blend yeast
1 tbsp caster (superfine) sugar
½ tsp salt
3 large eggs, lightly beaten
75 g / 2 ½ oz / ⅓ cup butter, softened
150 g / 5 oz / 1 cup apple, peeled and chopped
For the soaking syrup
450 g / 1 lb / 2 cups caster (superfine) sugar
240 ml / 8 fl. oz / 1 cup dark rum

- Oil 12 pudding tins and sit them on a baking tray.
- Combine the flour, yeast, sugar and salt in a bowl and gradually whisk in half of the beaten egg with an electric whisk.
- Continuing to whisk, incorporate half of the butter, followed by the rest of the egg.
- Beat the remaining butter in with a wooden spoon and incorporate the chopped apple, then divide the mixture between the moulds.
- Leave the babas to prove in a warm, draught-free place for 1 hour or until they have doubled in size.
- Preheat the oven to 200°C (180° fan) / 400 F / gas 6.
- Bake the babas for 10 – 15 minutes or until golden brown and cooked through, then turn them out onto a wire rack.
- Put the sugar in a saucepan with 675 ml water and stir over a medium heat to dissolve the sugar.
- Boil the sugar water for 5 minutes or until it starts to turn syrupy, then stir in the rum
- Transfer the babas to a mixing bowl, pour over the syrup and leave to soak for 10 minutes, turning occasionally.

891

MAKES 12

Pineapple Cakes

Pineapple and Lime Cakes

892

Try adding a tsp of finely grated lime zest to the cake mixture.

PREPARATION TIME: 15

COOKING TIME: 20 MINUTES

INGREDIENTS

110 g / 4 oz / 1 cup self-raising flour, sifted
110 g / 4 oz / ½ cup caster (superfine) sugar
110 g / 4 oz / ½ cup butter, softened
2 large eggs
225 g / 8 oz / 2 cups pineapple, drained

- Preheat the oven to 190°C (170° fan) / 375 F / gas 5 and line a 12-hole cupcake tin with paper cases.
- Combine the flour, sugar, butter and eggs in a bowl and whisk together for 2 minutes or until smooth.
- Divide the mixture between the paper cases and press a piece of pineapple into the top of each, then transfer the tin to the oven and bake for 15 – 20 minutes.
- Test with a wooden toothpick, if it comes out clean, the cakes are done.
- Transfer the cakes to a wire rack and leave to cool completely.

893

MAKES 12

Individual Rhubarb Pies

- Sieve the flour into a mixing bowl then rub in the butter until the mixture resembles fine breadcrumbs.
- Stir in just enough cold water to bring the pastry together into a pliable dough, then leave to rest in the fridge for 30 minutes.
- Preheat the oven to 200°C (180° fan) / 400 F / gas 6.
- Divide the chopped rhubarb between 12 ramekin dishes and sprinkle with the sugar.
- Roll out the pastry on a floured surface and cut out 12 circles. Score a cross-hatch pattern in the top of the pastry circles.
- Brush the edges of the ramekin dishes with a little beaten egg, then mould the pastry over the top.
- Make a little chimney for each pie out of rolled up tinfoil so that the steam can escape.
- Brush the pies with beaten egg then bake in the oven for 30 minutes or until cooked through and golden brown.

PREPARATION TIME: 30 MINUTES

COOKING TIME: 30 MINUTES

INGREDIENTS

225 g / 8 oz / 1 ½ cups plain (all purpose) flour
110 g / 4 oz / ½ cup butter, cubed and chilled
350 g / 12 oz rhubarb stems, chopped
55 g / 2 oz / ¼ cup caster (superfine) sugar
1 large egg, beaten

Individual Plum Pies

894

Try this recipe with any seasonal fruit – plums are particularly good. Alternatively, sprinkle the pastry with caster sugar before baking for an extra crunchy topping.

895

MAKES 36

Fruit Jewel Mini Cakes

- Preheat the oven to 190°C (170° fan) / 375 F / gas 5 and oil a 36 hole silicone mini cupcake mould.
- Combine the flour, cocoa, sugar, butter, eggs and vanilla extract in a bowl and whisk together for 2 minutes or until smooth.
- Divide the mixture between the paper cases and press a berry or cherry into the top of each one.
- Transfer the tin to the oven and bake for 10 – 15 minutes.
- Test with a wooden toothpick, if it comes out clean, the cakes are done.
- Transfer the cakes to a wire rack and leave to cool completely.

PREPARATION TIME: 15 MINUTES

COOKING TIME: 15 MINUTES

INGREDIENTS

110 g / 4 oz / ½ cup self-raising flour, sifted
110 g / 4 oz / ½ cup caster (superfine) sugar
110 g / 4 oz / ½ cup butter, softened
2 large eggs
1 tsp vanilla extract
12 raspberries
12 cherries, stones
12 blackberries

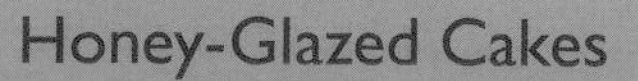

Honey-Glazed Cakes

896

Brush the cakes with honey when they come out of the oven for a sweet sticky glaze.

897

MAKES 6

Chocolate, Coconut And Almond Cakes

PREPARATION TIME: 20 MINUTES

COOKING TIME: 20 MINUTES

INGREDIENTS

55 g / 2 oz / ½ cup self-raising flour, sifted
55 g / 2 oz / ½ cup ground almonds
28 g / 1 oz / ¼ cup unsweetened cocoa powder, sifted
28 g / 1 oz / ¼ cup desiccated coconut
110 g / 4 oz / ½ cup caster (superfine) sugar
110 g / 4 oz / ½ cup butter, softened
2 large eggs

TO DECORATE
2 tbsp desiccated coconut

- Preheat the oven to 190°C (170° fan) / 375 F / gas 5 and oil a 6-hole silicone tartlet mould or 6 individual tartlet tins.
- Combine all of the cake ingredients in a bowl and whisk together for 2 minutes or until smooth.
- Divide the mixture between the tins then transfer the cakes to the oven and bake for 20 – 25 minutes.
- Test with a wooden toothpick, if it comes out clean, the cakes are done.
- Transfer the cakes to a wire rack to cool, then sprinkle over a little desiccated coconut.

Extra Almond Cakes

898

To increase the almond flavour in these cakes, add ½ tsp of almond essence to the cake mixture and sprinkle the cakes with flaked almonds before baking.

899

MAKES 12

Wholemeal Dairy-Free Banana Cakes

PREPARATION TIME: 25 MINUTES

COOKING TIME: 25 MINUTES

INGREDIENTS

3 very ripe bananas
110 g / 4 oz / ⅔ cup soft light brown sugar
2 large eggs
120 ml / 4 fl. oz / ½ cup sunflower oil
225 g / 8 oz / 1 ½ cups wholemeal flour
2 tsp bicarbonate of (baking) soda

TO DECORATE
dried banana chips

- Preheat the oven to 200°C (180° fan) / 400 F / gas 6 and line a 12-hole cupcake tin with paper cases.
- Mash the bananas with a fork then whisk in the sugar, eggs and oil.
- Sieve the flour and bicarbonate of soda into the bowl and stir just enough to evenly mix all the ingredients together.
- Divide the mixture between the paper cases, then transfer the tin to the oven and bake for 15 – 20 minutes.
- Test with a wooden toothpick, if it comes out clean, the cakes are done.
- Transfer the cakes to a wire rack and leave to cool completely.
- Top with dried banana chips to finish.

Dark Chocolate Banana Cakes

900

For a touch of luxury, stir in 110g / 4oz / ⅔ cup dark chocolate chunks before baking.

901

MAKES 12

Apple Crumble Cakes

- Preheat the oven to 190°C (170° fan) / 375 F / gas 5 and line a 12-hole muffin tin with paper cases.
- Whisk the sugar, eggs and oil together for 3 minutes until thick.
- Fold in the flour, baking powder and cinnamon, followed by the grated and chopped apple and the sultanas.
- Divide the mixture between the paper cases.
- To make the crumble topping, rub the butter into the flour until the mixture resembles fine breadcrumbs. Stir in the sugar, then clump the mixture together in your hands and crumble it over the top of the cakes.
- Transfer the tin to the oven and bake for 20 - 25 minutes.
- Test with a wooden toothpick, if it comes out clean, the cakes are done.
- Transfer the cakes to a wire rack and leave to cool.

PREPARATION TIME: 20 MINUTES

COOKING TIME: 20 MINUTES

INGREDIENTS

175 g / 6 oz / 1 cup light brown sugar
2 eggs
150 ml / 5 fl. oz / ¾ cup sunflower oil
175 g / 6 oz / 1 ¼ cups wholemeal flour
3 tsp baking powder
2 tsp ground cinnamon
110 g / 4 oz apples, coarsely grated
110 g / 4 oz apples, chopped
175 g / 6 oz / ¾ cup sultanas

FOR THE CRUMBLE TOPPING

55 g / 2 oz / ¼ cup butter, cubed and chilled
110 g / 4 oz / ¾ cup plain (all purpose) flour
2 tbsp caster (superfine) sugar

Rhubarb Crumble Cakes

902

This recipe works brilliantly with rhubarb too – substitute the chopped and grated apple for 150g / 5 oz finely chopped rhubarb.

903

MAKES 12

White Chocolate and Frangipane Cakes

- Preheat the oven to 190°C (170° fan) / 375 F / gas 5 and line a 12-hole cupcake tin with paper cases.
- Combine the flour, ground almonds, sugar, butter, eggs and almond essence in a bowl and whisk together for 2 minutes or until smooth.
- Divide the mixture between the cases.
- Melt the chocolate in a microwave or bain marie and spoon it into a small piping bag.
- Pipe a design on top of the cakes then transfer the tin to the oven and bake for 15 – 20 minutes.
- Test with a wooden toothpick, if it comes out clean, the cakes are done.
- Transfer the cakes to a wire rack to cool.

PREPARATION TIME: 20 MINUTES

COOKING TIME: 20 MINUTES

INGREDIENTS

55 g / 2 oz / ½ cup self-raising flour, sifted
55 g / 2 oz / ½ cup ground almonds
110 g / 4 oz / ½ cup caster (superfine) sugar
110 g / 4 oz / ½ cup butter, softened
2 large eggs
1 tsp almond essence
110 g / 4 oz white chocolate, chopped

White Chocolate Apricot Cakes

904

Try pressing half a fresh apricot into the centre of each cake before baking.

905

MAKES 12

Mini Apple Pies

Pear Pies

906

Replace the apples with pears and cook in the same way.

PREPARATION TIME: 30 MINUTES

COOKING TIME: 25 MINUTES

INGREDIENTS

225 g / 8 oz / 1 ½ cups plain (all-purpose) flour
110 g / 4 oz / ½ cup butter, cubed and chilled
375g can / 13 oz can Bramley apple pie filling
1 large egg white, beaten
2 tbsp caster (superfine) sugar

- Preheat the oven to 200°C (180° fan) / 400 F / gas 6.
- Sieve the flour into a mixing bowl then rub in the butter until the mixture resembles fine breadcrumbs.
- Stir in just enough cold water to bring the pastry together into a pliable dough.
- Roll out the pastry on a floured surface and cut out 24 circles then use 12 of them to line a 12-hole cupcake tin.
- Add a tbsp of pie filling to each pastry case, then top with the remaining 12 pastry circles and crimp round the edges to seal.
- Brush the pies with egg white and sprinkle with sugar then bake in the oven for 20 – 25 minutes or until cooked through and golden brown.

907

MAKES 36

Mini Rum Babas

Rum Babas

908

Use the above recipe to make 12 normal size babas by oiling 12 individual baba ring moulds. Bake them for 10 – 15 minutes.

Cinnamon Rum Babas

909

Add 2 tsp ground cinnamon to the baba dough. Add a whole cinnamon stick to the soaking syrup.

PREPARATION TIME: 1 HOUR 15 MINUTES

COOKING TIME: 5 MINUTES

INGREDIENTS

150 g / 5 oz / 1 cup plain (all purpose) flour
2 tsp dried easy-blend yeast
1 tbsp caster (superfine) sugar
½ tsp salt
3 large eggs, lightly beaten
75 g / 2 ½ oz / ⅓ cup butter, softened

FOR THE SOAKING SYRUP
450 g / 1 lb / 2 cups caster (superfine) sugar
240 ml / 8 fl. oz / 1 cup rum

TO DECORATE
225 ml / 8 fl. oz / 1 cup whipped cream
Summer berries
Gold leaf

- Oil a 36-hole silicone mini cupcake mould.
- Combine the flour, yeast, sugar and salt in a bowl and gradually whisk in half of the beaten egg with an electric whisk.
- Continuing to whisk, incorporate half of the butter, followed by the rest of the egg.
- Beat the remaining butter in with a wooden spoon, then divide the mixture between the moulds.
- Leave the babas to prove in a warm, draught-free place for 1 hour or until they have doubled in size.
- Preheat the oven to 200°C (180° fan) / 400 F / gas 6.
- Bake the babas for 5 minutes or until golden brown and cooked through, then turn them out onto a wire rack.
- Put the sugar in a saucepan with 675ml water and stir over a medium heat to dissolve the sugar.
- Boil the sugar water for 5 minutes or until it starts to turn syrupy, then stir in the rum.
- Transfer the babas to a mixing bowl, pour over the syrup and leave to soak until cold, turning occasionally.
- Remove the babas from the syrup and put on a serving plate.
- Spoon the whipped cream into a piping bag fitted with a large star nozzle and pipe a star on top of each baba.
- Top with summer berries and apply the gold leaf with a dry brush.

910

MAKES 12

Mini Pavlovas

Mini Chocolate Pavlovas

911

Dip the base of the meringues in melted white or dark chocolate.

PREPARATION TIME: 20 MINUTES

COOKING TIME: 35 MINUTES

INGREDIENTS

4 large egg whites
110 g / 4 oz / 1 cup caster (superfine) sugar
1 tsp cornflour (cornstarch)

TO DECORATE

225 ml / 8 fl. oz / 1 cup double (heavy) cream
2 tbsp icing (confectioners') sugar
½ tsp vanilla extract
4 tsp raspberry jam (jelly)
4 raspberries
4 tsp chocolate spread
4 tsp white chocolate spread
white and dark chocolate curls, to garnish

- Preheat the oven to 140°C (120° fan) / 275 F / gas 1 and oil and line a baking tray with greaseproof paper.
- Whisk the egg whites until stiff, then gradually whisk in half the sugar until the mixture is very shiny.
- Fold in the remaining sugar and the cornflour then spoon the mixture into a large piping bag fitted with a large star nozzle.
- Pipe 12 small swirls onto the baking tray, then bake in the oven for 30 minutes or until the meringues are crisp on the outside, but still a bit chewy in the middle.
- Leave to cool completely.
- To make the topping, whisk the cream with the icing sugar and vanilla until thick.
- Spoon the mixture into a piping bag fitted with a large star nozzle and pipe a ring on top of each meringue.
- Fill the centres with jam or chocolate spread and add a corresponding topping of raspberries or chocolate curls.

912

MAKES 24

Mini Mincemeat Tarts

- Sieve the flour into a mixing bowl then rub in the butter until the mixture resembles fine breadcrumbs.
- Stir in just enough cold water to bring the pastry together into a pliable dough.
- Roll out the pastry on a floured surface and cut out 24 circles then use them to line a 24 mini tartlet tins and crimp around the edges.
- Leave the pastry to chill the fridge for 30 minutes.
- Preheat the oven to 200°C (180° fan) / 400 F / gas 6.
- Fill the pastry cases ¾ full with mincemeat then bake for 15 – 20 minutes.

PREPARATION TIME: 35 MINUTES

COOKING TIME: 15 MINUTES

INGREDIENTS

225 g / 8 oz / 1 ½ cups plain (all-purpose) flour
110 g / 4 oz / ½ cup butter, cubed and chilled
225 g / 8 oz / 1 cup mincemeat

Mini Mincemeat Tarts with Marzipan Stars

913

Roll out 225g / 8 oz / 1 cup marzipan and cut out 24 stars and put on top of the tarts before baking.

914

MAKES 6

Rum and Raisin Giant Babas

- Oil a 6-hole silicone muffin mould.
- Combine the flour, yeast, sugar and salt in a bowl and gradually whisk in half of the beaten egg.
- Continuing to whisk, incorporate half of the butter, followed by the rest of the egg.
- Beat the remaining butter in and incorporate the raisins, then divide the mixture between the moulds.
- Leave the babas to prove in a warm, draught-free place for 1 hour or until they have doubled in size.
- Preheat the oven to 200°C (180° fan) / 400 F / gas 6.
- Bake the babas for 15 – 20 minutes or until golden brown and cooked through, then turn them out onto a wire rack.
- Put the sugar in a saucepan with 675ml / 1 ¼ pints / 3 cups water and stir over a medium heat to dissolve the sugar.
- Boil the sugar water for 5 minutes or until it starts to turn syrupy, then stir in the rum
- Transfer the babas to a mixing bowl, pour over the syrup and leave to soak until cold, turning occasionally.

PREPARATION TIME: 1 HOUR 15 MINUTES

COOKING TIME: 20 MINUTES

INGREDIENTS

150 g / 5 oz / 1 cup plain (all purpose) flour
2 tsp dried easy-blend yeast
1 tbsp caster (superfine) sugar
½ tsp salt
3 large eggs, lightly beaten
75 g / 2 ½ oz / ⅓ cup butter, softened
75 g / 2 ½ oz / ½ cup raisins
For the soaking syrup
450 g / 1 lb / 2 cups caster (superfine) sugar
240 ml / 8 fl. oz / 1 cup rum

915

MAKES 6

Peach Melba Cakes

PREPARATION TIME: 25 MINUTES

COOKING TIME: 20 MINUTES

INGREDIENTS

110 g / 4 oz / ½ cup self-raising flour, sifted
110 g / 4 oz / ½ cup caster (superfine) sugar
110 g / 4 oz / ½ cup butter, softened
2 large eggs
6 canned peach halves, drained
110 g / 4 oz / ½ cup raspberry jam (jelly)
Icing sugar (congfectioners') for dusting

- Preheat the oven to 190°C (170° fan) / 375 F / gas 5 and grease a 6-hole silicone Yorkshire pudding mould.
- Combine the flour, sugar, butter and eggs in a bowl and whisk together for 2 minutes or until smooth.
- Cut each peach half into thirds and arrange in the bottom of the moulds.
- Add 3 dollops of raspberry jam and top with the cake mixture.
- Transfer the mould to the oven and bake for 15 – 20 minutes.
- Test with a wooden toothpick, if it comes out clean, the cakes are done.
- Un-mould the cakes onto serving plates and dust with a little icing sugar.

Peach Melba Cakes with Raspberry Sauce

Try serving the cakes with a hot raspberry sauce: press 150g / 5 oz / ⅔ cup of raspberries through a sieve to remove the pips and heat the pulp in a saucepan with 2 tbsp of caster sugar. Stir until the sugar dissolves.

917

MAKES 6

Rose Jam Cakes

PREPARATION TIME: 25 MINUTES

COOKING TIME: 10 MINUTES

INGREDIENTS

4 plain cakes
55 g / 2 oz / ¼ cup desiccated coconut
75 g / 2 ½ oz / ½ cup walnuts, chopped
75 g / 2 ½ oz / ½ cup currants
110 g / 4 oz / ½ cup rose petal jam (jelly)
To decorate
55 g / 2 oz / ¼ cup rose petal jam (jelly)
6 rose petals

- Put the cakes in a food processor and process to fine crumbs.
- Stir in the coconut, walnuts and currants then bind together with the rose petal jam.
- Press the mixture into the bottom of 6 ring moulds and chill until firm.
- Remove the moulds and top with rose petal jam and a fresh rose petal.

Hazelnut Chocolate Cakes

918

Replace the walnuts with chopped hazelnuts and leave out the currants. Bind the mixture with 110g / 4 oz / ½ cup chocolate hazelnut (cob nut) spread instead of the rose petal jam.

919

MAKES 12

Chocolate Chip Madeleines

- Heat the butter until it foams and starts to smell nutty, then leave to cool.
- Combine the flour, ground almonds and icing sugar in a bowl and whisk in the eggs whites.
- Pour the cooled butter through a sieve into the bowl and whisk into the mixture until evenly mixed.
- Fold in the chocolate chips.
- Leave the cake mixture to rest in the fridge for an hour.
- Preheat the oven to 170°C (150° fan) / 325 F / gas 3 and oil and flour a 12-hole Madeleine mould.
- Spoon the mixture into the moulds, then transfer the tin to the oven and bake for 10 – 15 minutes.
- Test with a wooden toothpick, if it comes out clean, the cakes are done.
- Transfer the cakes to a wire rack to cool for 5 minutes before serving.

PREPARATION TIME:
1 HOUR 30 MINUTES

COOKING TIME: 15 MINUTES

INGREDIENTS

110 g / 4 oz / ½ cup butter
55 g / 2 oz / ⅓ cup plain (all purpose) flour
55 g / 2 oz / ½ cup ground almonds
110 g / 4 oz / 1 cup icing (confectioners') sugar
3 large egg whites
2 tbsp chocolate chips

White Chocolate Chip Madeleines

920

Replace the milk chocolate chips with white chocolate chips.

921

MAKES 12

Plain Madeleines

- Heat the butter until it foams and starts to smell nutty, then leave to cool.
- Combine the flour, ground almonds and icing sugar in a bowl and whisk in the eggs whites.
- Pour the cooled butter through a sieve into the bowl and whisk into the mixture until evenly mixed.
- Leave the cake mixture to rest in the fridge for an hour.
- Preheat the oven to 170°C (150° fan) / 325 F / gas 3 and oil and flour a 12-hole Madeleine mould.
- Spoon the mixture into the moulds, then transfer the tin to the oven and bake for 10 – 15 minutes.
- Test with a wooden toothpick, if it comes out clean, the cakes are done.
- Transfer the cakes to a wire rack to cool for 5 minutes before serving.

PREPARATION TIME:
1 HOUR 30 MINUTES

COOKING TIME: 15 MINUTES

INGREDIENTS

110 g / 4 oz / ½ cup butter
55 g / 2 oz / ⅓ cup plain (all purpose) flour
55 g / 2 oz / ½ cup ground almonds
110 g / 4 oz / 1 cup icing (confectioners') sugar
3 large egg whites

Chocolate Madeleines

922

Melt 110g / 4oz / ½ cup of milk chocolate and dip the Madeleines in as you eat them.

MAKES 12

Almond and Summer Fruit Loaf Cakes

Home-made Apple Pies

924

To make these cakes extra moist, add 1 grated apple to the mixture.

White Chocolate Mini Loaf

925

Alternatively, drizzle the tops with melted white chocolate for a touch of luxury.

PREPARATION TIME: 25 MINUTES

COOKING TIME: 25 MINUTES

INGREDIENTS

1 large egg
120 ml / 4 fl. oz / ½ cup sunflower oil
120 ml / 4 fl. oz / ½ cup milk
375 g / 12 ½ oz / 2 ½ cups self-raising flour, sifted
1 tsp baking powder
200 g / 7 oz / ¾ cup caster (superfine) sugar
150 g / 5 oz / 1 cup mixed summer fruits
75 g / 2 ½ oz / ½ cup flaked (slivered) almonds

- Preheat the oven to 180°C (160° fan) / 350 F / gas 4 and line 12 mini loaf tins with paper cases.
- Beat the egg in a jug with the oil and milk until well mixed.
- Mix the flour, baking powder, sugar, fruit and almonds in a bowl, then pour in the egg mixture and stir just enough to combine.
- Divide the mixture between the paper cases, then bake in the oven for 20 – 25 minutes.
- Test with a wooden toothpick, if it comes out clean, the cakes are done.
- Transfer the cakes to a wire rack and leave to cool completely.

926

MAKES 12

Chocolate and Coffee Fondants

PREPARATION TIME: 30 MINUTES

COOKING TIME: 8 MINUTES

INGREDIENTS

2 tbsp unsweetened cocoa powder
150 g / 6 oz / ⅔ cup dark chocolate, minimum 60% cocoa solids, chopped
150 g / 6 oz / ⅔ cup butter, chopped
85 g / 3 oz / ⅓ cup caster (superfine) sugar
3 large eggs
3 egg yolks
1 tbsp plain (all purpose) flour
2 tsp instant espresso powder

- Oil 6 mini pudding basins and dust the insides with cocoa.
- Melt the chocolate, butter and sugar together in a saucepan, stirring to dissolve the sugar.
- Leave to cool a little then beat in the eggs and egg yolks and fold in the flour and espresso powder.
- Divide the mixture between the pudding basins, then chill them for 30 minutes.
- Preheat the oven to 180°C (160° fan) / 350 F / gas 4 and put a baking tray in to heat.
- Transfer the fondants to the heated baking tray and bake in the oven for 8 minutes.
- Leave the fondants to cool for 2 minutes, then turn them out of their moulds and serve immediately.

927

MAKES 12

Honey and Date Madeleines

Oriental Madeleines

928

Try adding 1 tsp of orange flower water for a taste of the Middle East.

Honey and Apricot Madeleines

929

Alternatively, replace the dates with chopped apricots for honey and apricot Madeleines.

PREPARATION TIME:
1 HOUR 30 MINUTES

COOKING TIME: 15 MINUTES

INGREDIENTS

110 g / 4 oz / ½ cup butter
55 g / 2 oz / ⅓ cup plain (all purpose) flour
55 g / 2 oz / ½ cup ground almonds
110 g / 4 oz / 1 cup icing (confectioners') sugar
3 large egg whites
2 tbsp dates, chopped
2 tbsp honey

- Heat the butter until it foams and starts to smell nutty, then leave to cool.
- Combine the flour, ground almonds and icing sugar in a bowl and whisk in the eggs whites.
- Pour the cooled butter through a sieve into the bowl and whisk into the mixture until evenly mixed.
- Fold in the dates and honey.
- Leave the cake mixture to rest in the fridge for an hour.
- Preheat the oven to 170°C (150° fan) / 325 F / gas 3 and oil and flour a 12-hole Madeleine mould.
- Spoon the mixture into the moulds, then transfer the tin to the oven and bake for 10 – 15 minutes.
- Test with a wooden toothpick, if it comes out clean, the cakes are done.
- Transfer the cakes to a wire rack to cool for 5 minutes before serving.

930

MAKES 12

Custard and Frangipane Cakes

Plum Custard Frangipane Cakes

931

Cut 6 plums in half and remove the stones. Press a plum half into the centre of each cake before baking.

PREPARATION TIME: 20 MINUTES

COOKING TIME: 20 MINUTES

INGREDIENTS

55 g / 2 oz / ½ cup self-raising flour, sifted
55 g / 2 oz / ½ cup ground almonds
110 g / 4 oz / ½ cup caster (superfine) sugar
110 g / 4 oz / ½ cup butter, softened
2 large eggs
1 tsp almond essence

FOR THE CUSTARD
2 large egg yolks
55 g / 2 oz / ¼ cup caster (superfine) sugar
2 tbsp plain (all purpose) flour
2 tbsp cornflour (cornstarch)
1 tsp vanilla extract
240 ml / 8 fl. oz / 1 cup milk

- Preheat the oven to 190°C (170° fan) / 375 F / gas 5 and line a 12-hole cupcake tin with paper cases.
- Combine the flour, ground almonds, sugar, butter, eggs and almond essence in a bowl and whisk together for 2 minutes or until smooth.
- Divide the mixture between the cases.
- To make the custard, stir the egg yolks, sugar, flours and vanilla extract together in a saucepan, then gradually add the milk.
- Heat the mixture until it starts to boil, stirring all the time, then take off the heat and beat vigorously to remove any lumps.
- Spoon the custard into a piping bag and pipe a design on top of the cakes then transfer the tin to the oven and bake for 15 – 20 minutes.
- Transfer the cakes to a wire rack to cool.

965

MAKES 12

Wholemeal Raisin Cakes

PREPARATION TIME: 25 MINUTES

COOKING TIME: 20 MINUTES

INGREDIENTS

55 g / 2 oz / ½ cup self-raising flour, sifted
55 g / 2 oz / ½ cup wholemeal flour
1 tsp bicarbonate of (baking) soda
110 g / 4 oz / ½ cup caster (superfine) sugar
110 g / 4 oz / ½ cup butter, softened
2 large eggs
75 g / 2 ½ oz / ½ cup raisins

- Preheat the oven to 190°C (170° fan) / 375 F / gas 5 and line a 12-hole cupcake tin with paper cases.
- Combine the flours, sugar, butter, eggs and raisins in a bowl and whisk together for 2 minutes or until smooth.
- Divide the mixture between the paper cases, then transfer the tin to the oven and bake for 15 – 20 minutes.
- Test with a wooden toothpick, if it comes out clean, the cakes are done.
- Transfer the cakes to a wire rack and leave to cool completely.

Orange Raisin Cakes

966

Try adding the grated zest of an orange to the cake mixture and brushing the cakes with marmalade when they come out of the oven.

967

MAKES 12

Hot Chocolate and Raspberry Cakes

PREPARATION TIME: 25 MINUTES

COOKING TIME: 25 MINUTES

INGREDIENTS

1 large egg
120 ml / 4 fl. oz / ½ cup sunflower oil
120 ml / 4 fl. oz / ½ cup milk
375 g / 12 ½ oz / 2 ½ cups self-raising flour, sifted
55 g / 2 oz / ½ cup unsweetened cocoa powder, sifted
1 tsp baking powder
200 g / 7 oz / ¾ cup caster (superfine) sugar
110 g / 4 oz / ⅔ cup dark chocolate, minimum 60% cocoa solids, chopped
150 g / 5 oz / 1 cup raspberries

- Preheat the oven to 180°C (160° fan) / 350 F / gas 4 and oil 12 small ramekin dishes.
- Beat the egg in a jug with the oil and milk until well mixed.
- Mix the flour, cocoa, baking powder, sugar and chocolate in a bowl, then pour in the egg mixture and stir just enough to combine.
- Divide half the mixture between the ramekins and top with the raspberries.
- Spoon the rest of the muffin mixture on top then bake in the oven for 20 – 25 minutes.
- Test with a wooden toothpick, if it comes out clean, the cakes are done.
- Serve the cakes warm with a dollop of whipped cream and some extra raspberries on the side.

Hot Chocolate Cakes with Raspberry Sauce

968

Try serving these cakes with a hot raspberry sauce: press 150g of raspberries through a sieve to remove the pips and heat the pulp in a saucepan with 2 tbsp of caster sugar. Stir until the sugar dissolves.

MAKES 12

Sultana and Walnut Mini Loaf Cakes

Spiced Mini Loaf Cakes

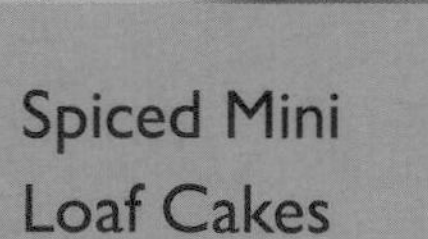

Try spicing up the muffin mixture with 1 tsp each of ground cinnamon and ground ginger and ½ tsp of ground cloves.

Sultana and Almond Mini Loaf Cakes

971

Replace the walnuts with flaked almonds.

PREPARATION TIME: 25 MINUTES

COOKING TIME: 25 MINUTES

INGREDIENTS

1 large egg
120ml / 4 fl. oz / ½ cup sunflower oil
120ml / 4 fl. oz / ½ cup milk
375 g / 12 ½ oz / 2 ½ cups self-raising flour, sifted
1 tsp baking powder
200 g / 7 oz / ¾ cup caster (superfine) sugar
75 g / 2 ½ oz / ½ cup sultanas
75 g / 2 ½ oz / ½ cup walnuts, chopped
12 walnut halves

- Preheat the oven to 200°C (180° fan) / 400 F / gas 6 and line 12 mini loaf tins with paper cases.
- Beat the egg in a jug with the oil and milk until well mixed.
- Mix the flour, baking powder, sultanas and chopped walnuts in a bowl, then pour in the egg mixture and stir just enough to combine.
- Divide the mixture between the paper cases and top each one with a walnut half, then bake in the oven for 20 – 25 minutes.
- Test with a wooden toothpick, if it comes out clean, the cakes are done.
- Transfer the cakes to a wire rack and leave to cool completely.

987

MAKES 24

Chocolate and Coconut Cake Balls

Double Chocolate Coconut Balls

988

Replace the plain cupcakes with chocolate cupcakes.

White Chocolate and Almond Balls

989

Replace the coconut with 1 tbsp of almond extract and the plain chocolate for white chocolate.

PREPARATION TIME: 25 MINUTES

COOKING TIME: 20 MINUTES

INGREDIENTS

6 plain cupcakes
225 g / 8 oz / 1 cup plain chocolate, minimum 60% cocoa solids, chopped
55 g / 2 oz / ¼ cup desiccated coconut

- Put the cakes in a food processor and process to fine crumbs.
- Melt the chocolate in a microwave or bain marie and mix ⅔ of it with the cake crumbs to form a dough.
- Roll the dough into balls, then coat them in the rest of the chocolate and roll them in the coconut.
- Leave in a cool place for the chocolate to set.

990

MAKES 12

Pear and Chocolate Mini Loaf Cakes

- Preheat the oven to 180°C (160° fan) / 350 F / gas 4 and oil a 12 mini loaf cake tins.
- Beat the egg in a jug with the oil and milk until well mixed.
- Mix the flour, cocoa, baking powder, sugar, chocolate and pears in a bowl, then pour in the egg mixture and stir just enough to combine.
- Divide the mixture between the paper cases, then bake in the oven for 20 – 25 minutes.
- Test with a wooden toothpick, if it comes out clean, the cakes are done.
- Transfer the cakes to a wire rack and leave to cool completely.

PREPARATION TIME: 25 MINUTES

COOKING TIME: 25 MINUTES

INGREDIENTS

1 large egg
120 ml / 4 fl. oz / ½ cup sunflower oil
120 ml / 4 fl. oz / ½ cup milk
375 g / 12 ½ oz / 2 ½ cups self-raising flour, sifted
55 g / 2 oz / ½ cup unsweetened cocoa powder, sifted
1 tsp baking powder
200 g / 7 oz / ¾ cup caster (superfine) sugar
110 g / 4 oz / ½ cup dark chocolate, minimum 60% cocoa solids, chopped
2 pears, cored and chopped

Mini Loaf Cake with Hot Chocolate Sauce

991

Make a hot chocolate sauce to serve with the loaf cakes: heat 225ml / 8 fl. oz / 1 cup double (heavy) cream until boiling then pour over 225g / 8 oz / 1 cup chopped milk chocolate and stir until smooth.

992

MAKES 12

Orange Syrup Cakes

- Preheat the oven to 190°C (170° fan) / 375 F / gas 5 and line a 12-hole cupcake tin with paper cases.
- Combine the flour, sugar, butter, eggs and orange zest in a bowl and whisk together for 2 minutes or until smooth.
- Divide the mixture between the paper cases, then transfer the tin to the oven and bake for 15 – 20 minutes.
- Test with a wooden toothpick, if it comes out clean, the cakes are done.
- While the cakes are cooking, mix together the caster sugar, lemon juice and marmalade with 2 tbsp water in a small saucepan. Stir over a medium heat to dissolve the sugar then boil for 3 minutes or until syrupy.
- When the cakes come out of the oven, flood the moulds with the syrup and leave them to cool completely and soak up the syrup.

PREPARATION TIME: 20 MINUTES

COOKING TIME: 20 MINUTES

INGREDIENTS

110 g / 4 oz / ½ cup self-raising flour, sifted
110 g / 4 oz / ½ cup caster (superfine) sugar
110 g / 4 oz / ½ cup butter, softened
2 large eggs
1 orange, zest finely grated

TO DECORATE
110 g / 4 oz / ½ cup caster (superfine) sugar
2 lemons, juiced
2 tbsp marmalade

Lemon Syrup Cupcake

993

Try this recipe with lemon zest in the cake mixture and replace the marmalade with the grated zest of 1 lemon to make lemon syrup Cakes.

Index